**making money
from property**

Go make money from
property!

All the best

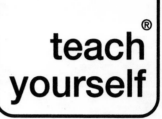

**making money
from property**
martin roberts

Launched in 1938, the **teach yourself** series
grew rapidly in response to the world's wartime
needs. Loved and trusted by over 50 million
readers, the series has continued to respond to
society's changing interests and passions and
now, 70 years on, includes over 500 titles,
from Arabic and Beekeeping to Yoga and Zulu.
What would you like to learn?

be where you want to be with **teach yourself**

For UK order enquiries: please contact Bookpoint Ltd, 130 Milton Park, Abingdon, Oxon OX14 4SB. Telephone: +44 (0) 1235 827720. Fax: +44 (0) 1235 400454. Lines are open 09.00–17.00, Monday to Saturday, with a 24-hour message answering service. Details about our titles and how to order are available at www.teachyourself.co.uk

Long renowned as the authoritative source for self-guided learning – with more than 50 million copies sold worldwide – the **teach yourself** series includes over 500 titles in the fields of languages, crafts, hobbies, business, computing and education.

British Library Cataloguing in Publication Data: a catalogue record for this title is available from the British Library.

First published in UK 2008 by Hodder Education, part of Hachette Livre UK, 338 Euston Road, London, NW1 3BH.

This edition published 2008.

The **teach yourself** name is a registered trade mark of Hodder Headline.

Typeset by Transet Limited, Coventry, England.
Printed in Great Britain for Hodder Education, an Hachette Livre UK Company, 338 Euston Road, London NW1 3BH, by Cox & Wyman Ltd, Reading, Berkshire.

The publisher has used its best endeavours to ensure that the URLs for external websites referred to in this book are correct and active at the time of going to press. However, the publisher and the author have no responsibility for the websites and can make no guarantee that a site will remain live or that the content will remain relevant, decent or appropriate.

Hachette Livre UK's policy is to use papers that are natural, renewable and recyclable products and made from wood grown in sustainable forests. The logging and manufacturing processes are expected to conform to the environmental regulations of the country of origin.

Impression number   10 9 8 7 6 5 4 3 2 1
Year   2012 2011 2010 2009 2008

contents

acknowledgements

This book is dedicated to Kirsty, without whose tireless dedication, help and support it would not have been written.

Special thanks also go to the following people:

The Art of Bathrooms in Bath (**www.theartofbathrooms. co.uk**) for lending me the bath for the front cover photo.

Alison Frecknall – who became hooked on *Homes Under the Hammer*, and asked me to write the book.

Mel Eriksen and the production team of *Homes Under the Hammer*, for all their hard work to make the programme such a success.

Julian Humphries of Robson Taylor in Bath (**www.robson taylor.co.uk**) for all his help and support over the years.

Mark Broughton for all his invaluable advice and guidance.

Dave Hughes for being my best mate through thick and thin.

My mum and dad – for encouraging and supporting me in all things – including buying my first house.

Scott – for bringing such joy into our lives.

Egbert and the Bed Gang.

My angels – who surround and protect me through life's ups and downs.

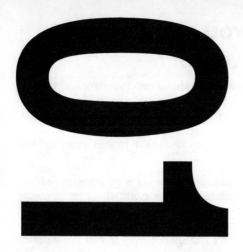

01

introduction ...

In this chapter you will learn:
- a bit about my background
- how property can help you achieve financial freedom
- the advantages of investing in property

... why do you want to be a property investor?

Property has been one of the financial success stories of the last decade. Many 'normal' folk have made the transition from being 'employed' to being 'self-employed' property investors/developers. This trend shows no signs of abating. The purpose of this book is to show how you can make money (a living) out of property.

The fact that you have picked up this book and begun reading indicates that you are interested in joining the ever growing throng of people in the UK who have decided to invest in property. Perhaps you are tired of being stuck in a boring job and are looking for a career change, or maybe you are worried about how you are going to save for your retirement? You could even be a bit of a DIY enthusiast and fancy your chances at turning your hobby into something more serious, or a plain old money-maker wanting to learn the tricks of the trade in the world of bricks and mortar.

Whatever your reasons for wanting to learn about how to make money from property, this book is essential reading. It will help you to avoid making expensive mistakes, point out to you where to focus your time and money and suggest to you different strategies to follow to make a profit. I can't guarantee you success, but by reading this book and applying the information I pass on to you to your property investing activities, you will have the odds well and truly stacked in your favour.

Let me introduce myself. I am Martin Roberts and I present the BBC1 daytime property programme *Homes Under the Hammer*. As the title suggests, the show is all about people who buy property at auction in the UK. We follow the successful bidders to find out what their plans and motivations are for the purchase and at the same time take a look at the property that they have bought. We then go back to the property in 3–6 months' time, to see if the plans have worked out and if so what the results have been. The stories that unfold are incredible and I have been astounded at the response that the programme has received. I think the fact that it attracts close to 2 million viewers each morning says something about this nation's attitude towards all things property related. It's true, we have a love affair with property ... and this shows no signs of abating.

In the five years since I started presenting *Homes Under The Hammer*, I have met literally hundreds of people who now make their living out of property investing and renovating. Some of them have appeared on the programme when they have first dipped their toe into the water – so their first project has been watched by millions of people! Others are more experienced property developers who have been at it for years and now treat each project on its financial merits alone. One thing that has struck me is the great range of ages, backgrounds and personalities of people who we have followed. I find it hugely inspiring to see such a great breadth of people now making a success out of property investing – everything from young first-time buyers to grandmothers, ex-farmers to city bankers, builders to market traders!

Of course, not all the stories that we cover end up with the buyer making money. Some sadly do not. Some pay well over the odds for the property, others simply don't do their research thoroughly and fail to identify inherent (and usually costly) problems with the property. However, I am pleased to say that the vast majority of cases that are featured do end up with the buyer making at least some profit.

It is also extremely fulfilling when people stop me and say that as a result of the programme, they have now given up their previous careers and become property investors! This is a huge compliment and I always feel very honoured to think that I have touched (and hopefully improved) so many people's lives in this way.

I should also point out that I am a property developer and investor myself. Like many people who we feature in the programme, I realized the benefits of buying property and renting it out, and have a portfolio of residential and commercial property both here in the UK and overseas. In building this portfolio, I have learned many lessons myself – made the mistakes and had the triumphs – and this experience, along with the knowledge I have gained from making the TV programme, means that I have come across most of the common issues associated with buying, renovating and selling houses. I also run my own overseas property consultancy – PropertyQC – and have guided many people through the process of investing abroad.

I have tried to condense these years of experience into this book so that you can learn how to make money from property without some of the setbacks that I and our programme contributors have experienced. Contained within these pages is a wealth of knowledge spanning a whole range of property related topics – from cracking the 'buy to let' market, identifying hotspots, buying property at auction, buying land and commercial property to how to manage renovation projects. I've tried to highlight **what not to do** as well as **what to do** in tackling certain issues. If you follow the advice here, keep your head and learn from your own experiences, you will be well on track for property investment success.

But first, let's understand why the thought of making money from property is so appealing. After all, there are lots of other things that you could be doing with your time and other things that you could spend your money on or make money from.

I think it is fair to say that while there may be lots of individual reasons why someone chooses to invest in property, the vast majority of us are motivated by a few key thoughts:

The pension crisis

Unless you've been living on Mars for the last few years, you couldn't fail to realize that we have a massive problem with pension funding in the UK. There are lots of reasons for this:

1 People are living longer in retirement – so the government has to pay out more money in the form of state pensions. We have an overall ageing average population thanks to medical improvements and this is putting a strain on government finances.

2 There are fewer young people working to contribute to the state pension 'pot'. Imagine the state pension as being a bucket with a tap on the bottom. The workers in the population pay into the bucket by means of National Insurance contributions and personal tax. The retired population draw out from the tap at the bottom by means of state pension. Due to young people carrying on their education into their 20s, there are fewer contributions going into the bucket at the top and yet because pensioners are living longer, the money is flowing out quicker from the tap at the bottom.

3 Employers cannot afford to provide pensions for their employees. In the past employers (particularly the large ones) have provided pension schemes for their staff. Often these schemes were 'non-contributory' which meant that the employees didn't have to pay any money themselves into the pension. On retirement, the employee could look forward to continuing to receive an income from the employer – often up

to two-thirds of what they earned while employed. These schemes are extremely expensive to the employer though and, partly due to poorer stock market performance, many companies simply can't afford to offer them any more. Employees, therefore, have to make their own pension arrangements.

4 Lower stock market performance. Even where someone has been making payments into a pension plan, falling investment returns means that this money isn't generating such a healthy pension as in previous decades.

The crux of all of this is that unless we personally take control of our own destiny and save for our own retirement we face a situation of living in poverty in old age. Employers and the government will not be able to take care of us. We have to do it for ourselves. The need to generate enough investments to produce a healthy income in retirement has been a major factor in driving people to get involved in property investment. If, during our active working lives we can acquire enough property, by the time we retire we hope that we can look forward to an income from it. Property is an ideal medium for saving in this long-term way. It has the potential for steady, continuing growth and it isn't as volatile as stocks and shares.

Passive income

How cool would it be to think that you are making money even when you sleep? Or if you do work already, that you can be generating a second income when you are at the office, working on your primary income? This is what we mean by 'passive income' – a way of having an income that comes to you without you having to actually toil at the grindstone for it. One of the wonderful things about property investment is that you can be making money even when you sleep. Thanks to market forces at work (rather than you), the value of property increases over time, so although this isn't money trickling into your current account all day, you are in effect making money 24 hours a day, 7 days a week.

Career choice

I have met so many people who have used property as a means of getting themselves out of a rut. People who have been stuck in jobs that they don't enjoy, but are frightened to leave because to retrain for another profession may take years and, in the meantime, they still have to live. Property can provide them with the key to release themselves. The key to financial freedom.

Lifestyle choice

Property investment allows you to be your own boss. You can choose what hours you work and what you wear to the office. In our busy, hectic twenty-first-century lives, many people have opted to develop property because it gives them the freedom to make choices for themselves. As someone who makes sufficient money out of property to support yourself and your family, you can choose when to work, where you work and who you work with. This is tremendously liberating and for some people has meant that they can spend more time with the children/wife/dog etc.

Property investing can be great fun. For those investors who get their sleeves rolled up and stuck into the renovation work, it is very hands on – drawing on practical and creative skills which may not be utilized by doing an office job. Despite the fact that, like anything else, property investing has its challenges, overall it is very rewarding. Anyone who has renovated a house themselves will be able to relate to the great sense of achievement in standing back and looking at the finished project.

So what are the advantages of investing in property?

Advantages of investing in property

It's a Steady Eddy

Property will always rise in value over the long term. Average house prices have fallen just four times in the past 50 years. According to Nationwide, at the end of 2005 the FTSE 100 index was 10 per cent below its 1999 level, yet house prices were more than twice as high. Figure 1.1 illustrates how property values have consistently risen over the years.

Of course, as we all know, past performance is not necessarily a guide to the future, so you have to weigh up lots of factors (which I cover in this book) to decide whether you believe that a particular property will increase in value in the future. But if you take the view that average prices will always increase over the long term, then it is just a question of whether the amount of increase is sufficient for you, compared with other forms of investment.

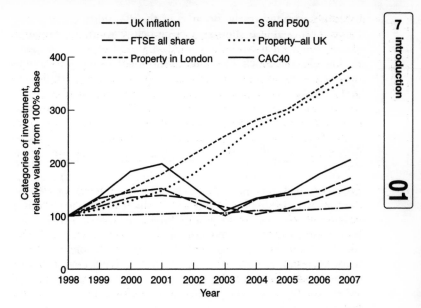

figure 1.1 property versus stocks – growth and income in the UK

It has many uses

One of the reasons why property will rise in value over the longer term, is that there will always be a demand for it. There are lots of reasons why people want or need to buy or rent property – and it's not all about investment returns. We all need somewhere to live. This is a basic living requirement which won't go out of fashion or fall out of favour with the pundits. Similarly, businesses need premises within which to operate, so demand for property on a practical level will remain.

It can be purchased 'below market value'

This is a term that I will return to later in the book, but for now the concept of buying 'below market value' is born out of the fact that a property may be bought or sold by someone who can pay or accept whatever they decide, and who may not have full knowledge of the property's actual worth. Unlike stocks and shares, which are traded openly by people who have all the market information at their fingertips, property is usually a transaction between just two people – a buyer and a seller. It is an *illiquid* asset – which means that it cannot be bought and sold quickly – unlike stocks and shares which are highly liquid and can be traded freely. Because of the illiquidity of property, it may be possible to buy at a price below what the property would achieve if it could be traded in an efficient, fast-moving market like the Stock Exchange. Emotional factors also come into play. A seller of a property may place more importance on *liking* the buyer than getting the maximum possible price, or they may be forced to sell quickly in which case they may have to accept whatever offer a buyer is willing to make.

It can be leveraged

One unique feature of property that sets it apart from stocks and shares, is that it is possible to leverage property to create a greater return on investment. I talk in more detail about leverage later in this book, but essentially it means using 'other people's money' to increase your buying power. If you believe that property is going to increase in value, then you will want to put as much money as you can into it to reap as much profit as possible. If you can borrow money to do this and yet keep the profit for yourself, then this is using leverage to maximize your returns. It is very easy to find companies (banks, building societies and mortgage companies) that will lend you money secured against property to allow you to buy more of it. This isn't the case with more traditional forms of investment such as stocks and shares (unless you employ sophisticated techniques) and so property has an overriding advantage because it is easy to leverage.

It's easy to understand

As an asset class, property is relatively easy to understand. We all live in property of some description and so can relate easily to it and can establish why someone would want to buy it. This is unlike stocks and shares which have a whole bunch of complex business reasons why their price might rise or fall. This is beyond the knowledge of many people – whose only way of being able to gain exposure to these markets without substantial risk is to use a stock broker or analyst.

Residential property investment can also appear a safer bet than the more volatile financial markets.

Once again, the very fact that you have picked up this book to read indicates that you are one of a growing number of people who like the idea of creating wealth for themselves through property. The good news is that property is no longer the privilege of the cash-rich investor or institutions with very large coffers – it has become the talking point of the last decade and investment vehicle of choice for many thousands of people. For many who have already embarked on a vocation of property investment, it has already become the catalyst to financial freedom and independence. With the help of my book, you can join them!

02 ... understanding your objectives

In this chapter you will learn about:
- goal setting
- different types of investor profile
- deciding on your strategy
- managing a portfolio
- kinds of exit strategy

... beginning with the end in mind

> 'Begin With the End in Mind'
>
> Stephen R. Covey; *The 7 Habits of Highly Effective People.*
>
> Covey calls this the habit of personal leadership – leading oneself that is, towards what you consider your aims. By developing the habit of concentrating on relevant activities you will build a platform to avoid distractions and become more productive and successful.

So you've decided to become a property investor. Congratulations! You have now taken the first step into a world which could prove to be exciting, dynamic, financially rewarding and fun.

Before embarking on a property shopping spree, it is important to identify your property investment goals and form a strategy so that you know which properties to look to buy and at what price.

This chapter takes you to the starting point with goal setting and planning your strategy and then moves on to cover various forms of property investment strategy and their relative merits.

But before you go and order your business cards saying 'Property Investor' it is important to think about what property investment is going to mean to you. People get into property for all sorts of reasons, but if you know now what you want to achieve from embarking on this vocation, then it is likely you'll have far greater success at it. Later in this book we will be discussing where to find the right properties to buy, how to know what price to pay for them and various strategies for making money from property. But the chances are they are not all going to be right for you. And while having a bit of a spread of investments in your portfolio is good, trying to be a 'jack of all trades' will inevitably result in you being a 'master of none'. You need to think about what you want to achieve from buying, selling, renovating, renting or developing property. You need to be realistic about your own abilities and the resources you have available to you. While the idea of owning a portfolio of commercial property might suit your desires to generate a long-term, low-risk rental income, if you have limited capital available to buy such properties, then it may take you a very long time to achieve your goal. Similarly, if you are working full time and because of family pressures or other commitments you have limited time available at weekends to embark on a strategy of property renovating where you do most of the work, again it just isn't realistic. Chances are you'll fail and either run out of time and enthusiasm or you'll end up drafting in help which you might not have budgeted for.

Having an effective strategy and following it will greatly increase your chances of success. As Stephen R. Covey, author of *The 7 Habits of Highly Effective People* says: 'Begin With the End in Mind'. So at this stage you don't need to worry about the detail and how you are going to achieve wealth from property, but concentrate on the end result and what that will mean to you.

Goal setting

At this stage you need to do a bit of goal setting. You need to have a clear mental picture of what you want to achieve. Research has found that people who have personal goals are more likely to achieve more, have a greater level of concentration or focus, suffer less stress and anxiety and generally lead much more fulfilling lives.

The more precise and specific you can be about your goals, the better. In fact, many professionals swear by a simple mnemonic for goal planning. Their rule is to make all goals SMART. A SMART goal is one that is:

- Specific – You can state the goal clearly.
- Measurable – You have some measurement tool to tell you how close you are to achieving your goal.
- Achievable – There is no point in setting yourself a goal that you haven't got a hope in hell's chance of achieving.
- Realistic/relevant – The goal needs to be important to you.
- Timebound – You need to set yourself some timescales of when you want to have achieved your goal.

People who have SMART goals tend to be people who achieve things. This is because they have a route map for their lives and wake up each morning knowing exactly why they need to get out of bed. Usually a long-term or big goal can then be broken down into smaller, more manageable chunks, so you know exactly what you need to do each day, week or month to get you to your goal.

Let's suppose that your objective is to replace your current earned (salary) income with income from property so you can afford to give up your employed work. (Incidentally, this is a very common objective and one of the main reasons why people get into property investing – they see it as a way of making a living so they can 'give up' their existing work.)

A SMART goal for someone with this broad objective might read something like this:

'In the next five years I want to build a property portfolio of ten buy to let properties that will generate a combined net rental income of £25,000 per annum, so I can give up work.'

- Specific – It is specific. It tells the reader exactly what the goal is about.
- Measurable – We know that the person has to buy ten properties.
- Achievable – Buying ten properties in five years is certainly achievable – especially when you read about some of the 'creative buying strategies' later in this book.
- Realistic/relevant – If £25,000 p.a. is enough to replace this person's existing earned income, then it is definitely realistic and relevant.
- Timebound – The person wants to do this within five years.

At the end of the five years, the person will be able to look back at the number of properties they have bought and how much rental income they are generating to know quite accurately whether the goal has been reached and, if not, how far they still have to go.

Spend some time NOW thinking about your own objectives and writing down your own SMART goals. The rest of this book will then help you to crystallize your plans.

☺ Did you know?

The most successful and effective people are those who **write down** their goals and **share them** with their friends, spouse or partner. Committing yourself to your objectives should include discussing them 'publicly' with someone else close to you and writing them down. Keep your list of objectives with you so that you can refer to it regularly.

What kind of investor are you?

Once you have set your personal goals, you should also consider what kind of investor you are. This will have an influence on which kind of property investment strategy is going to best suit you. The different types of investor that I come across are:

The armchair investor

You are the kind of person who is either too busy or (let's be honest) too lazy to take an active involvement in property. Yet, you understand and appreciate the financial benefits of investing. The thought of buying run-down property to renovate yourself fills you with dread – it just isn't how you want to spend your time. You are more likely to want to invest in 'hands off' type deals such as land investments, property funds or properties which have an active management company in place (i.e. condo hotels). The main risk to you is that you are too passive and don't carry out sufficient research or visit properties that you intend to buy.

The financial analyst

You are interested only in the numbers and will analyse the merits of any deal based purely on financial information. You probably carry out lots of research on prices and rental values of comparable properties, and on the expected returns of any investment you consider. You may also analyse economic data about the region, country or market that you are considering, and only when you are satisfied on the financial case will you decide to invest. The main risks to you are that you spend all your time analysing but you never actually take action. They call this 'analysis paralysis'.

The DIY enthusiast

You love watching TV programmes about property development (hopefully *Homes Under the Hammer* of course!) and are taken with the interior design and creativity aspects of developing property. You see 'great potential' in any renovation project and aren't afraid to get your hands dirty doing restoration works yourself. You are far more drawn to the 'ugly duckling' properties as you have a desire to make them good and are less motivated by land deals, commercial properties and those which are already in good repair. The main risk to you is that you let your heart rule your head and may find it difficult to stick to your budget on renovation projects.

These profiles may be a little over simplistic and in reality most property developers will have traits of all three, but it is likely that one profile will be dominant and it is important for you to know which one you veer towards and what are likely to be your greatest challenges.

So, once you know what your objectives are and the type of investor you are, you are in a position to consider various different investment strategies and analyse which will work for you.

Deciding on your strategy

There are a number of property investment strategies that you might choose to employ. Each of these is discussed in more detail later in this book, but for now, let's just look at some of the most popular strategies and consider some of the pros and cons of each.

Buy to let

This area of the property arena has exploded over recent years. And it's easy to understand why. If you are able to buy the right property at the right price, even if you have a mortgage on the property, your tenants paying you rent each month can be sufficient to cover the mortgage payments. Or at least that's the theory! You as the landlord have someone else paying your mortgage for you and you can benefit from the long-term capital growth of owning the property.

Traditional long-term residential let

Pros – If you buy at the right price and your rental income covers your mortgage payments, then you effectively have a property for free and can look forward to the capital appreciation of the asset. The availability of buy to let mortgages in the past 10 to 15 years has made this strategy accessible to 'normal' folk (i.e. you don't have to be a high-flying property developer to own buy to let property in this way). If you have long-term tenants, they are responsible for the service and utility charges along with council tax.

Cons – Because of the substantial increase in house prices in the UK in recent years, the prices of properties are now often out of balance with the rental income potential, so the scenario described above where the rent covers the mortgage payment is more difficult to achieve, and you may find that you have to supplement the mortgage payments each month.

🍴 Food for thought

Even if you have to supplement your monthly rent to meet your mortgage payments, if the value of the property is rising by an amount more than this then you are still getting a return on this money. So in a rising market, you might still wish to buy properties even if they do not have positive cashflow.

Many inexperienced buy to let investors fail to take into consideration upkeep and maintenance costs of the property when they work out their sums, and you should also factor in the likelihood that, even in a popular rental area, you may have void periods. Nowadays there is far more rental property for tenants to choose from, so you should be prepared to make your property stand out from the crowd.

Student accommodation

Another form of buy to let is student lets. The trick here is not to get emotional at all about your purchases. Student accommodation will be very different from a traditional home. Living areas such as sitting rooms and lounges will be converted to bedrooms. The key here is to consider how many 'rental rooms' you can get out of the property. Students will require their own room (with enough space for a desk and somewhere to sit) but aside from a kitchen and bathroom, you don't need to provide separate living areas.

Pros – A large property split into rental rooms for students can generate more combined income per month than if you let it as a whole house. Also because you have several tenants in the same property, if one decides to move out it doesn't have such a detrimental effect on your cashflow, as you will still have the rental from the remaining tenants. Often existing students who are renting from you will act as good advertisers for your property and help you find tenants.

Cons – It is vital to buy in the right location. Property slightly out of town or off a main transport route will be enough to deter your would-be tenants. Students are sometimes also messy and destructive. If you are the type of landlord who puts your heart and soul into picking out fixtures and fittings for each property then student lets may not be for you. You also need to do your sums on a 10- or 11-month rental year rather than 12 since students will usually vacate the property completely during the summer months.

HMOs

These are 'houses in multiple occupation' and come under special government rules. There are specific definitions of what is considered a HMO and, if your property falls within the definitions, you will be required to abide by special rules. For some landlords, this is a lucrative niche and if you buy HMOs and know the rules, you may be able to buy property at a keen price because others are put off by the thought of extra red tape.

Under the changes in the Housing Act 2004, if you let a property which is one of the following types it is considered a HMO:

- An entire house or flat which is let to **three or more** separate tenants (i.e. they form **two or more** households) who share a kitchen, bathroom or toilet.
- A house which has been converted entirely into bedsits (or other non-self-contained accommodation) and which is let to **three or more** separate tenants who share kitchen, bathroom or toilet facilities.
- A converted house which contains one or more flats that are not wholly self-contained (i.e. the flat does not have a kitchen, bathroom and toilet) and which is occupied by **three or more** separate tenants.
- A building which is converted entirely into self-contained flats if the conversion did not meet the standards of the 1991 Building Regulations and more than one-third of the flats are let on short-term tenancies.

Additionally, property must be used as the tenants' main residence and it should be used solely or mainly to house tenants. Properties let to students and migrant workers will be treated as their main residence and the same will apply to properties which are used as domestic refuges.

However, HMOs are further subdivided into licensable HMOs, where you are legally required to fulfil certain Building Regulations, and non-licensable HMO's, where you are not. This depends on certain criteria – such as number of rooms, occupants and floors. You local council will confirm which category any property you are considering falls into.

So, for example, a three-storey townhouse that has been modified to provide six bedrooms all let to separate tenants, would fall within licensable HMO rules, whereas a two-storey townhouse with six bedrooms may not.

Pros – Once you know the guidelines, HMOs like student lets can be more profitable than letting the entire property to one tenant. Many of the requirements of HMOs are common sense anyway and will make for a safer home for your tenants.

Cons – If your property is a HMO you will be expected to abide by certain rules. These can vary between different councils and are legally enforceable, with heavy fines if you don't comply.

We cover the topic of HMOs in more detail later, in Chapter 5.

Corporate lets

This is where you let your house out to employees (often from the same company). The company itself may actually be the tenant.

Pros – Corporate bodies generally make good tenants. By their very nature the likely occupants are working professionals and so should conduct themselves in a responsible manner. Chances are they will be using the property only from Monday to Thursday night since they will have their own homes to return to for the weekend. Corporate lets can also command higher levels of rent than a comparable straightforward residential let.

Cons – You can expect the duration of the tenancy to be shorter. Often the employee is on a fixed-term contract and the let therefore may be only for a few months. You should be prepared to be flexible on terms. You will also be restricted on the kind of property that has a corporate let on it.

Holiday lets

The idea of owning your dream holiday home and then letting it out for part of the year to cover costs is extremely appealing. However, if you do venture into this arena, make sure that it does actually fit with your investment objectives and goals. It is easy to let the heart rule the head with this type of investment because it is more emotive than other types of purchase.

Pros – If the financial case stacks up, buying holiday let properties is a fantastic way to free holidays! You own the holiday property and let other people pay for its annual upkeep through rents. Holiday let properties can also command far higher levels of rent per week/month than a comparable long-term residential let property.

Cons – Unless you are buying in a resort with an onsite management company, the logistics of renting a holiday property can be difficult to manage. Unlike long-term residential lets, you are responsible for the payment of utilities and services and you will also need to have in place arrangements for the property to be cleaned and laundry changed at the beginning/end of each let. Depending on where you buy, the season for generating rent might be quite limited – so you will need to work hard to maximize occupancy during these periods to carry you through the rest of the year.

We discuss more about short-term holiday lets in Chapter 13.

Buy to restore

This is an altogether different way of making money from property. Although you might eventually rent the property out as a buy to let, the initial strategy is to buy a property in poor repair at a low price and do it up, and then either sell it at its true market value or rent it out. Years ago there were plenty of older properties in need of restoration available for property developers to take on. However, nowadays they are harder to find. And they don't always come cheap.

Pros – A great way to get into property investing if you have the vision and project management skills to actually do the renovation required. Many developers follow this strategy because they are builders or tradespeople themselves and, can therefore, do the works at a fraction of the cost to another person. There are also developers who do it for the buzz. It is a very hands-on and rewarding way of making money.

Cons – Getting the property at the right price is crucial to this strategy working – and in today's market this is getting harder to do. Many inexperienced developers also underestimate the costs and time of works to be done, so underbudget and then lose out on profit.

Chapters 8 and 9 of this book examine in more depth the topic of buying property to renovate or restore.

Buy to sell

This might be a buy to restore project as well, but here your strategy is to buy a property with the sole intention of selling it on again to make profit. The key to your success with this strategy is doing your research thoroughly and making sure you buy at the right price. If you are intending to sell the property on very quickly, then the price you pay is even more key as you are reliant on the fact that you are buying at *below market value* to make any money ... otherwise you might have to hold the property for longer and wait until the market moves sufficiently for you to generate your margin. In Chapter 7 we cover how to negotiate the best deal and buy at the right price.

Pros – You can move your money around quite quickly with this strategy and it isn't tied up in a property for a long period of time, as is often the case with renovation projects. Literally, you can buy and sell on again as fast as the conveyancing process will allow – so you can make a profit very quickly. I have met people who have bought and sold on the same day and made many thousands of pounds in the process. It's nice work if you can get it!

Cons – If you are unsuccessful in finding a buyer for your property then you may have to consider other options such as renting. In the worst-case scenario, you have an empty property on the market which is tying up your capital and costing you money on a monthly basis.

Own use

You may, of course, be buying property with the intention of making use of it yourself for at least a proportion of your time. Even though you have your own personal needs and requirements to consider, this doesn't mean that you have to take off your 'property investor' hat. With careful thought, you will be able to find properties that serve your own needs perfectly well and that can still make you money. For example, you may wish to buy a holiday home. Your primary objective is to buy something which suits you but if you buy shrewdly, you may also be able to rent out the property as a holiday let and generate income from it. Similarly, small business owners looking for shop or office premises may want to buy a property rather than lease one, and if so they could sublet part of the building to another party. The trick with any 'own use' purchase is to make sure that you have a balance between what makes sound commercial sense and what you desire. You must be strict with yourself and may have to forgo some of your personal choices for what makes more financial or commercial sense.

Martin's tip

Combining own use with investment return

If you are buying a property that you intend to use yourself, make a list of your needs and requirements. Be as specific as you can. Then subdivide this list into factors which are essential and which are 'nice to have'. You may have to compromise on some of the less essential features for a property that stacks up better as an investment.

Managing a portfolio

As part of the exercise in setting your objectives, you should also consider whether you are going to roll up your sleeves and get stuck in yourself or let the professional property management agents do things for you. There are reasons for and against both options. The most important thing is for you to be realistic about what you can achieve. Don't commit yourself to fully managing a property portfolio if you work full time and have little spare time – managing rental properties can become time consuming.

There are plenty of management agents around who concentrate on just that – managing property. They will often have good connections themselves with tradespeople and builders, so a burst pipe or other potential catastrophe can be dealt with quickly, wherever you happen to be.

The downside of using a property management company is that you will be paying up to 15 per cent of your rental income to them. So if your cashflow is tight, this might be the thing that pushes you from a positive to a negative cashflow.

Kinds of exit strategy

Whatever your strategy is, you must also think about your exit strategy (i.e. how are you going to actually extract the profit from your property). Remember Stephen Covey's words: 'Begin with the end in mind'. Whatever properties you decide to buy, you should always consider how you are going to make money from them. It's all very well owning a property that has increased in value by £100k, but if you can't get your hands on that value by either liquidating (selling) it, refinancing or renting then it may as well be held in a locked safe. Remember: property is a very illiquid asset class – you can't just go and cash it in or make a withdrawal as if your money was invested in the bank or building society. You need to plan your exit strategy with any property deal before you commit to it.

Generally speaking, the more exit strategies you have available to you, the more options you have for getting your money out of the property. Common exit strategies are:

1 Selling the property – clearly in the case of the buy to sell route, this is the primary objective.
2 Renting the property – you generate your money from the rental income being paid to you.
3 Refinancing – rather than selling the property (which can be done only once) you could refinance it. This allows you to take some (but not all) of the value out of the property by means of a loan secured against it. You still own the property and can, therefore, benefit from future growth, but now you have a mortgage (or a bigger mortgage) on the property.

Summary

In this chapter we have looked at:

- Goal planning and the importance of setting yourself clear goals at the outset.
- Various property investment strategies and the pros and cons of each.
- Ways to manage a property portfolio.
- Various types of exit strategy.

03 where to find properties to buy ...

In this chapter you will learn:

- the advantages and disadvantages of available tools and strategies
- general top tips for buying properties

... sorting the wheat from the chaff

In this chapter we look at a whole range of options and ideas to help identify the right properties to buy to meet a chosen investment strategy, and highlight the advantages and disadvantages and the best ways of dealing with each.

Once you have decided on your chosen strategy for property investing, clearly the next thing is actually to find some properties to buy. Nowadays, the UK property market is an enormous, sophisticated and information-rich marketplace with lots of sources of reference available to purchasers. No longer are you restricted to just making friends with your local estate agent – although this is still a very valid and important way of buying.

Successful property investors are always on the lookout for good deals – and even if they are not in the market to buy at a particular time, they will still be evaluating current deals as part of their ongoing research. They will more than likely also employ a range of tactics and methods to find and buy their properties. In this chapter we are going to look at the various ways in which you can find properties to buy, and consider their relative pros and cons. We will also highlight which *type* of properties to buy. As you will see me reiterate throughout this book, effective and diligent research is the key to getting it right, and even though you might find that one particular route to buying suits you best, other methods should not be ignored as they will form the backbone of your research.

In today's market, property investors have a number of tools and strategies available to them to find the right properties to buy.

Estate agents and letting agents

On my travels around the UK, I have realized that a sure-fire way of knowing if a particular area has a buoyant property market is to look at the number of estate agents and letting agents in the high street. Twenty years ago, a village, small town or neighbourhood of a larger city might have had the odd one or two trusty estate agents who dealt with the house buying and selling needs of the local residents. In those days, people bought houses only to live in and tended to stay in the same property for many years (sometimes their whole life!). They saw fit to move only if family or work requirements forced them to do so. Nowadays, it is becoming increasingly common for a family group to own more than one property, either as a second home or as an investment property. This is partly due to changing socio-demographics as well as the compelling financial reasons that surround buying property.

Drive down the main high street of a neighbourhood where the property market is thriving and you will see that many of the shops are now estate agents or letting agents. (Take Mutley Plain in Plymouth, for example. When I drove through the neighbourhood recently, a typical rank of shops was almost entirely given over to property in some way. Out of 14 units I counted in one stretch, 12 were either estate agents or letting agents and one was a mortgage shop. Tell me that Mutley Plain doesn't have a rampant property market!)

Estate agents and letting agents will be your staple diet for doing your research and for helping you find and evaluate the best properties for you to buy. As a successful property investor, you should be making yourself known to all the agents in the area where you want to buy and letting them know that you are in the market to make a purchase. Be exact about what you want from them – that way they will be better able to help you. Take some time educating them about your requirements – the kind of property you are looking for, the condition of property you want, the postcode, the price range and any other 'must' or 'mustn't' haves. The more information you can give them, the better chance they will have of showing you only opportunities that are right for you. You won't be sent details of things which are irrelevant, and the agent won't feel that you are wasting their time because you never progress to a purchase.

I know it's easy to bad-mouth estate agents, as a profession – they sometimes seem to be up there with traffic wardens on the list of people we love to hate – but remember: they have to earn a living too. Many (in particular the independent companies) are commission only salespeople. They often earn only when a deal is closed, so they are not going to take too kindly to having their time wasted. As an investor wanting to get first bite at the cherry on good deals in an area, the last thing you want to do is cheese-off estate agents – the very people most likely to be able to help you reach your goals. Don't make empty promises you can't keep. Telling them you're a cash buyer and can exchange in two weeks might get your low offer accepted this time, but you are guaranteed to fall out of favour with the agent (who, remember, works for the vendor) if you don't hold to this. They are going to be less motivated to call you next time a hot deal lands on their desk.

Be professional and treat estate agents as you would professional colleagues. Keep in close regular contact and build up a rapport with them as you would with other work associates. Over time, your estate agent contacts will become like business partners, so treat them as such. Show them your appreciation and reward them when a deal goes through.

It's worth taking into consideration that there are different types of estate agent:

- Independents – smaller firms with one or a few offices concentrated around an area. Often owner-managed, and commission from sales is their only revenue – which pays staff wages, vehicles and rent on the business premises. Generally very motivated to sell property because if they don't then they don't eat!
- Networks – many independents are part of larger networks for cross-marketing opportunities. The local agent still has control over how his or her practice operates but has a wide network of similar firms through which to access properties and buyers.
- Nationals – estate agency arms of larger businesses (e.g. building societies and banks). Many offices spread throughout the country or a region. Usually staff will be salaried and the business premises will be paid for by 'head office'. Advantages are that they have broader reach and can network with other offices of the same company. Disadvantages are that they can be more rigid enterprises with less room for negotiation on charges.

Most estate agents will advertise regularly in local newspapers and specialist property newspapers and magazines. They, therefore, showcase their property inventory very readily and freely, so as an investor it is easy to find out what properties they have for sale at any time.

Pros – You can build up a good rapport with estate agents and they can do much of the 'filtering' for you, finding properties that will suit your requirements. They should have in-depth knowledge of the area in which you are investing, and can be invaluable sources of information. They will have first-hand knowledge of how an area or property market is performing. Their services to you as a buyer are 'free'.

Cons – The agent works for the vendor, not you as a buyer, and so their loyalties will lie in getting the best deal for the seller not you. They have only a limited number of properties on their books at any one time and it can be quite labour intensive and time-consuming to sift through them. They are usually available to you only during normal office hours.

Letting agents are also a good source of information about property that is, or is going to be listed for sale since they will know where notice has been given to tenants to vacate a property. They will also know of landlords who are selling up and may even be able to introduce you to a whole portfolio of properties from a single landlord. If you promise to give them your lettings business if you are successful in buying the property, lettings agents are more likely to want to help you and will more readily introduce you to properties – perhaps even before they are put on the market.

Property finders/consultants

These are property professionals (very often individuals, but can be small firms too) that you employ to act on your behalf to find you suitable properties. They tend to be expert in one particular area and, given your requirements, will find properties and often negotiate with the vendor on your behalf. Like estate agents, the more information you can give property finders as to your requirements, the more effective they will be.

Some consultants will also act in an advisory capacity to you. They will take the time to find out about your exact requirements and goals and then make recommendations to you about which areas and markets you should consider investing in. This can take a lot of the time and effort associated with researching out of your hands – although this doesn't mean that you can just put your feet up. I recommend that even if you are using a consultant or property finder you still remain diligent until you are completely satisfied with the deal on offer. Consultants and property finders are particularly worthwhile when you are investing in an area with which you aren't familiar and where physically visiting to check out things yourself would be difficult. They are definitely worth considering if you are going to be investing in another part of the country from where you live, or overseas.

Property finders and consultants will charge you a fee for finding property for you. This fee can sometimes be a fixed amount (e.g. £5,000), or a percentage of the value of the property that you then buy – typically 3 to 5 per cent. This covers the time, effort and expense of doing the research and locating properties for you. They may receive some commission on the deal should you eventually buy, but this is not necessarily the case. It is worth asking the consultant or property finder what they stand to earn out of the deal over and above your fee. It may influence which properties they put forward to you! A good consultant or property finder will be completely independent of any agent or developer so they can honestly work on your behalf. Be prepared to be asked to pay the fee even if you decide not to buy the property that they put forward to you. At the end of the day, they will have done their work and will expect to be paid – irrespective of whether you decide to proceed or not. In fact, some property finders or consultants will actually charge all or part of the fee upfront before doing any work to prevent them spending a lot of time and effort and then not getting paid for it.

You can also find people who come into contact with property during their daily lives but who aren't strictly 'property people', yet make very good property finders. For example, architects, interior designers, gardeners, etc. They tend to be good networkers and are well known within the business community in the area where you want to invest. They are likely to just introduce you to deals but won't check them out or negotiate on your behalf. A finder of this type might expect to receive a fee of 1 per cent of the purchase price of any deal they refer you to, or they may just want you to buy the next round at the local pub!

---

⑪ Food for thought

Think Win:Win

If you want to develop long-lasting relationships with estate agents, property finders and other partners, ensure that they get something out of the deal as well. If you build in something for them, they will be more motivated to help you. For example, reward people who bring you deals and opportunities – either financially or by sending referral business to them. Make sure your rental properties are always maintained in good condition, and listen to concerns and feedback from your tenants. You will develop a reputation with your tenants and agent as a professional and thoughtful landlord. If you are selling and have made a good profit, leave some profit in the deal for the next buyer – it will create enormous goodwill. Finally, have integrity, honesty and honour in everything you do. Here endeth the lesson!

Auctions

Buying property at auction is now more popular than ever. I'd like to think that my TV show *Homes Under the Hammer* has a lot to do with that. But anyway, it's easy to see why. An auction creates a true market. The property will be sold there and then to the person who is prepared to pay the most for it. Gone are the 'politics' of buying and negotiating through an estate agent and, of course, there is no chance of being gazumped! In some countries (e.g. Australia), 90 per cent of properties are sold in this way. A property that is being sold there will have an advertised Open Day and the auction is held at the property itself. Auction is a very reassuring process for both the buyer and seller because, once the hammer falls, both parties know that the deal is done.

On that note, if you do decide to buy at auction, it's even more critical that you do all your research beforehand. If you are the successful bidder, you can't suddenly withdraw your offer because you have found out something about the property that you're not happy with. It really is 'Buyer Beware'. Once that hammer goes down, you are contractually bound to buy the property and the vendor is contractually bound to sell it to you at that price – in the condition and state that it was presented at the time of the auction.

In my time presenting *Homes Under the Hammer*, I have been amazed at the number of people who buy 'blind' at auction. They bid on property without having actually seen it beforehand! This is a very foolhardy approach. Some, of course, do okay. They pay a realistic price and execute their chosen strategy without too much trouble. But I have to say that these are people who know the market very well and, although they may not have actually visited the specific property, they have enough experience and knowledge of the area to know what price to pay and make it work. The people who lose out are those who believe that in a rising market, they can buy ANY property and make money. While this may have been true in the past, it certainly isn't the case now, and I strongly discourage anyone from buying blind at auction.

Buying at auction can be a very exciting and rewarding way to buy. You can find details of autions on www.makingmoney fromproperty.tv. Alternatively, at the back of this book is a list of auction houses in the UK. If you want to pursue this method of purchase, I suggest that you make contact with the auction houses that operate in the area in which you want to invest and get on their mailing lists. They will then send you their catalogues for forthcoming auctions.

On the day of the auction you need to have cleared funds available to you for the 10 per cent deposit if you are the successful bidder. You can expect completion to be 28 days after the auction, so if you are going to take out a mortgage on the property, you will need to have an agreement in principle at least before you bid. If as the successful bidder you are unable to complete, you stand to lose the 10 per cent deposit paid and could be fined other costs associated with the vendor relisting the property. You could also end up paying the difference if a lower price is achieved for the property at a subsequent auction.

Later in this book there is a whole chapter (Chapter 10) dedicated to buying at auction, with hints and tips that I have built up over the many years I have been presenting *Homes Under the Hammer*.

Pros – It is a very 'clean' sale and purchase. Once the hammer goes down, if you are the successful bidder you know that the property is yours. Completion will normally take place 28 days later, so it's all done and dusted. There are no long and protracted purchase process shenanigans and endless negotiation. You buy as seen and the seller sells as so.

Cons – On the day of the auction, you need to have cleared funds available to you for the 10 per cent deposit if you are the successful bidder. It can also be quite a nerve-racking experience and some investors don't like the fact that everyone else in the room is watching them make their purchase. You have to have a clear idea of your absolute maximum price beforehand and you have to avoid overbidding. If someone bids higher than you, it could be a wasted journey to the auction.

Newspapers, magazines and specialist publications

Local and national newspapers often have classified ad sections which list a variety of properties that are for sale, either in your local area or countrywide. Sellers who place these ads may well be organizing the sale process themselves and may be motivated to accept a lower price for the sake of dealing directly with the buyer. There are also many specialist property publications and free-ad newspapers such as *Daltons Weekly*, *Exchange & Mart*, or *Trade-It* that will have property sections which may have interesting opportunities.

When it comes to the overseas property market, specialist magazines will not only contain properties for sale privately but will have numerous advertisements for developers and agents offering a wide variety of deals and purchase opportunities.

Pros – A straightforward way to see properties that are available for sale. Private sellers may offer discounts as they do not have to pay commission to an estate agent.

Cons – You may not be dealing through a professional intermediary who can offer you some level of protection and advice.

Investment clubs

These are becoming increasingly popular in a country where property investing has become so widespread. Investment clubs usually meet regularly and will discuss various opportunities that are available. The larger clubs will also often arrange for guest speakers to give talks on relevant topics (e.g. 'No money down' schemes, overseas property, mortgages, etc).

Most investment clubs will charge a joining fee – even if it is only a nominal amount to cover administration costs associated with keeping everyone in the club in touch with what's going on. They are great networking opportunities – a chance to meet and talk to like-minded individuals and share their ideas and strategies, and this in turn could lead to syndicated purchases (see below). Often deals become available to investment clubs that you wouldn't otherwise come across through other means. This is because sellers – in particular developers who have a whole project to sell – know that there is a critical mass of purchasers all in one place. Despite the fact that they might have to offer the properties for sale at a discount, they could potentially sell most or all of the project through one route. This is great news if you are a developer who has to factor marketing costs into the overall build budget.

Pros – You can learn a great deal from other investors and gain access to deals not generally available on the high street. They offer great networking opportunities and you can share experiences with other like-minded people. Investment clubs can also be a good catalyst for the formation of syndicates, where groups of investors join together to buy property.

Cons – Some 'clubs' aren't all they seem and are only routes to market for developers pushing overpriced properties. Don't get pushed into purchasing by 'hard sell' tactics. If you like the idea of joining an investment club, please visit www.makingmoney fromproperty.tv.

Syndicates

The idea of syndicates has certainly come to the fore recently – spurred on by the recent changes in pensions legislation that allows property to be held within certain types of pension plan, for example SIPPs and SSASs.

If you believe that diversification in a portfolio is a good thing – and you should – then buying through syndicates is a great way of achieving this. You can have a part share in a number of properties without needing to have the money available to buy them all. For example, if you have £30,000 to invest, this could be enough to give you a deposit on one or two properties – with the remainder of the purchase price coming from a mortgage. If, on the other hand, you were to club together with four other people, each with £30,000 each to invest, then this investment 'pot' is increased to £150,000. This would then allow you to buy say, six or seven properties in a variety of locations – including some overseas. You own a 20 per cent share in each of these properties, so benefit from 20 per cent of the growth. You are liable for 20 per cent of the costs associated with managing and maintaining these properties, but you also get only 20 per cent of the hassle, and you have diversified your portfolio and spread your risk.

Clearly, if you are buying a property with the idea of making use of it yourself, then a syndicated purchase may be far too restrictive (you would be able to use the property for only 20 per cent of the time, if at all) but if you are totally unemotional about your purchases and want to do it only for financial reasons, then syndication can be a good idea.

The key is to find other people who are like-minded and have similar levels of deposit available to them. Ideally, they will also be following the same strategy as you, so that there aren't any conflicts of interest in terms of the type of properties to buy. Investment clubs, specialist property lawyers, property finders and consultants can all act as catalysts for syndicates to be formed. Forward-thinking independent financial advisers (IFAs) may also be a source of potential syndicates – with the IFA putting some of his or her clients in touch with one another for this purpose.

¶⃰ Food for thought

You may also want to check out the syndicate section of the website that complements this book – www.makingmoneyfrom-property.tv – where we bring together people who are looking to invest in property through a variety of means, including syndicates. You may find other people with whom you could work, or just advice from people who are doing it for themselves.

Clearly, at the outset it will be important for a syndicate to agree its investment parameters – what sort of properties to buy, what locations, what prices, what exit strategies to pursue – so that anyone joining the syndicate will know what to expect from the investment decisions taken. It's also important to have agreements in place covering what happens if one member dies or just decides they want to leave the syndicate. A good lawyer will create a suitable syndicate document, and details of some suggested firms are listed in 'Taking it further' at the back of this book.

Pros – A great way of diversifying your portfolio. Can give you access to a wider range of purchases than may be possible from your own funds. A good way to reduce risk and it can be fun.

Cons – Not a choice for someone who wants great flexibility and who wants to have a particularly active involvement in the properties or who wants to make use of the property themselves. It also might not suit a control freak. You may also dilute gains from higher performing properties.

The Internet

I couldn't write a chapter on where to find property to buy without making reference to the massive wealth of information and opportunities that can be found on the Internet. Any self-respecting estate agent, property consultant or auction house will have their property inventory listed on the Internet as part of their overall marketing plan.

The great thing about the Internet is that it is available to you 24/7 unlike traditional shop-based estate agents, so you can browse properties without getting up from your chair and the filtering process is streamlined. Lots of UK properties are now listed with a gallery of photos so you can 'view' the property and some even have video 'virtual tours'. This is all very helpful to a property investor and can save lots of wasted journeys to see properties which simply aren't suitable.

Some companies – especially those which specialize in investment property either in the UK or abroad – don't actually have an office or shop, but simply have a 'virtual' shop window on the Internet. They will invest time and resources into their website, rather than have a conventional high-street presence, in the knowledge that their customer base is huge and worldwide.

The Internet is also a fantastic tool for research. If you are looking to find out whether the price you are considering paying for a property is reasonable, then within a few minutes surfing the Net, you will be able to find lots of comparables. You can find out what other properties are available for sale.

As well as locating properties to buy and using the Net as a comparison tool for prices, you can also use the Internet for, among other things:

1 Subscribing to newsletters from property websites that give factual information about areas of interest.
2 Researching areas of high government and local authority spending so you can find areas of regeneration or pockets where prices are potentially below market value.

The Internet is also used by niche companies to sell properties that you wouldn't necessarily find elsewhere, for example repossessions. Buying repossessed property is one strategy for finding property at below market value but it is becoming increasingly difficult to find. However, there are specialist online companies which have databases of repossessed property available for sale.

In 'Taking it further' I have listed a number of property-related websites that I find useful and you'll also find links to these on www.makingmoneyfromproperty.tv

Pros – Masses of information readily available at your fingertips. You can 'view' any number of properties without actually stepping out of your own home. Also great for researching price comparisons and general information relating to property investing.

Cons – There is nothing quite like seeing property 'in the flesh', so while using the Internet can help you to filter which properties you are interested in, it is no substitute for actually visiting them yourself.

Networking and exhibitions

In today's marketplace there are numerous property seminars, exhibitions, tradeshows and other networking opportunities. For the price of entry into any of these events (usually less than £10 and very often free) you can gain access to a wealth of information about property investing. While they can seem a bit overwhelming at first, and you should be prepared for a whole host of salespeople keen to tell you that their product and location is the best thing since sliced bread, they can provide an invaluable opportunity for research.

Some of the property shows are now so large that you could easily spend an entire day scouring the aisles for information and listening to the various debates and presentations taking place. Many of the shows also run a programme of seminars throughout the day – fronted by experts in their field. For the price of entry into the main event, you can often take part in the seminars too and fill up on all sorts of useful information.

Pros – Opportunity to get lots of information all under one roof. Ability to talk directly to people who are expert in the product they are selling and to hear from industry experts.

Cons – You may be subject to hungry salespeople keen to sell you property. The sheer breadth of information available can be overwhelming and confusing.

Advertising and leafleting

One proactive approach which you can take to finding property is to place adverts in local newspapers or magazines saying that you are keen to buy and that people should get in touch with you if they have property to sell. This can often encourage people who may have been thinking about it for some time into actually doing something.

Alternatively, you can create a leaflet saying the same thing and deliver this to the properties in an area in which you are interested in buying – whether they are for sale or not. Again, people can often be tempted into selling if they think a good offer is on the table.

Pros – You may unearth properties which otherwise may not come onto the market. You will deal directly with the vendor and therefore may be able to negotiate a better price. You can be very targeted about areas in which you want to invest.

Cons – It's quite labour intensive and time-consuming and you need to be able to act quickly if you get a positive response. You need to be sure of the price that should be offered, since you will often be driving the negotiation.

£ Martin's tip

Buying property

Whichever methods you decide to employ to help you find properties to buy, there are certain general things which you should look for in the property itself. Here are just some of the things that may help in narrowing down your choice of properties:

- Look for properties that you can improve either in terms of internal layout and arrangement of accommodation or by means of redecoration or refurbishment. This way you can add value to the property if you are aiming to sell on.
- Try to buy properties on large plots or that have outbuildings which could be converted. This adds extra versatility to a property and can make it stand out from the crowd. There could be an option to build other properties on the land.
- If you are buying a property in an area where there are lots of similar houses, choose properties that are differentiated in some way such as end of terraces, corner plots or properties that can be easily extended. Once again, this will give you the

chance to add value to your property and for it to rise above the competition.

- Buy in areas where it is increasingly popular to live. Regeneration and other investment into the area are good indicators of things being 'on the up'. We'll discuss more about location in the next chapter.

Summary

In this chapter we have looked at the pros and cons of buying property through:

- Estate agents
- Property finders/consultants
- Auctions
- Investment clubs
- Syndicates
- The Internet
- Networking and exhibitions
- Advertising and leafleting.

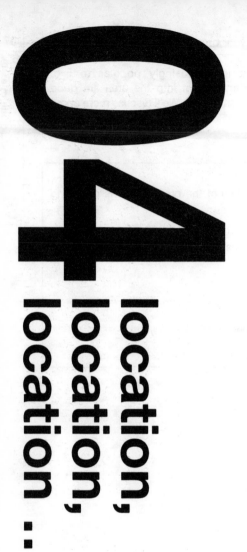

04

location, location, location...

In this chapter you will learn about:
- Concentric Ring Theory or the 'ripple effect'
- buying near 'tenant pools'
- regeneration zones
- how to value property effectively
- the importance of postcodes

... the Golden Rule and how to break it

Everybody knows that the golden rule of property investment is location, location, location. In this chapter we talk about what to look for in terms of location of property and what strategies the experts adopt.

Hopefully, you now know what resources are available to you to help you find properties to buy. Most property developers will employ more than one approach, they might speak regularly to estate agents in the area where they invest, but will also attend property auctions, and are most likely to be members of investment clubs or at the very least on the mailing lists of property companies.

Soon you will be in a position where all sorts of property opportunities are presented to you. The trick is to filter through all these 'possibles' to find those which are 'probables' and then ultimately those which are certainties. It's worth mentioning here that it is really important not to get too emotional or hung up on a certain deal or property. If you think you want to buy a particular property, have done your research as far as you are able and start down the route of buying it, sooner or later you will come across a deal from which you have to walk away. It's inevitable. Lots of things can change from when you start to research a property, to you actually closing on the deal. There are so many variables and it is vitally important that you keep your head. Sometimes, after further research, the deal may simply not stack up – or perhaps someone else is interested in the same property as you and the price gets pushed up. Stick to your budget, objectives and what your research has revealed to you, and, whatever you do, don't be hell bent on buying a property at any cost. If it's a good deal and you lose it ... chill out – there will always be others. There are literally hundreds and hundreds of properties on which you could spend your hard earned cash, all of which may fit with your chosen strategy. So don't kid yourself that the renovation project that is getting lots of bids at auction is the only deal for you. One of the key traits of a successful property investor is knowing when to walk away.

So, on to the process of sifting through all the possible opportunities and whittling them down to ones to actually pursue.

The first rule of property investing

So, the first rule of property investing is location. But what actually makes a good location? This goes back to your chosen strategy. For example: if your chosen strategy revolves around holiday lets, then a good location is going to be a place which already attracts lots of holidaymakers. This might sound obvious, but you'd be surprised by the number of people I have come across who have invested in a holiday let property that is tucked away in the back of beyond, miles off the beaten track. Yes, it's got a lovely view, a fantastic natural well in the garden and is really peaceful, but romantic as this may be, chances are, it's not going to attract the quantity of holidaymakers to make it viable. Again, it's all about not letting your heart rule your head.

Rarely does a property fit within more than one camp when it comes to choosing the right location. To give you an example, take my home city of Bath: a wonderful historic city which is a World Heritage Site and a thriving tourist destination, but which also has its fair share of industry and commerce, and a university too. Bath as a location could work for me if my strategy is holiday lets, student lets, corporate lets and even traditional residential buy to let. Sounds like I can't lose. I could buy any property in the city and if I can't make it work as a holiday let, I can just stick in some tenants and 'Hey presto', I've got a student let, right? Wrong. While this sounds good in theory, in practice these markets are all distinct and the location *within a location* becomes critical. Tourists will want to holiday in a central part of the city. They'll be drawn to an older, historic building that is more authentic, and ideally it will be somewhere with views. A corporate tenant is more likely to prefer a quieter, residential suburb where there is ample parking and facilities nearby; a student will need to be in close proximity to the campus, on public transport routes and have shops close at hand; and a residential buy to let tenant might have proximity to schools and work to consider. So while it *might* be possible to find a property that fits all three markets, it is better to stick to your chosen strategy and find a property that works REALLY well for that market, rather than QUITE well for all markets.

Martin's tip

When deciding what properties to buy, look for those that suit your chosen strategy and are the best that you can find for this purpose. Long term they are likely to provide a better investment than properties that are just okay for a number of different objectives.

What makes a good location?

The 'des res'

You probably know within your own home city or town which areas have and will always be popular. 'The Posh End of Town' will always command a premium price over other areas. Sometimes, these higher prices are down to the fact that this area has better facilities or maybe the pattern of development here has led to a better environment: wider roads and green spaces, for example. The style of architecture and age of the buildings can also impact on a particular area's desirability. If you know which areas are the most sought after, then property in these areas should always be on your radar – providing you buy at the right price (more on this in Chapter 7). If the area has been and continues to be popular, then unless something unexpected happens, it will always be so. These 'des res' areas become a self-fulfilling prophecy. Because people want to live there, businesses will locate themselves there. Nicer shops and restaurants will open, safe in the knowledge that they have a catchment of well-heeled customers close by. If your property falls within the right postcode, then you will find that it holds its value better in these locations. Owner-occupiers will aspire to live in this area and tenants will feel privileged to rent here, so you will always find buyers and renters for your property.

The trick is not to get too carried away and pay too much for your property in these locations. If it is a desirable area, sellers may be inclined to pitch the price above what even the local market can command, and chance that they may get lucky. Do your research and know what price to pay, and don't get swayed into paying a premium over and above what the location commands.

In prime locations, keep your eyes open for:

- New build projects – where you may be able to buy 'off plan' and therefore get in at a discounted or undervalued price (we talk more about buying off plan in Chapter 6).
- Renovation projects – perhaps a change-of-use property (i.e. a shop, church, school or commercial building that can be converted into residential use).
- Land to develop – you may be able to buy a plot of land where you can build a property (see Chapter 12 about buying land).

Schools

Anyone with children will tell you how important it is to live in the catchment area of a good school. Parents will readily relocate their whole lives to live in a property that falls within the catchment area of their preferred school. Even if you are not a parent, it is worth taking some time to research which schools are the most sought after in any given location. Clearly, if your strategy is for corporate lets or even student lets, the proximity to the best schools in the area is going to be irrelevant. But it will be important if you are going down the route of traditional buy to let. And if you are investing in a large home suitable for a family, then this factor should be high on your list of things to consider.

If you don't live in the area then you can find out about local schools from the estate agents and letting agents who operate in the area. They should be able to tell you where the most popular schools are and identify the catchment area.

Universities, hospitals and employment pools

Universities, hospitals and other large employers have one thing in common: they bring with them an abundance of would-be tenants, all looking for property close to where they study or work. In the case of universities, students will want to live within very close proximity to their university, among fellow students. They will not want to travel very far and so if your property isn't in walking distance, it must be on a regular public transport route for it to work as a student let. The same is largely true with hospitals. The very nature of the work (shift patterns) means that many hospital staff will prefer to live within easy reach of the hospital site. Again, the location of the property must fit with your chosen strategy, but in short, buying in areas that are close to universities, hospitals and large employers will prove beneficial if you are investing in:

- student lets
- HMOs
- corporate lets
- traditional buy to let.

Regeneration zones

The really shrewd investor is one step ahead of the game. They will have knowledge of where new commercial and business parks are being built and regeneration is happening, and will buy in these areas before prices rise.

Many UK city centres have undergone massive urban regeneration programmes over recent years. Take the likes of Birmingham, Manchester and Cardiff: years ago the city centres were run-down areas with numerous vacant and boarded up properties. Following local and national government investment of literally millions of pounds for redevelopment, these cities now boast modern, trendy city centre accommodation ripe for purchase with lifestyle and leisure facilities on hand. Old buildings have been either pulled down and replaced with modern, state-of-the-art apartment buildings, or refurbished to what in most cases are exceptionally high standards. Property in these new developments is fashionable and desirable, and values have therefore stood up well. So, again to really make the most out of the market, you should be looking to invest in these types of locations before or during the regeneration programme, not afterwards when the area has already increased in value.

However, a note of caution. Some city centre developments have seen stagnation and even falls in property prices in recent years. This is partly due to supply and demand: too much supply of new properties, particularly one and two bedroom apartments, and not enough demand. Many of these developments were also sold to pure investor clients who all wanted to sell up their investments at the same time – again weakening prices. A safer investment opportunity may be to buy traditional terraced property which has enduring appeal, rather than apartments in a large complex.

Be on the lookout for local authority initiatives that are aimed at regenerating a particular area. It might be that the government body is redeveloping retail, entertainment or other commercial property and not getting involved in residential projects. However, if they are leading the way in regenerating an area, private construction companies will undoubtedly come in to build residential projects.

Consider looking further afield than just the UK market. Many UK cities have already been transformed, and the opportunities that existed 10 years ago are no longer there unless you are particularly diligent with your research.

However, if you open your eyes to city centres elsewhere in Europe and the world, you can find regeneration areas where it is still possible to buy in at very low prices and be at the start of the regeneration process. In particular, consider Central and Eastern European capitals which are now members of the EU and are therefore scheduled to receive massive EU handouts to modernize their main cities. Old communist-style blocks of flats are readily being replaced with twenty-first-century apartment buildings suited not only to ex-pats but the new wealthy local market. This is happening in places like Budapest, Prague and Bucharest. If you can do your research and manage to apply the same diligence that you would to your UK purchases, then these locations offer great potential.

Supply and demand

This is a very simple rule to follow. Buy in areas where the supply of property is less than the demand. Very obvious, I know, but again inexperienced investors still get this wrong. Maybe the location is right but their timing is all wrong. If you had bought city centre Birmingham before, during or shortly after the massive urban regeneration programme, you would have probably seen a good increase in the value of your property. Even if rents are no longer what they used to be (rents in city centre Birmingham have actually fallen) you will probably still be doing all right because you bought at the right time and at the right price. Roll the clock forwards a few years and there is a glut of buy to let property, because everyone jumped on the bandwagon, causing rent and prices to fall. Quite simply, supply exceeds demand.

If you are looking to rent out your property, find out what competition you will have from other landlords. The same goes if you are buying to sell. You need to know that there is more demand for property in the area you are considering than there is supply. This will put upwards pressure on prices.

We look more at the factors influencing supply and demand in Chapter 6.

Buy near water

There are some property investors who always look to buy near water. This may not seem to be an obvious strategy, but it is one which makes a lot of sense. The thing about water is that there will be a limited number of properties that can be located near it (and when I say near it, I mean within walking distance). Properties with sea views will always be in higher demand than those without. People like looking out at water. It is aesthetically pleasing and, of course, guarantees that you aren't going to be overlooked by other buildings.

Obviously issues such as coastal erosion and flooding need to be assessed, but in general there are profits to be had in being by the sea or river.

Now let's break the rules and apply another theory.

Concentric Ring Theory – the 'ripple effect'

I really like this strategy. It's a way of breaking the rules and still making the deal work. Concentric Ring Theory is about buying in locations that are *outside* of the 'prime' area (i.e. 'des res' but which are close enough to benefit from price increases in that area). Imagine dropping a stone into a pool of water and watching the ripples. Where the stone hits is the prime area – the 'des res' where prices are at their highest and property is most sought after. As the ripples expand outwards, these 'rings' mark the areas which aren't right in the centre but which will still benefit from above average demand and growth. This principle also applies to city centre locations that are being extensively regenerated.

As prices in the prime area continue to rise and become expensive relative to incomes in the area, some people will get priced out of the market but they still aspire to living in the 'des res' area. Because they can't afford it, they will buy in a secondary location very close to the 'des res' area – possibly where they can still tap into the services and community of the prime location. Owner-occupier buyers will compromise on

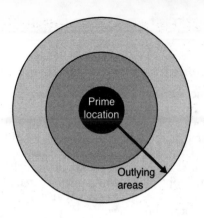

figure 4.1 Concentric Ring Theory

where they live in order to buy a larger, better property and so they move out to this secondary location. Prices in this outer 'ring' will rise as a consequence until they also become too expensive, at which point buyers will move out further. A good example of this is the Clifton area of Bristol city. Years ago, the 'posh' place to live was Clifton. It was considered fashionable and desirable but as prices increased many people couldn't afford it, so they bought property in neighbouring Redland. Nowadays, both districts command high property prices. Redland got pulled up by Clifton and has benefited from its proximity to Clifton. Now the influence is spreading even further to other neighbouring areas.

So, if you are a property investor wanting to buy shrewdly, these neighbouring areas that fall within the 'concentric rings' of the prime location offer some interesting possibilities. It is important to do your research and don't look at any one consideration in isolation. Just because a property is in a neighbouring district and has the chance to be pulled up by the prime location alone isn't a ticket to property investment success. It should still be in a location that sits with your chosen strategy (i.e. have buy to let tenants, holidaymakers, corporate clients or whatever is your target rental).

How to value property effectively – knowing how much to pay

When buying any property it is vital that the price you pay is either a true reflection of the current market value or, better still, a genuine discount. You should gather as many like-for-like comparables as you can in the immediate vicinity of any property that you are considering buying. The quickest and easiest way to evaluate the value of a property is to scour estate agents and the Internet for similar properties for sale in the area. However, be aware that the price at which a property is offered for sale doesn't necessarily reflect its true market value – anyone selling a property is probably looking for the highest price they can achieve and a common complaint against estate agents is that they will place properties on the market for too high a price in order to be given the business by the seller.

A better way of gauging the right price to pay for a property is to use a slightly more analytical approach and dig out comparable properties that have actually SOLD recently in the area. In the language of chartered surveyors and estate agents, this is known as the 'comparable sales' method of valuing property.

The comparable sales method is sometimes also referred to as the 'inferred analysis' of property values. Basically it involves estimating the value of a house by comparing it with the prices of similar properties that have been sold in comparable locations within a recent period of time. This is a far more realistic guide to the value of a property than looking at the prices at which properties are listed on the market. It works on the principle that a property is worth only what someone is actually prepared to pay for it!

To value a property in this way, you need to collect data on comparable properties. By far the most accurate source of data is the Land Registry which records details of all property transactions that occur. Their website is an invaluable tool (www.landregistry.gov.uk – the official website of the UK Land Registry). Another useful tool is an up-to-date property transaction database such as www.mouseprice.com which is fed with information from the Land Registry. You could also use any of the following websites:

www.upmystreet.com Helps you find out everything from actual property prices in a neighbourhood to its favourite newspaper.

www.rightmove.co.uk Quotes asking prices, not the price at which homes sell. It's valuable to show trends in the current market, but should be looked at in conjunction with other data.

www.hometrack.co.uk Reports are based on prices agreed by agents between sellers and buyers. They may be open to renegotiation. As with Rightmove they're a useful guide to current trends.

www.nethouseprices.com Provides access to UK house prices in England, Scotland and Wales, as recorded by the Land Registry (since April 2000) and the Registers of Scotland (since May 2000).

www.nationwide.co.uk This details the Nationwide House Prices survey which is often reported in the press.

www.halifax.co.uk Another benchmark used to indicate how property is performing is the Halifax House Price Index. This survey is useful for showing national and regional house price information and how prices have changed over time.

You can find details of all these sites and more on www.makingmoneyfromproperty.tv.

We take another more analytical approach to evaluating the price of property in Chapter 7.

The importance of postcodes

It is vital that you do your research on postcodes and find out the postcode of your property before you decide to buy it. In some parts of the country, for example London, the postcode can literally add or detract thousands of pounds to/from a property's value. To complicate matters, the boundaries for postcodes can literally be one side of the street or the other. People are sometimes sensitive that certain postcodes have an association with a given area and property values can therefore benefit. A property located in a very desirable postcode, even if it is right on the boundary of the postcode, can command a higher price than an identical property across the road that falls into another postcode. Likewise, a poor postcode will have a detrimental effect on property prices and it may take a long time to lose the stigma of such.

Summary

In this chapter we have looked at:

- Concentric Ring Theory or the 'ripple effect'.
- Buying near schools, hospitals, employment hotspots and other 'tenant pools'.
- Regeneration zones.
- How to value property effectively – knowing how much to pay.
- The importance of postcodes.

05

rental strategy ...

In this chapter you will learn about:
- how to work out rental yields
- long-term lets
- your responsibilities as a landlord
- short-term holiday lets
- guaranteed rental income programmes

... helping your purchase bear fruit

As we have already discussed, buying property to rent out is an excellent strategy for making money from property. Buy in the right areas, where demand is strong, and buy at the right price and you could find yourself generating a good, healthy profit from owning rental property. The 'buy to let' model has seen a massive upsurge in the UK in recent years and there are a number of reasons for this.

First, the mere fact that property has increased so much in value has meant that it is increasingly difficult for people to actually be able to afford to buy property. Nowadays, the first-time buyer has to have a pretty sizeable chunk of money as a deposit to get themselves onto the property ladder. This has meant that young people are forced to rent for a number of years while they either save up the cash for the deposit or manoeuvre themselves into a financial position that allows them to buy. The time taken for young people to buy their own house after moving out of the family home has increased substantially and this has therefore created enormous demand for rental property. It's not uncommon for young people to rent for many years and first-time buyers can be in their mid-thirties. And while there's demand, there will be supply – property investors happy to buy houses to rent out to these people.

Similarly, the changing demographics of the UK has meant that there is more demand for rental property, particularly at the lower end of the market (i.e. the 1–2 bed flats and smaller houses). People are putting off getting married and settling down until they are older compared with previous generations. The young are now more likely to go to university, travel, live with friends or cohabit with a partner before actually settling down permanently and committing to buying a house. At the other end of the spectrum, sadly couples are more likely to divorce or separate (thus having a requirement for say, two smaller houses rather than one large family home) and financial circumstances will often dictate that at least one party rents. Finally, the population of the UK is on the increase as a result of immigration. Migrant workers also create a pool of tenants. All of this has led to a greater demand for rental property than has ever been experienced before.

Another factor fuelling the buy to let market over the past decade or so, has been the availability of money to buy investment property. Over the last 10 years we have experienced lower interest rates than have been on offer for half a century. People are wooed into taking out mortgages to acquire buy to let property because loans have become cheap. It has been very easy to borrow, with lenders falling over themselves to offer the cheapest rates. While interest rates are low, it is easy to make the maths work and so more people have been tempted to go for it – working on the simple principle that if they can borrow at, say, 5–6 per cent p.a. and yet generate a net yield greater than this, then they are going to be 'quids in'. We cover working out rental yields later in this chapter.

The availability of specific 'buy to let' mortgages has also made this whole process so much easier, with lenders developing specific mortgage products to satisfy the demands of such property investors.

The idea of buying property, renting it out, letting someone else effectively pay your mortgage for you while you profit from the capital growth, makes a lot of sense. However, before you get carried away by how simple it all sounds, you should remember that being a landlord isn't just about buying rental properties. There are legal obligations placed on you to keep the property in good working order and if you buy a HMO (houses in multiple occupation) there is other red tape of which you need to be aware, which we discuss later. Many first-time landlords also underestimate the costs of maintaining and managing the property and, once this has been taken into consideration, the investment may not always be so attractive. There is also the question of the commitment and responsibility that you will need to take on.

In this chapter, we are going to look at how to get a rental strategy right. Among other things, I've provided a list of costs to consider when buying property to let, and tips on what type of property to look for. I'm also going to teach you how to present your property for rental so you can differentiate yourself from other similar properties and we'll also take a brief look at short-term lets as a rental strategy.

Before I start explaining about ways of executing a successful rental strategy, let's just consider its merits against buying property to sell. Think of property being like a fruit tree. The fruit (let's say apples) is the rental income that you derive on a regular basis from the investment. To keep the tree producing rosy, juicy apples we must look after the tree – ensure it gets water and sunshine so that it can grow and thrive. Provided that I 'manage' my investment well, it will continue to produce apples for evermore. The profit I make on apples may not be as much as if I were to chop down the tree and sell the wood, but it is a continuing stream of income that will keep coming in for as long as I want. If I wanted to maximize my profits from the tree all in one go, I might choose to chop down the tree and sell the wood. This way I get one big hit of profit but once that is gone, it is gone for good and I can no longer benefit from the apple harvest. The same principles apply to property.

As a property investor, you will be aiming to build a portfolio of properties (how big or small is entirely up to you) like the apple orchard. There may be times when you chop down one or two trees (i.e. sell some properties), but the majority of the portfolio should remain intact to continue to produce a return.

Successful property investors rarely sell property. They will always buy and hold. There is no point growing an orchard and then chopping it all down for the quick hit when you can get a very good return from selling the continuing supply of apples!

How to work out rental yields

Being a buy to let investor, it is important to understand a very important term: *yield*. This is the term used to describe your profit. To work out your gross rental yield, you divide the annual rental income by the purchase price of the property. So very simply, if you had a property worth £100,000 that generated £10,000 of rent per year, then your gross yield would be 10 per cent (£10,000 divided by £100,000).

gross yield = <u>annual rental</u>
purchase price

However, a more accurate indicator of the return you are going to get is to work out the **net** rental yield. This is the return after property management, lettings fees, maintenance and repair and other running costs have been taken into consideration, and gives you a far more realistic view of your return. If you have a mortgage on the property though, you do not take the mortgage payments into consideration when working out net yields. Net yields are also a better way of comparing properties since while on the face of it a given property might produce a better annual return, if the running costs are high, the net yield may not be so attractive. In the example above, if the annual gross rent is £10,000 but you have agency fees of 10 per cent and various other monthly outgoings of say £200 per month, then:

Gross annual rent	£10,000
Less agency fees @ 10 per cent	£1,000
Less outgoings of £200 per month	£2,400
Net rental income is	£6,600

£6,600 divided by £100,000 is 6.6 per cent. This figure represents the net rental yield.

net yield = <u>annual rental less running costs</u>
                        purchase price

🍴 Food for thought

Gross yield is vanity. Net yield is sanity.

Just to say, yields anywhere from about 6 per cent to 10 per cent are considered good and provided that everything else about the property stacks up, if a property is achieving this level of return then it is worth investing in. The UK buy to let market currently averages a little less than this – around 4.5 per cent.

Long-term lets

When you talk about buy to let, most people take this to mean buying property that is then let out on a residential basis over a long term (minimum six months). If you are going to buy this type of property, you should first consider your target market and then look for properties that will suit this type of tenant. Nowadays, tenants can come from a cross-section of society: everyone from students, young couples, working professionals and families to people on housing benefits, migrant workers, divorcees and people relocating. However, as previously discussed you need to decide on your strategy and which sector of the market you are going to aim for, and then buy properties that will suit them.

As a general rule, the type of properties that you should be considering for long-term let purposes are:

- **Studio flats** – particularly in inner city areas. These will appeal to working professionals (who may want a base just during the week) and students (who may not be able to afford anything larger). Don't buy studios in rural locations though as the tenant pool here will be too restrictive. Also be careful that you are not buying on a development with literally hundreds of identical properties unless there is a good demand. Tenants can be remarkably disloyal and will move out of your property into a new one if it comes onto the market at the same or a lower price.

- **One-bedroom flats** – Again these appeal to young professionals (couples and singles) and corporate lets if located in an inner city area close to retail, leisure, entertainment and commerce. They have a wider appeal than studio flats given that they offer more accommodation.

- **Two-bedroom flats** – although more expensive than one-bedroom flats and studios, two-bedroom flats offer more versatility. As well as appealing to young professionals as before, they may also attract sharers and young families. Try to buy only two-bedroom flats that offer car parking since it is highly likely that your tenants will own cars.

- **Two- and three-bedroom houses** – smaller houses are very desirable with families and divorcees as well as working professionals. They can also work for students and sharers, although if this is the market you are aiming at, it is better to buy low-maintenance properties (without a large garden, for example).

- **Larger houses** – These lend themselves well to students and sharers if they are located close to city centres and/or universities. Larger houses in more rural or residential locations will appeal primarily to families so here the size of the garden, availability of parking, proximity to schools and shops become important considerations.

So, going back to what we have already discussed in Chapter 2, it is crucial to know your strategy and only buy properties that are suitable for your target market.

Finding good tenants

As a landlord, you will want to attract good tenants. There is no point in pursuing a buy to let strategy if all you are doing is providing free board and lodgings to non-paying tenants who don't look after the place. My aim is to identify 'A1' tenants. These are tenants who are financially stable, capable of paying above-average rents and who respect and look after the property. If you want to attract A1 tenants, you should commit to ensuring that your properties are well maintained and any appliances supplied are in good working order. If you have high standards then you will generally be rewarded with respectful tenants.

£ Martin's tip

Ten tips for avoiding problem tenants

1 Compile an application form that includes details of the last three years' previous residences.

2 Ask for a copy of a driving licence, passport or other proof of identity.

3 Consider using a tenant credit referencing service. You can get a full reference carried out on potential tenants for less than £30.

4 Ask for a copy of the last three or six months bank statements.

5 Trust your instincts. Poorly dressed and poorly behaved tenants may require further investigation. Beware of people who seem to be in a rush to move in and are not forthcoming with references and information.

6 Make unannounced visits to the property to see how it is being looked after. You can also confirm that the tenant is actually living there, as some tenants use property as a post drop for benefit and other fraud.

7 Insist they take out insurance to cover their own belongings and the house's contents.

8 Take six weeks' deposit to avoid the scenario where the tenant does not pay the last month's rent, then leaves but there is damage to the property which needs to be paid for.

9 Make sure you have adequate and specific rental property insurance in place that includes cover for injury to people residing in or visiting the premises.

10 Always make sure you have a fully signed 'Assured Shorthold Tenancy Agreement' in place before the tenant moves in.

Assured Shorthold Tenancy Agreements (AST's)

An AST is a legally binding agreement that gives rights to both you and the tenant. It allows you easily to evict them if they do not follow certain rules and regulations, and legally protects your position in other ways. You should not allow a tenant to move into your property before one of these has been signed. You can pick up standard ASTs from stationery shops, or have your lawyer draw up something specific.

Here are a number of rental markets that you could consider:

Corporate lets

Here you let your property out in its entirety to a company for use by its employees. Very often the company will sign up for a long period (typically up to three years but can also be as short as six months) and they are responsible for paying the rent rather than the individual tenants. The kind of individual you can expect to be living in your property will be a working professional and it is not uncommon that the tenants are only resident from Monday to Thursday evening – returning to their own homes for weekends.

Your property should be very well presented and offer modern appliances and quality fixtures and fittings to attract corporate lets, and be located close to business/industry with good transport links. A garden is less important for this type of let, but close proximity to leisure facilities, good restaurants and entertainment will attract better lets.

Very often, it will be a condition of the let that the property is professionally managed, so you will need to take into consideration management fees when working out your budgets.

Large luxury homes make good corporate lets, as do modern apartments that perhaps offer onsite leisure facilities.

Professional lets

These are also highly desirable tenants since they are in paid employment and can, therefore, usually demonstrate that they are financially stable. However, most buy to let landlords aim at this sector of the market and so the competition is tough. While years ago a working professional wanting to let a house or flat might have had to choose from a small number of poorly maintained and poorly decorated properties, nowadays they can pick from a large number of modern, well-presented houses or flats. To make your property stand out from the rest, you should provide modern appliances and high-quality fixtures and fittings. Modern technology such as broadband or wireless Internet and digital TV are also an advantage and a modern kitchen and white goods are essential. It is better to be located near some good restaurants and shops, supermarkets and entertainment facilities and car parking is also a must in this sector.

Student/hospital lets

One of the main considerations here is the location of the property. Without stating the blindingly obvious, it needs to be near a university, school or college, or hospital if you are planning on renting out to medical people. Many students will rely on walking, cycling or public transport, so you need to be mindful of this. Larger properties with good-sized kitchens are best. Forget gardens: they probably won't be maintained, but it is a bonus if there is some outdoor storage space for tenants to keep bicycles, etc. Focus on the size of the bedrooms, since they will serve as both sleeping and studying areas for your tenants. You don't really need to provide a lounge (very often the downstairs reception rooms are utilized as bedrooms) but it is helpful if there is more than one bathroom. Clearly, don't waste money on putting in luxury fixtures and fittings – durable and 'fit for purpose' are best.

Houses in multiple occupation (HMOs)

There has been lots of talk in recent years about HMOs or houses in multiple occupation. The legal definition of a house in multiple occupation is a 'house which is occupied by persons who do not form a single household'. The term also includes any purpose-built or converted flat whose occupants do not form a single household.

If you have property that you are renting out which is divided into a number of separate accommodation units (such as bedsits or flats) the property is probably a HMO. If so, then as an owner of a HMO, there are various requirements that you must satisfy. These are legally enforceable and cover standards of fire safety, general management and upkeep of the HMO's common parts.

It's important to note that HMOs are divided into those which require a licence and those that do not. A property can be in multiple occupation and yet not be classified as a licensable HMO. If it sounds complicated, that's because it is, and there are some very specific criteria, rules and regulations surrounding HMOs.

If you are unsure whether your property falls under HMO rules, then you should contact your local authority and speak to the HMO department. They will be able to advise you if the property is a HMO and what you need to do if it is.

Categories of houses in multiple occupation

There are various categories of HMO which are listed below. It must be stressed that the inclusion of a particular class of premises in the list (e.g. guesthouse) does not mean that it is necessarily a HMO. The circumstances of the occupancy will determine this.

Category A

Houses occupied as individual rooms, bedsits and flats which are considered to have a number of rooms for individual rent. There may be shared amenities such as bathroom and/or toilet and kitchen. In these types of properties, each room, bedsit or flat is rented out separately.

Category B

Houses occupied on a shared basis, for example where students live as a single household unit for some activities (i.e. they share kitchen and living room facilities), but for others they are separate (i.e. they have their own rooms for sleeping and studying). Although most common among students, it is now becoming more popular for other groups of people such as working professionals to come together in the house and share some amenities, but individuals have their own bedrooms.

Category C

Houses described as 'houses let in lodgings' (i.e. catering for lodgers on a small scale). The lodger does not live as part of the main household. Normally the owner of the property will live there as well.

Category D

This category applies to houses generally referred to as hostels, guesthouses, and bed and breakfast accommodation. They will provide accommodation for people with no other permanent place of residence. This category would also include hotels, guesthouses, and bed and breakfast establishments used by local authorities to house homeless persons whose only financial support is state benefits.

Category E

Hostels, homeless shelters, nursing homes or other homes that provide board and personal care for people in need due to old age, disablement, dependence on alcohol or drugs, or mental disorder. These houses require registration under the Registered Homes Act 1984. Unlike Category D houses, these houses would provide permanent accommodation for people with nowhere else to go; this would be their only home and would include a level of support not normally present in Category D accommodation which provides a home only for the short term.

Category F

Houses which have been converted to provide self-contained accommodation, usually via an access door off a common area. There would be no sharing of amenities with occupiers of other dwellings except that they may share a main entrance.

There is no clear boundary between each of these categories and a house (or even part of a house) might move between categories over a period of time.

Additional requirements of HMOs

Guidelines on what additional measures need to be put in place for HMOs vary between different local authorities so it is worth checking this out early on in your property search if you believe that you may fall under this legislation. However, as a minimum you can expect to have to consider:

- installing fire doors
- self-closing mechanism on all internal doors
- integrated smoke and heat detectors
- emergency lighting
- fire escapes and fire extinguishers
- upgraded ceilings, floors and staircases.

It is vital that a landlord of a HMO complies with the necessary requirements. Failure to do so is a criminal offence and can result in prosecution and heavy fines.

Shared occupancy properties

Properties that are rented out to a number of different people under separate tenancy agreements but which do not fall under the government HMO definition, will be shared occupancy properties. You can expect a property to be split up into rooms, which are then rented by separate individuals on a weekly or monthly basis. There is a fine line between shared occupancy properties and HMOs and it is important to check with the relevant authorities to determine into which category your property falls.

Shared occupancy properties will require certain standards of safety and Building Regulations but may avoid some of the more onerous requirements needed for a full HMO licence. They can, therefore, be potentially easier to establish.

Additional costs of buy to let property

Many first-time landlords make the mistake of not factoring in the additional maintenance and running costs of buy to let property and then wonder why they are not making a good profit. Before committing to buy, try to get accurate figures for the ongoing running costs, and use these to work out your net rental yield. Likely ongoing costs include:

- **Maintenance and repairs** – Ultimately you as landlord are responsible for ensuring that the property is in a good state of repair and appliances are in working order. You should set aside an amount from the rental to create an emergency fund to cover the cost of putting things right should they go wrong.
- **Insurance** – You will need to maintain suitable buildings insurance and optional contents insurance.
- **Utilities** – Whether or not your rental figure is to include gas, electricity and water or not is up to you, but even if you pass on the monthly or quarterly bills to your tenants for the amount they use, you are still likely to have to pay for annual inspections and standing charges.
- **Service charges and ground rent** – In the case of flats, you are often still responsible for the service charges paid to the management company for the upkeep of communal areas and ground rents.
- **Agents' fees and set-up costs** – Depending on the level of service you receive from your letting agent, you may be paying up to 12–14 per cent of the monthly rent to them for the management of the property. Alternatively, you could pay a one-off fee for them to find and vet tenants for you. In both cases you will need to cover expenses for providing references and putting rental agreements in place.
- **Void periods** – An easy thing to overlook, but a savvy investor will also take a view on how many void periods they are likely to experience over a given period of time. Your monthly charges (and mortgage payments) will still be due even when you have no tenants in the property.
- **Council Tax** – Typically your tenant will pay council tax, but you are liable to pay it when the property is vacant albeit

📓 Martin's tip

Top ten tips for buying to let

1 Research the market thoroughly before making any decisions to buy. Analyse local rental demand and what type of tenant is most prevalent in your area. Decide on your chosen rental strategy based on what the area offers (e.g. large company offices nearby, a hospital or university nearby, good schools or trendy bars and restaurants).

2 If your strategy is renting to working professionals then ideally you should have double bedrooms in the property.

3 Choose properties that are near to large sources of potential tenants such as universities, teaching hospitals, commercial centres and industrial science parks.

4 Buy close to transport links if you are renting to working professionals or students. Off-street parking will pay dividends as will some outdoor storage space.

5 If your target market is families, buy properties that offer lots of storage space and have a garage. A garden is a plus for this market, but otherwise avoid large gardens that will require lots of upkeep.

6 Be prepared for hard work – especially if you are going to manage the property yourself.

7 Low-maintenance properties, such as those that have been recently renovated, can be a better bet, particularly if you don't live nearby. If you are new to buy to let, buying your first properties close to home means you are on hand if things go wrong.

8 Ensure that any common parts of the building are well maintained and clean. If you are the freeholder, then this is your responsibility, otherwise ensure that arrangements are made through the leasehold management company. The entrance to the property creates the first and most lasting impression.

9 Consider whether your chosen market will prefer furnished or unfurnished properties. Often unfurnished is more desirable and is certainly less hassle and cost to you.

10 Don't underestimate the additional costs incurred and make sure you do your sums properly before investing.

often at a reduced rate. However, some accommodation let to students is exempt from council tax. Speak to the local council for more details.

Your responsibilities as a landlord

Even if you are going to be using a letting agent to take care of the day-to-day management of your property, there are some responsibilities which you as the landlord still need to cover. These are:

1 You must ensure that there are sufficient fire escapes and fire extinguishers within the property. These must be in good working order. Your local council will be able to give you information on what is required.
2 You will need to show a certificate proving that all gas appliances such as fires and boilers are safe and in good working order, and that the electrical circuits are up to current standards.
3 All soft furnishings and upholstery must be made of fire-retardant material and comply with current fire regulations.

Short-term lets

An alternative rental strategy is to consider short-term lets or holiday lets. There is a huge demand for self-catering holiday rentals of villas, apartments and cottages to supply the growing number of independent travellers keen to take advantage of low-cost airline offers, and organize their own holidays without using a travel agent. The demand is growing every year as broadband Internet connections expand giving quicker web access and more people enjoy a good experience from direct online booking.

What you can charge for a weekly let for a holiday property is far greater than what you could charge in a comparable property on a long-term let. However, it is highly unlikely that you will get 52 weeks of the year rented out and so it is unrealistic to compare income in this way. You should look at overall annual income from any potential holiday let that you are considering and, as with long-term lets, calculate what your gross and net yields are likely to be. This way you can do a more realistic comparison between properties.

Another reason why investors buy holiday let properties is because of the lifestyle attraction of owning a property in an area where you like to go on holiday yourself. Essentially this can mean 'free holidays'. Lots of investors have purchased property abroad with this in mind, and traditional tourism hotspots like Spain and France have, therefore, been a popular choice for the overseas buy to let investor, as well as UK holiday lets. However, if you are going to be using the property yourself during your peak weeks this will have a detrimental impact on your overall return. If you are buying strictly for investment, the own-use element should be secondary to securing the best possible financial return.

There are a number of important considerations to work through when you are considering holiday lets:

Location, location, location

This primary rule doesn't change when you are looking at short-term holiday lets. The location of the property remains the No.1 criteria. If your target market is tourists and holidaymakers, then clearly you need to buy property that is in a popular tourism location. This might sound obvious, but you'd be surprised by the number of people I have come across who have invested in holiday lets that are located away from tourist spots. While this might suit the landlord, if the property is too far away from main attractions and tourism centres, then you'll struggle to get the required level of bookings to justify it. Proximity to major motorways or local airports will be another powerful attraction, as will additional features such as the view, location, swimming pool and accommodation.

Property management and 'meet and greet'

The chances are your rental property won't be in the same vicinity as where you live, so you will need to employ the services of a local lettings company to manage the property for you when you aren't there. They will be responsible for checking over the property at the end of each let and ensuring that all appliances are in working order. They should do a full inventory check and report to you any breakages or damage. Usually a property management company will also subcontract out cleaning and laundry services so you can deal with this aspect at the same time.

Another important role of the property management company will be offering a key holding facility and a meet and greet service, ensuring that there are clear instructions for your arriving guests about how to gain entry to the property.

Clearly, there is a charge for this kind of property management service and the rate varies enormously. You can expect to pay anything from 20 to 40 per cent of your rent depending on the level of service that is being provided. At the upper end of this scale you would expect the property management company to also handle bookings for you and be responsible for finding customers.

Cleaning and laundry

This isn't a consideration when you are doing long-term lets, as tenants will be responsible for their own cleaning and laundry. That changes with a holiday let, and you cannot cut corners on this aspect of your offering. A well-presented property that is spotlessly clean will create a good first impression, and rental guests will be quick to criticize if they find anything that is not up to standard. If you are providing laundry such as bedding and towels, choose high-quality products since these will not only give a better impression but last longer as well. Keep it simple and opt for plain white linens; it is easier to replace and match up and creates a crisp, clean image.

If laundry is being done within the property, you will need to invest in a good quality washer and dryer. The people doing this work will have a lot to do to turn your property around for the next rental (sometimes just a few hours) and so they will need to be able to wash and dry linen quickly. Some management companies offer a 'towel service' whereby you pay an annual charge per towel to have them cleaned before each let.

Advertising for rentals

Some property management companies will also offer an advertising and booking service. If you pass your property over to a tour operator, then they may take on the whole service from inspecting your property prior to letting and grading it accordingly, to advertising for rentals, handling the booking, sending out necessary paperwork to guests, meet and greet, cleaning and laundry and all property management. The charges you will have to pay can amount to 50 per cent or more of the rental income received, but it gives you a true armchair investment as all the responsibility for the property is handed over to them. If you can make it work financially, this option is attractive, as getting involved in the advertising and marketing of your property for rentals can be time-consuming and may not be playing to your strengths. However, if you do decide to take on the marketing and advertising yourself, then there are many and varied ways that you can generate bookings. These could include:

Listing your property with an 'Accommodation only' Internet portal site

Here you will pay an annual fee to have your property listed and the website will then generate traffic. Usually there are no guarantees of the number of enquiries that will be generated, but once you have paid the annual fee (which is typically £100–£200 per property) you don't have to pay for each enquiry that comes to you. You set your own rental rates and come up with your own terms and conditions, which offers far greater flexibility and control to you as the owner than if you contract the property to a tour operator. However, you will be responsible for all aspects of servicing the booking such as meet and greet, cleaning and laundry, etc. Some of the most popular portal sites listing owner-managed holiday properties are:

www.holidaylettings.co.uk
www.ownersdirect.co.uk
www.interhome.co.uk
www.holiday-rentals.co.uk
www.holidaybank.co.uk

See www.makingmoneyfromproperty.tv for more advice.

Developing your own website

The costs of building and hosting your own website have come down considerably. In fact there are website design and build packages that you can use to create extremely professional looking sites free of charge. You just pay the monthly hosting fee.

The trick with websites is to ensure that they are found by people who want what you have to offer. This requires you to invest a certain amount of resources in driving traffic to your site. This is not a straightforward process and is a science in itself; you may want to employ the services of a specialist web design and promotion company.

For details of companies that can help with website design, build and hosting, please refer to Taking it further.

Placing advertisements in national papers and/or relevant publications and on the web

A small advert in a well-chosen magazine, newspaper or website needn't cost a lot but could generate significant booking enquiries. If you know the kind of people who are likely to rent your property, target magazines, websites or newspapers that they are likely to read.

Friends and family

Make sure that you let all your friends and family know that you have a property that is available for rent. Produce some form of simple brochure that they can see and also hand out to their own circle of friends. Make sure that the pictures, in particular, are very attractive. It may be worth investing in professional photography of your property so that it is shown in the best possible light.

Placing advertisements at local clubs

Sometimes the most simple strategies are the best. If you are a member of a gym, sports club or social club then it is worth putting together an advert for your property and displaying it in a prominent location. The fact that you are local and a member of the same club means that anyone interested in the property can talk directly to you.

Featuring your property on a large employer's intranet site

If you work for a large organization or know someone who does, this can give access to a market of possible tenants.

Insurance

You will need to have adequate buildings and contents insurance cover, plus insurance that covers you for any claims that are made against you for any negligence or injury incurred when the client is in your property. It is vital that your insurance company is aware that the property is being used for short-term lets. You will probably have to take out a specialist policy and it is, therefore, worth consulting a specialist insurance broker. Some property management companies may also be able to recommended insurance companies.

Companies specializing in holiday homes insurance are:

- Schofields (www.schofields.ltd.uk), a specialist company offering insurance on UK holiday lets and second homes
- Hiscox (www.hiscox.co.uk) have policies for overseas holiday homes
- Lloyd & Whyte (www.lloydwhyteintl.com) is a specialist provider of insurance solutions for property overseas.

Tax and corporate structure

As with long-term lets, you will be required to pay tax on rental income that you receive but you will able to offset any costs, such as maintenance and management charges, plus 10 per cent of any rental income to allow for wear and tear. It is therefore important to keep good book-keeping records and accounts. The tax you pay will depend on your personal circumstances and you should seek specialist advice from your accountant.

For tax and liability reasons, it might be advisable to operate your holiday lets through a limited company that you set up. You will then be personally protected in case of any legal or liability claims against you. It could also help to create a more professional appearance to your business. Setting up a limited company is not difficult or expensive and your accountant or one of the specialist corporate set-up firms can advise you.

Visit www.companieshouse.gov.uk for more information.

What type of property

Once again you need to do your research and decide what kind of market you are aiming for. This will dictate the most suitable type of property. The location and availability of local attractions will also have an influence on the type of guest who is likely to want to holiday in your property. To give you an example, you could buy a country cottage in a lovely picturesque location in, say, the Lake District. This is likely to attract couples, families and groups who enjoy the outdoors and who will most likely be taking part in outdoor pursuits. It therefore makes sense to buy property that lends itself to this kind of guest – a quaint cottage would appeal to couples and small families yet a large family property with a big kitchen/dining area will be snapped up by groups (say two families holidaying together). Here a large garden with games in it would give you the edge over other properties for rent because it will offer something to entertain children staying at the house.

On the other hand, an investor wanting to do short-term holiday lets in my home city of Bath, could quite happily buy a period flat and still make a good return from renting it to couples and singles. In this case, having a garden would be a negative because it will need tending to – something that holiday renters are not going to do. But it will need to be tastefully furnished in a style in keeping with the period of the property.

Go for luxury

My experience has been that if you aim for a high-quality, 'luxury' property, it will pay dividends. Go for properties that would be the equivalent of four- or five-star rated. It is a false economy to buy low quality property even if you rent it out as a cheap option. These days, holidays are considered essential to surviving the rest of the year rather than being an extravagance, and people are far more discerning when it comes to their choice of accommodation. Our overall standard of living is high; we live daily with modern furnishings and appliances and this is also what we expect when we rent a holiday property. So, don't scrimp on the furnishings and, if you can afford to, add in some luxury items such as a wide-screen TV, a DVD player, PlayStation and/or other games. Air conditioning or central heating (depending on the climate) are essential, and satellite TV, Internet access and outdoor facilities such as a swimming pool will help. If your property doesn't have a pool, you might consider installing a hot tub, which is a very appealing feature.

£ Martin's tip

Research shows that holidaymakers demand clean, well-maintained properties with comfortable facilities and modern safety features. Well-equipped kitchens, bathrooms and bedrooms and efficient central heating or air conditioning systems are accepted as standard. Beds should be clean and in good condition with quality duvets and new bed linen.

There is a holiday rentals market for older, more basic properties (for walkers, people with pets and children, students and lower income families) but you may not be able to demand a high enough rental or attract the right quality of client to make the economics stack up.

Think about the type of activities people are likely to take part in while on holiday in your property. It will help you establish what sort of property is going to be best suited to your target market. In my portfolio, I have properties in a Canadian ski resort (www.bigwhitechaletrental.com). While they all offer very high-end accommodation, it is the larger chalets, which can sleep up to 15 people, that are in most demand. My two-bed apartment which is also beautiful and well located, is requested less. Part of the reason for this is that skiing is an activity in which people tend to take part in groups, either extended families or groups of friends. Remember also the changing social demographics. When divorcees remarry there are often children from both sides of the relationship and they may all get together on holidays.

How to market your property effectively for rental

Some investors will choose to adopt the DIY approach to managing and letting their property. They will take on the responsibility of marketing the property for rental and handling enquiries themselves. Clearly, this saves on charges and fees, but this saving needs to be balanced with the amount of time and effort that will have to be put in to generate the required level of bookings. This might not be your core strength. Don't forget, you are a property investor, not a tour operator. However, if you do decide to adopt the DIY approach, here are some useful pointers on how to maximize your enquiries and bookings:

- Are you able to cater for short breaks, especially to destinations served by low-cost airlines? UK holidaymakers are taking fewer two-week holidays and are taking more short breaks (two to four days), weekends and one-week holidays than ever before, and they're often booking within just a few weeks of departure. The logistics of cleaning and organising the changeovers is more demanding, but the income to be made is far more lucrative if you are able to be flexible.

- Make the 'out-of-season' possibilities more appealing by finding out what your guests could be doing in the local area. Are there nature reserves, national gardens, good quality golf, walking, traditional festivals or annual fairs? What are the local highlights or places of entertainment that your guests might like to seek out when the season is less busy? The more ideas you give to your renters, the more they will want to experience it for themselves and the more likely they will be to return.

- If you find you have vacant periods you could offer a discount on the standard price three to four weeks before the vacant dates.

- Stairgates, highchairs, travel cots and other child safety measures are imperative if you wish to attract families. A box of 'rainy-day' and beach toys is also a thoughtful touch that holidaymakers appreciate. Provide heating/air conditioning, hairdryers, outdoor furniture and barbecues where required.

- Most people have mobile phones nowadays but it is still advisable to have a telephone landline open for incoming calls but blocked for all but emergency outgoing calls. In some countries, this might be a legal requirement. Many holidaymakers also expect an Internet access point.

- Provide a Visitor Book and encourage people to leave comments. It can not only give you valuable feedback, but often people write positive things in Visitor Books which you can use as quotes from satisfied guests in future marketing initiatives.

- Develop your own website and make sure that you have lots of photographs of the property on there for people to see. It may be worth getting a professional photographer to take these shots for you. Pictures of the surrounding area are also helpful and can be obtained from the local tourist board websites as long as you check copyright issues first. If you have access to drawings of the layout of the accommodation, these can help people visualize the internal space. You don't have to be a techno genius to develop a professional looking website. There are lots of online tools that enable you to develop one yourself with very little technical expertise. You will have to pay for a company to host the site, but this should cost no more that about £20 per month.

Guaranteed rental income programmes

One final word on buy to let investments. If you start actively looking for properties to buy on the Internet, in specialist property publications or at trade shows you will undoubtedly come across companies offering guaranteed rental income schemes. Here the vendor (usually a developer or agent selling new build properties) will offer a set level of return in the early years, say 6 per cent per annum for two years. This is to compensate for the fact that it can be difficult to generate rents on the open market on a property that is brand new and in an area which might still be developing. The local infrastructure and facilities might still be in their infancy (or not there at all yet) and so the ability to rent out may be hindered.

My thoughts on guaranteed rental schemes in general are: 'beware'. Treat any offer of a guarantee with caution, and get the small print checked out before you commit yourself to buying. While many schemes are perfectly genuine, offering you a guaranteed return during the first couple of years of ownership, there are others which are no more than a marketing gimmick to sell more properties. You need to ask the person or company promoting the property:

1 What is the anticipated rental return once the guaranteed rental period is over? Can you be provided with evidence of this by way of comparables?
2 When is the rent paid to you? Some developers will pay out only annually or six-monthly in arrears which presents a cashflow problem if you have a mortgage on the property that needs to be paid.
3 Are you able to make use of the property yourself at all. Sometimes, own use will be limited to, say, four weeks per year if you are part of a guaranteed rental scheme.
4 Is the guaranteed rental scheme optional or is it a requirement of purchase that you enter into this contract?
5 Who is underwriting the rental? Is it being provided by the developer, which in effect means that they are offering you cash back?
6 How financially secure and legally protected is the company offering the guaranteed rental. I have seen examples of non-trading or 'shell' companies offering guaranteed rentals.

Remember that the money for the guaranteed rental has to come from somewhere. Often it is added to the price of the property, creating a property that is sold at more than its true market value. This will lead to problems if you try to obtain a mortgage or sell in the future.

Summary

In this chapter we have looked at:

- How to work out rental yields.
- The pros and cons of various long-term let strategies
  - Corporate lets
  - Professional lets
  - Student lets
  - Houses in multiple occupation (HMOs)
  - Shared occupancy properties.
- Your responsibilities as a landlord.
- Short-term holiday lets.
  - Considerations for this market
  - What type of property?
  - How to market your property effectively for rental.
- Guaranteed rental income programmes.

06

capital growth strategy ...

In this chapter you will learn about:

- factors to maximize potential for growth
- buying properties below market value
- conversion projects
- emerging foreign markets
- undervalued and regeneration areas

... show me the money

One way investors make money from property is by way of the increase in the value of property over a period of time. The period in which various forms of property investment can deliver capital growth can vary – from a matter of months to many years. Here we take a look at various strategies for maximizing the potential for capital growth from property.

The increase in value of a property over time is one of the major routes to making loads of money from bricks and mortar. While renting a property out and benefiting from the income that this produces is a valid method of making money from property, the real big bucks come from capital growth. Some investors that I know base the whole of their investment strategy on buying properties that they consider to be below market value, sprucing them up a bit and then refinancing them or selling them on. They are not particularly interested in the rental potential of the property. Every few years or so, they remortgage the property in order to release further equity from it, and this is what they live on! If you have enough properties in your portfolio, refinancing them over a number of years can produce a regular income stream just from the equity that the properties generate. The rental income received from renting out the properties is just considered a means of helping pay for the finance on the properties and so these investors are not bothered if the rental income produced each month doesn't actually cover the costs of the mortgage. In other words, this strategy doesn't rely on every property having a positive cashflow, provided that the value of the property is increasing more each year than the deficit between rental income and running costs (including mortgage repayments).

Example

I buy a property for £80,000. Having spent £20,000 on refurbishment, the property is valued at £130,000. My total outlay of £100,000 is therefore rewarded by the fact that I have now got £30,000 of equity in the property. I decide to rent out the property. I can achieve £525 per month rental – or £6,300 per year which nets down to £462 per month/£5,544 per year after agency fees. Because I have borrowed money to purchase the property, my mortgage interest is £450 per month and I also have another £100 per month running costs. So my total monthly outlay is £550 per month – £88 per month more than I am receiving in income per month. This deficit amounts to £1,056 per year, but I know that property prices in the area are rising at 5 per cent per annum, which based on a value of £130,000 is £6,500. So, in effect, I am making £6,500 per annum profit on the property, it costs me £1,056 to service this, giving me a 'paper profit' of £5,444.

As you can see, there is far more money to be made through increases in property value, so this chapter aims to help you identify areas and properties that offer the best opportunity for this growth.

Factors to maximize potential for growth

Supply versus demand

The successful property investor understands supply and demand, and looks to invest in locations where this dynamic benefits them. Essentially, the ideal situation is finding a location where supply is limited for whatever reason and yet demand is strong and increasing. This will result in property prices rising and a good return on investment for property owners. Taking this one stage further, property investors seek to find locations where demand is currently static (and therefore prices are low) but where it is likely to increase substantially in the future and where supply is limited at the same time. This is very easy to illustrate in principle, but not so easy to achieve in practice! However, there are a few things to look out for that can determine whether the supply versus demand dynamic is set in your favour.

Demand increasers

These are factors which can give rise to an increase in demand for housing generally or in a specific area.

- **Economic growth** – If the economy is booming there is simply more money to go around and generally a more bullish attitude to spending. Looking at the bigger picture, countries that are experiencing above average GDP also have strong property markets.

- **Falling interest rates and availability of mortgage money** – Falling interest rates can have an effect on the demand for housing in two ways. First, mortgages become 'cheaper' and so individuals are able to afford more debt. Second, other forms of investment (i.e. gilts and bonds) become comparatively less attractive, steering more investment money towards property as a sector.
- **Wage and salary inflation** – If wages and earnings are increasing well, people will have more money with which to buy houses.
- **Decreasing unemployment** – If unemployment levels are falling, more people will have more money to spend on housing.
- **Changing demographics** – Higher divorce rates and internal migration will lead to greater demand for property. Divorced couples need two smaller properties to live in as opposed to one large family residence. People are also living longer, so there is a greater need for housing for the elderly. Migration into an area such as people moving out of the city to the country or vice versa also drives demand.
- **Changing legislation** – Changes in government policy can also lead to greater demand. Remember Margaret Thatcher's introduction of the Right to Buy scheme for council tenants? Similarly, current low-cost ownership schemes are designed to help first-time buyers enter the property market.
- **Political reform** – When looking at property on a worldwide scale, political reform is a major factor often underpinning these other demand increasers. Countries that have changed from communist to democratic states have seen substantial increases in demand for housing as the very nature of the economy changes.
- **Government and foreign direct investment** – Any large-scale investment into a country, region or area will spell good things for the economy and drive demand.
- **Improving transport and infrastructure** – New road, rail or air links will help to 'open' up areas and increase demand for housing there.

Supply limiters

These are factors which can reduce the supply of property generally or in a specific area.

- **Planning restrictions** – If the local or government policy is to restrict the development of new property, then supply will obviously be limited. This can also apply to building density and height restrictions.
- **Special Status Areas** – If an area is designated a World Heritage Site, an Area of Outstanding Natural Beauty, a Conservation Area, National Park or Site of Historical or Special Scientific Importance then the supply of property is likely to be limited. We discuss some of the rules surrounding property that is located within conservation areas or world heritage sites later in this chapter.
- **Lack of debt finance** – If developers can't borrow money to build, then the supply of houses will become limited. At the time of writing, we are in the aftermath of the 'Credit Crunch' in the USA. Time will tell how this will impact on property supply as developers struggle to secure bank funding.
- **Geographical restrictions** – There may be geographical restrictions to a particular area, such as an island. Take Manhattan, for example, where there is a geographical limit on the supply of land. Developers are forced to build upwards rather than outwards, but even then there is a limit to the number of properties that can feasibly be built there.
- **Legislation** – Government policy may also restrict supply. For example, restrictions on ownership by foreigners which occurs in some overseas countries.

Demand versus supply – areas to look for

There are some areas where supply will always be constrained or limited. These are great areas to invest in because as long as demand is good, the very fact that supply is limited will mean that there will always be upward pressure on property prices.

Areas where there is a finite supply of property and yet demand is destined always to remain strong are:

Waterfront

Be it near a beach, marina or inland waterway, the very fact that there are a limited number of properties in a location that enjoys the benefits of being 'waterfront' will result in good capital growth. The truth is that beaches, lakes and rivers are natural features that cannot be built elsewhere. Combine this with the fact that views overlooking water are intrinsically appealing ensures that you will always have buyers for your property.

Prime inner city areas

Buying within a particular inner city district or neighbourhood which is popular will always pay dividends. The prime location is usually limited by the postcode or physical boundaries such as roads, rivers, parkland or sea. Once the available land within the district has been accounted for it becomes difficult (or impossible) to build more properties there. However, there will always be strong demand for well-maintained inner city areas since they benefit from being in close proximity to retail, leisure and business centres.

Areas of outstanding natural beauty or heritage

Properties which are located within national parks and areas of outstanding natural beauty will always be in demand because they are, by definition, in pleasing locations. These areas will also have very strict controls on planning to prevent them becoming too built up, also ensuring that demand in these locations exceeds supply.

Fantastic views

Similar to properties that are located on a waterfront, any properties that benefit from a particularly spectacular or iconic view will always be in demand. The view itself cannot be replicated in another location. A property with a view of the Eiffel Tower, for example, will command a higher price than a comparable property in Paris without the view.

Architectural or historical importance

Properties that are 'listed' because of their architectural or historical importance are also primed for above average growth. Again, because they have something special about them they differentiate themselves from the rest of the market.

Migration factor

Where possible, buy in locations where there is a migration of people to the area. Some good examples of where the migration factor has played a part in property values rising are in some 'new' EU capital cities and areas popular for retirement. Capital cities like Sofia, Budapest and Prague have experienced strong capital growth over recent years as there has been a migration of workers from the country to the city, where employment and a wealthier standard of living beckon. Salaries and employment opportunities are greater in the capital cities and so workers will move there to enjoy these benefits.

The same is true for areas where new business parks or leisure facilities are being built. People will move to be closer to areas of high employment or a better quality of life.

For example, as new transport links have opened up more rural locations within the Home Counties, there has been a migration of people out of London to the surrounding countryside. Here, workers are searching for the peace and tranquillity associated with country living, yet need to still be able to commute to the city for work.

Finally, another example of the migration factor coming into play is within popular retirement hotspots such as Florida and Southern Europe. Due to the climate and lifestyle associated with these areas, retirees have migrated there in their droves, and properties there have increased in value accordingly – particularly those which have great views or are close to golf courses, beaches and main transport routes.

Concentric Ring Theory

We covered this in Chapter 4, but just to recap: Property is bought in a particular location close to an area which is already popular, and property values have grown. Working on the principle that by buying in neighbouring locations you can purchase a property at approximately 70–80 per cent of the cost of a similar property in the prime location, you can expect to see capital appreciation based on the fact that prices in the prime market will squeeze out some buyers who will happily buy in areas close by. Buyers will weigh up the advantages of being able to afford more property for their money in these 'secondary' locations and these neighbourhoods will therefore become popular, and prices will rise.

High yields

Areas which have a proven track record of achieving above average yields will also prove popular and therefore demand will be strong.

Communications and infrastructure

As part of your research into areas to buy property, find out about areas that are earmarked by local or regional government to receive government funding for upgrading or enhancing existing communication links and infrastructure. These areas can expect higher than average growth because the development of infrastructure will not only see an injection of government investment, but usually private sector investment will follow. If a new road network is planned, this will improve access to and from this area and you'll find that, subject to planning, retailers and other commercial enterprises will also spring up. Where there are new, modern retail and business facilities, residential interest will also follow, and so on. So you should always keep an ear to the ground to find out about new transport links, schools, hospitals, retail centres or business parks that are due to be built in areas you are considering.

On a slightly different scale, areas which are set to benefit from EU funding will also witness strong appreciation in prices. If you look at new EU countries which have received enormous grants from the EU for the development of their infrastructure, you'll see that these locations have also had strong GDP growth and property price increases.

Forced appreciation

In some instances there are factors at play other than pure supply and demand. Whether intentionally or not, councils, planning departments or even private land owners can have an effect on property values through 'forced appreciation'. Property prices are literally driven up by these factors. As an example, I own a skiing property in a smaller ski resort in British Columbia in Canada. The mountain itself is privately owned and so all planning decisions are passed through the family that owns the resort. This family creates the best possible price for land and property on the mountain so the supply of land released for new development is cut. This has had a positive impact on the capital values of privately owned property as it simply gets increasingly difficult to find new land to develop. This is an example of forced appreciation.

So, we have looked at various factors which can influence the rate of capital growth that a property can achieve and you should now be able to identify areas where capital values will increase at an above average rate. If you prefer to follow the lead of large business, corporations and developers who employ people to do all this research for them, then there are some easy-to-spot, tell-tale signs that an area is set to come into its own:

💰 Martin's tip

Identifying up-and-coming areas

- If larger property developers and housebuilding companies are interested in an area, usually you'll seen signage displayed on a site some months before building work actually commences. It's a good indication that things are happening if a large site is acquired by a major development company or builder.

- New estate agents appearing on the high street, particularly if they belong to one of the larger chains.

- New supermarkets opening. The big supermarket chains are major land owners in the UK and will develop new stores as they see fit to meet demand. They will have access to overall town plans and will know where the areas of further house building are planned.

- Large office developments, manufacturing plants or factories appearing. Companies opening new premises in an area will give a boost to local employment and create a demand for housing.

- Existing 'high street' premises being opened up as new, trendy restaurants and bars. Similarly, fashionable homeware and furniture shops appearing.

- Any large-scale development or conversion project to create modern, desirable accommodation. If an area is brought down by drab, run-down buildings and these are then converted into trendy flats or apartments, you can bet on the area seeing a surge in interest.

- New or improved transport links in an area.

- Local government or council-led regeneration programmes. Particularly if it involves the provision of new community facilities such as sports centres, libraries, local authority offices or healthcare centres, etc.

- The emergence of specialist retailers aimed at more affluent types, such as wine merchants, delicatessens, specialist coffee shops, art galleries, etc.

The other variable to take into consideration when looking at the capital return on a property investment is the price that you pay for the property. As a property investor, you should always aim to buy properties that are 'below market value'. In other words similar properties in a similar location at a given point in time are valued higher. The term 'below market value' is simply a way of describing properties that are sold at a discount to what the open market would dictate.

Below are a few strategies for buying properties at below market value.

Buying property below market value

Buying 'off plan'

One popular way of buying below market value and enjoying potential strong capital appreciation on a property is to buy 'off plan'. You reserve and pay a deposit on a new build property before it is constructed. You select your specific property based on architects drawings and plans – hence the term 'off plan'. You are likely to be buying a unit or units in a development where there are lots of identical or similar properties – rather than a bespoke house or flat. Depending on the developer and the stage which the project has reached when you decide to buy, you may have to commit to a purchase based on quite simple floor plans and artist's impressions of what the finished property will look like. However, this is no reason to cut corners on your own research and due diligence, and you should still ask for as much detail and information as possible from the seller. For this reason, it is not a method that will suit every investor – particularly if you find it difficult to visualize how something will look based on drawings and pictures alone – but if you can, then this can be a great way to buy.

The amount of information available can vary enormously between different sellers, who may be the development company themselves, an agent or a marketing company employed specifically to generate pre-build sales. Some will have quite sophisticated scale models of the finished project and computer generated tours, while with others you will have to rely on scale drawings or floor and site plans.

In recognition of the fact that you are buying before the property has been built, you can expect to buy at a discount. It is always worth asking what the completed sales price is likely to be so you can get a feel for the level of discount on offer. For larger developments, the project may be sold in phases. The developer can then control the amount of inventory on the market and once again, if you are buying in phase 1 then it is worth asking for the prices of subsequent phases. The phasing of projects will often coincide with the project reaching key milestones. For example, phase 1 might be launched when the project has been granted planning permission. Phase 2 may follow when initial foundations are laid and construction starts in earnest, and perhaps a later phase 3 will follow when the roof is on the building and only the internal refit is left to be done. Clearly, you can expect to pay more for a property that is partly constructed than something which is still a hole in the ground, but you get the added benefit of being able to actually step inside and 'view' the property while it is being built. Sometimes, if you are buying off plan and you get into the deal early enough, it is possible to negotiate an individual specification or design, provided it doesn't change the property so much that new planning permission needs to be applied for. But if you are buying for pure investment, don't get too carried away with personalizing the property to your own tastes.

If you are buying off plan, it is very important to find out if the planning permission has actually been fully granted and the appropriate Building Regulations or licences have been met. This is particularly important if you are buying an overseas property off plan (see Chapter 13 for more on this topic) because it is not uncommon for developers to try to generate pre-sales even before the final permissions have been received. This need not necessarily be a bad thing – you could get a substantial discount (say up to 20 per cent) off the launch price if this is the case – but you must make sure that there is provision for you to receive a refund of your deposit if planning permission is not granted or takes much longer than originally anticipated. In these circumstances, you also need to make sure that the deposit that you pay is held in a secure account (i.e. a solicitor's client account) or in Escrow (a protected bank account) pending the granting of planning permission. This means that the money is totally secure and can readily be refunded to you in the event that planning is severely delayed or worse still, refused. Whatever you do, don't pay anything more than a small reservation deposit directly to a developer on an off plan purchase if the final planning permission (or its equivalent in overseas jurisdictions) is still unconfirmed, without there being a clear written explanation of what will happen if the developer has difficulties with gaining planning consent. This is a recipe for losing your money!

You should also ask the seller to clarify exactly what the payment plan is. Sometimes, you will be asked to pay a deposit, say up to 20 per cent of the price of the property, and that will be all until completion, when the balance is paid. Clearly, if you plan to take out a mortgage on the property, then the later you have to pay the majority of the money, the better. If the property is completed, then it is probable that the mortgage company will be happy to advance you a loan in order for you to pay this final instalment to the seller. However, some deals require you to make stage payments to coincide with key milestones in the construction – for example, 20 per cent upfront, 30 per cent at first floor level, 30 per cent at roof level and 20 per cent at completion – and in these cases, you will need to ensure that you have access to the funds for the whole purchase from other means.

The fact that you can lock in on a purchase price for a property that is not due to be completed until, say two years' time allows for you to 'gear up' your investment. This is a great way to maximize your returns in a rising market. If, for example, you can buy a property off plan that is due to complete in two years time with a 20 per cent deposit and the market is rising by 10 per cent per annum, you can get a very good return on your money.

Example of gearing on off plan property

Let's say the property you are buying costs £200,000 and is completing in two years' time. Your 20 per cent deposit amounts to £40,000. By the time the property completes in two years' time, at a growth rate of 10 per cent p.a. the value at completion will be £242,000. So, your £40,000 investment has bought you £42,000 profit. That's a 105 per cent return on investment!

One final word on buying off plan. Your should examine the purchase contract that you will be issued in detail, and get this checked out by an independent lawyer. The purchase contract should cover what will happen in the eventuality that the construction timetable is delayed, or changes to the design and specification are required during the build. This is very important because there have been many occasions when purchasers have bought off plan overseas projects and paid the deposit, to then find that they have to wait years until the property is constructed. Not necessarily a problem if you know that this is going to be the case because you will have fixed your purchase price at the time of signing the contract and paying the initial deposit, but it will affect your cashflow if you are relying on the property to be finished to start renting or if you have borrowed money to find the initial deposit.

‖▷ Food for thought

A cautionary tale

Mr A is tempted to buy an off plan property with a very appealing £1,000 reservation fee. He is told that by the time the project completes, he will be able to get a mortgage based on the increased price of the property, but will have to pay only the original 'off plan' price. In effect, it is sold as a 'no money down' deal as the mortgage will cover the entire cost of purchase. He signs his purchase contracts. However, he hasn't done his research and doesn't realize that the property is already overpriced.

The market dips and in two years it's time for him to complete on the purchase of his property. Unfortunately, the price hasn't gone up as anticipated – in fact, it has dropped and the valuation for mortgage leaves him needing to find a hefty portion of the money required to complete for himself. He doesn't have this money. Never mind, he's only lost his £1,000 reservation fee, right? Wrong! He has signed a contract legally committing him to buy the property. If he reneges on the deal the property developer can sue him, so now he has to either pay the deposit monies and buy the property for, in effect, more than it is worth or be sued by the developer. Not a good scenario!

 **Martin's tip**

Buying off plan overseas

If buying off plan in an overseas destination, make sure that you have a specialist overseas property lawyer checkout the contract for you and provide you with a clear English explanation of what the contract contains. Details of UK based overseas property lawyers are contained within 'Taking it further' at the end of the book.

Renovation projects

One of the most talked about strategies for people to buy properties at below market value is that of buying property that is in need of renovation or modernization. Many of the properties featured on my TV programme *Homes Under the Hammer* fall into this category – although that's no coincidence, since auctions are an ideal source of property that needs some TLC (tender loving care!). While many people have made a success of this, sadly it isn't always as straightforward as it sounds, and more recently as we have experienced a slow down in property price increases I have come across examples of people who haven't managed to make any profit at all (and, in some cases, made a loss).

There's much more detail about renovation projects in Chapter 8, but for now I'll just say that this can be an excellent way of buying property below market value. The key to success is to make sure you do pay the right price for the property (i.e. you don't get carried away at the thought of becoming an overnight interior designer and pay too much) and you manage the costs of the renovation well. At all times, you need to be aware of what the finished property is likely to fetch on the open market because this will drive the rest of the project.

Repossessions

Setting aside the emotional issues and the personal, social and economic issues that have caused a property to be repossessed, buying repossessed property is an excellent way of picking up bargains and buying below market value. The sad truth is that lending institutions offering repossessed property for sale are just looking to get the property sold as quickly and easily as possible, and are not looking to achieve the maximum price. While government figures indicate that the number of repossessions has increased quite markedly in the last couple of years, it is actually still very difficult to find repossessed property. This is partly due to the fact that the mortgage companies have stopped revealing whether the properties they are selling have been repossessed.

Many repossessions end up at auctions, and those that do tend to be properties that are in need of refurbishment or repair. Often repossessed properties are found to be poorly maintained – so this is an opportunity for a property developer to buy stock at heavy discounts, work their magic in terms of renovation and then either resell, let or refinance the property on completion.

Conversion projects

Another popular way of pursuing a strategy for capital growth is to buy property that has the potential to be converted or have its usage changed. A typical example of this would be buying a large house that can be converted into several flats and each sold or rented independently, or acquiring, say, an old church or school building and changing it into a residential property. Both strategies will involve applying for planning permission and carrying out building works, which involves time, money and effort. If you are attracted to armchair investments, then this route is unlikely to appeal. That said, it has been a very popular choice for UK property developers and can be far more rewarding than just doing a cosmetic 'tart up' of an existing property.

The two major factors to consider with conversion projects are planning permission and Building Regulations. To convert a property from a single to multiple dwellings will always require planning permission and this is not guaranteed. You should find out from the local planning office if a property you are considering buying is likely to be granted planning permission for conversion, before you commit to buying it. Local planning officers will usually have a policy for which properties can be developed and which can't. They can often give you an informal indication of the likelihood of approval, or otherwise, over the telephone.

If you are intending to convert a property into flats then you will also need to consider Building Regulations to make sure that the finished units comply. You will therefore need to employ the services of an architect and discuss in detail with them what you want to do. They will be able to tell you if your proposals are feasible, bearing in mind that you will need to allow for:

- individual access to each flat – which may mean adding stairways and entrance halls. There are rules guiding the steepness and width of stairways which will need to be considered;
- kitchens and bathrooms in each flat – which has an impact on plumbing layout. You may need to upgrade the plumbing and water supply entering the property or add additional soil pipes;
- individual service supplies – such as electricity, gas and water to each flat.

However, if you are able to find a suitable property and can successfully convert it into flats then there is usually a good level of profit available. You should make a judgement on the maximum number of flats that you can get into the space and trade this off with the amount of space given to each unit. Clearly, the more flats you can create, the more profit there will be in the project, but that said, you will struggle to resell if you create pokey little 'rabbit hutches' – especially if you are pricing them at a level that is not competitive. You will need to consider car parking and general access to the property. If this is limited, and you are intending to turn one large house into, say, six flats, then you also need to think about where your eventual buyers or tenants are going to park their cars. Providing an area of communal parking (or allocated parking spaces) will be well received and of varying importance depending on the target market you are aiming for.

As with any renovation project (see Chapter 8) the success of a conversion project will depend on how well you plan and budget for works to be done, and how well you research the eventual resale value or letting income of the finished properties. Make sure you talk to a mixture of estate agents and letting agents about the anticipated value of the end product to ensure that all money spent in the conversion is recovered in the final price.

Finally, if you are buying a large freehold property and converting it, you will most likely offer these individual properties for sale on a leasehold basis so you will also need to employ a solicitor to draw up the leasehold agreement. You will also need to implement provisions for a management company to look after the communal areas.

If you are considering converting a non-residential property into a home then, once again, planning permission will be critical. Developers who have been fortunate enough to buy old chapels, churches, school buildings, warehouses and even offices and convert them into residential use have not only had very interesting projects to work on, but very often can make a tidy profit. Planning offices can be quite receptive to this type of conversion, depending on the location, since it relies on existing buildings being regenerated to provide housing rather than having to build on previously untouched land. You'll find this particularly achievable in inner city areas where older buildings have become derelict and you, as a private investor, will be converting them into new homes. The local authority may provide funding for your project in the way of a grant because you are contributing to the regeneration of an area. This is the case in certain parts of the UK.

Foreign emerging markets

With prices in the UK climbing beyond the reach of many people, the relative inexpensiveness of some overseas destinations has attracted both first-time buyers desperate to get themselves onto the property ladder and investors alike. The world has become a smaller place and the global property boom has inspired many to invest in foreign markets.

A good way to buy properties cheaply with a view to holding them for medium- to long-term capital growth is to explore new 'emerging' countries. There are many other things to consider when buying abroad, including the tax position, availability of mortgages and the legal situation, which we will cover in Chapter 13, but for now let's look at some of the reasons why emerging markets can achieve strong capital growth.

Factors driving emerging markets

Economic growth

Countries that are experiencing strong economic growth will also be increasing the standard of living for their population. The measure of economic growth is Gross Domestic Product (GDP) or the country's output including government spending and investments and what individuals spend in the shops. An emerging country that has above average GDP will be heralded as a country that is 'booming'.

Foreign direct investment

Another strong barometer of whether an emerging market is worth investing in or not is the level of 'foreign direct investment' (FDI). This is investment from other countries and corporations and is a signal that the economy of the country is growing. For the private investor, following the lead of other governments and multinational organizations is reassuring and since FDI also generally creates jobs and employment in the recipient country, the knock-on effect is that the economy improves further.

Interest rates and inflation

Interest rates are very important in an emerging market. If interest rates are falling, money becomes cheaper to borrow and as such, more buyers can afford to purchase property. This then drives demand and prices in the area. If interest rates are rising, property becomes more expensive and prices tend to cool off. The ability of locals to borrow money to buy property has been a recent development in many emerging countries and has also driven up demand and prices in these locations.

Inflation is also relevant because it affects interest rates and *ipso facto* the property market. If inflation is rising then it is likely that interest rates will also have to rise in order to control the cost of money (and in turn, inflation). So, when looking at an emerging market through the eyes of a property investor, you want to see an environment of low and controlled inflation.

Local wealth

The relative wealth of the local population is another important factor in evaluating an emerging market. If the locals are experiencing an increased level of wealth and generally higher standard of living, this will drive up property prices. In many European capital cities, the locals simply have not had the means to buy property for themselves and in Eastern Europe, they have often historically lived in government provided housing blocks. However, with the advent of membership of the EU, locals in cities like Budapest, Prague and Bucharest are now experiencing an unprecedented level of wealth, and the first thing they want to do as soon as they can afford to, is to buy their own home. This is all good news for property investors there.

The ability of the local population to buy property is fundamental to the attractiveness of any foreign market. At some point you may wish to sell your property, and if you have bought in an area where the locals have the willingness and ability to invest in property themselves, it greatly improves your chances of resale. Relying on foreign investors and tourists alone for resale limits your market and potential returns.

Employment

Employment is linked to the wealth of locals and growth in the economy. If FDI is creating new jobs and improved employment prospects, money is put into the local economy. More money means more demand for property.

Regional and local factors

Less scientific but equally important are local and regional events. Take the effect of the announcement that the 2012 Olympic Games would be held in London. Property prices in the historically deprived area of East London increased overnight. This is a great example of how these local factors can help drive prices. Similarly, property prices in Liverpool have risen dramatically not least because it was awarded the European City of Culture for 2008.

New tourism

The opening up of new tourism centres and transport links to reach them will have a huge impact on the local economy of an emerging destination. Turn the clock back 10 years or so and it's likely that most people would not have been able to tell you where the likes of Bratislava, Tallinn and Bucharest were. Yet with low-cost airlines operating to these destinations from UK regional airports, they are now experiencing a level of tourism that would have previously been unthinkable. Because it is very cheap and easy to reach these destinations, the short break holiday market has opened up, and with it, the property market.

---

⑪ Food for thought

Be careful when buying in destinations served by a low-cost carrier if you are relying on tourist lets. Some airlines operate routes only during the peak season and stop flying out of season. If so, your market for tourist tenants is severed drastically when the flights stop.

Tastes and fashion

The way people travel and spend their leisure time can also have an impact on property values, if you are considering investing in a location that is tourism led. As spending habits and trends alter, so can the demand for your property. For example, the growing popularity of golf as a pastime has really increased demand for properties that are located on or near golf courses, and the shift over the past two decades or so from package holidays to bespoke 'independent' travel has also driven demand for more luxury properties.

On this point, as a travel journalist and former travel TV presenter on *Wish You Were Here...?* and *Sky Travel* I have witnessed the changing trends in travel over the past 20 years. These days, we generally lead very busy lives, have high levels of stress and constant demands on our time, so we are now much more discerning when it comes to our annual holiday. Gone are the days of accepting poor standards of accommodation in the pursuit of a new experience. We now expect holiday property to be of at least equal standard to the property we live in at home. This means decent furniture, modern appliances and a few luxury items such as plasma screen TVs, swimming pool or hot tub. Because we are able to save money on our flights (thanks to low-cost airlines) we can justify spending a greater proportion of our holiday budget on the accommodation itself. The result is that four- and five-star properties are now in greater demand than mid-range three-star ones. Therefore, if you are considering buying property in a destination that is tourism led, you shouldn't scrimp on quality. Aim high: go for luxury and you will reap the rewards in higher rental rates and better yields.

 Martin's tip

Go for luxury

If you are buying property that is within a tourist destination, go for as high a specification as you can afford. If budget is limited, it is better to go for a smaller, more luxurious property than a larger property that has a low standard of finish.

Multiplier effect

This occurs when an increase in investment from local, regional, government or EU bodies has a knock-on effect on employment and local wealth. Because there is more money being injected into an area by way of this large-scale investment, individuals become more prosperous and they too can spend money buying goods and services from others, so further driving the economy. You'll also find that workers migrate to the area, which again brings more money into the economy, and so it goes on.

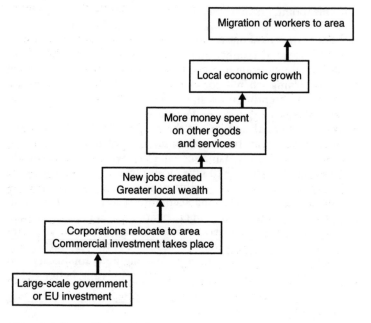

figure 6.1 the multiplier effect

Emerging markets worth considering

Countries that have just joined the EU offer some of the best opportunities for capital growth that exist today and have the benefit of being relatively close to home should you want or need to visit. Many of them now benefit from regular flights from the UK on low-cost airlines (another factor driving growth) and so they are sometimes just as easy to checkout as towns and cities in the UK. Consider:

- **Bucharest** – Capital of Romania, which joined the EU in January 2007 and which is now playing 'catch up'. Its own middle classes are pouring their new found wealth into property ownership and mortgages for locals are now available.
- **Riga** – Capital of Latvia, which joined the EU in 2004. The largest city within the three Baltic states and home to one-third of Latvia's population.
- **Tallinn** – Capital of Estonia, the most northerly of the Baltic states, which joined the EU in 2004. Tallinn is one of Europe's best preserved medieval cities and now enjoys strong tourism.
- **Vilnius** – Capital of Lithuania, which is the largest and most populous of the Baltic states, and which joined the EU in 2004. Vilnius is a picturesque city on the banks of the rivers Neris and Vilnia, and it has one of the most impressive and largest old towns in Eastern Europe with a thriving and unusual university.
- **Warsaw** – Capital of Poland, which joined the EU in 2004.
- **Bratislava** – Capital of Slovakia, which became an independent state in January 1993 after Czechoslovakia split. Slovakia is in the heart of central Europe, linked to its neighbours by the River Danube and is now experiencing new found tourism from Western Europe.
- **Prague** – Capital of Czech Republic. Prague is more than 1,000 years old and has a wealth of historic architecture of different styles. Because of this, the city has become a favoured location for tourists and property investors.
- **Budapest** – Capital of Hungary, which also joined the EU in 2004. Now experiencing unprecedented levels of foreign direct investment and record EU grants.

Also consider some of the long-haul destinations in countries where the economy is booming and property prices look set to increase over the short to medium term:

- **Brazil** – Set to become a major global economy.
- **Canada** – A strong economy which has historically played 'little brother' to the USA but which now is experiencing unprecedented levels of wealth.
- **Thailand** – Asia's leading tourist destination which is evolving from a backpacker's hideaway to a major five-star tourism spot.

- **Other South East Asian countries such as Malaysia,** which are benefiting from increased tourism within the region.

For more information on overseas property hotspots, visit www.propertyqc.com

---

 Martin's tip

When investing for capital growth, consider:

- Supply versus demand for property in the area. Try to aim for locations which have limitations on supply and strong demand.
- Whether there is any migration into the area.
- Whether you can buy more property for the same money in areas which are set to increase in value that appear in 'concentric rings' surrounding an existing hotspot.
- Researching locations that are already producing high rental yields.
- Areas that are earmarked for significant investment in communications and infrastructure.
- Looking to buy properties below market value by buying off plan, repossessed properties or properties that are ripe for renovation.
- Achieving added value by converting property and changing its use.
- Investing in foreign emerging markets to find bargains where growth is likely to be strong.

Summary

In this chapter we have looked at:

- Factors to maximize capital growth: supply v. demand; migration; concentric ring theory; high yields; communcation infrastructure; forced appreciation.
- Buying property below market value: off plan; renovation projects; reposessions; conversion projects; foreign emerging markets.

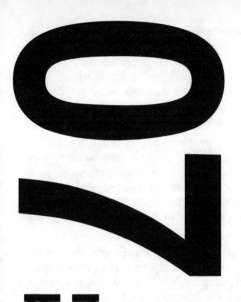

07

negotiating the best deal ...

In this chapter you will learn about:

- understanding how property pricing works
- negotiating the best deal
- how to structure the deal – making the offer
- fees and disbursements
- Home Information Packs

... the price is right

Equally important as location, growth potential and income yield, is the price of the property. All your potential profit can be wiped out if the property is acquired at too high a price. This chapter aims to give you some commonsense advice on how to establish and negotiate the right price for a property.

The price that you pay for a property has as much impact on your potential profit as the level of growth and income yield that can be achieved. It is vitally important that you, as a property developer, understand property pricing and how to spot when a property is priced competitively in order to ensure that you don't pay over the odds and better still, only buy bargains.

There are lots of theories about how to value properties – some more technical than others – and it is up to you to decide how much analysis you are prepared to do to ensure that you pay a fair price for any deal you are contemplating. If you immerse yourself in the market where you want to buy, keep scouring the local estate agents, newspapers and Internet looking at properties in the area, you will develop a good feel for general pricing and will be able to spot a bargain more readily.

However, as a starting point, let's look at some of the methods of evaluating the 'right' price for properties.

Understanding how property pricing works

The price/rent ratio

If you were to invest in the stock market, you would soon become familiar with a term called the 'price/earnings ratio' (P/E ratio). This is a commonly used calculation which measures how high the company's net earnings are, in relation to the price of the shares. For an ordinary company, a price/earnings ratio of between 9 and 18 would be considered within the 'normal' range. Anything above that is considered high. In other words, the value of the shares would seem 'expensive' compared with their future earnings (or yield).

The other factor to look at is the yield itself. This is the amount of money that is paid out as a dividend against each share. Yields from company shares of between 5.5 per cent to 10 per cent are considered normal.

☺ Did you know?

Information about the shares of a company, the price/earnings ratio (P/E ratio) and yield (dividend) are quoted in the *Financial Times*. If this is the first time you have heard about price/earnings ratios and yields, I recommend that you buy a copy of the newspaper and look at the shares of companies that you have heard of. See what the price of the shares is, what price/earnings ratio (P/E ratio) they are at and what yield (dividend income) they receive.

This same theory can be applied to the housing market, particularly the buy to let arena, to help you to evaluate current prices of property, but instead of a price/earnings ratio, we evaluate the price/rent ratio.

As rental yields fall, you should expect the price of property to also adjust to reflect the 'earning power' of the property; if it doesn't, then the price starts to look expensive. The table below illustrates how the rental yield and price/rent ratio work in tandem.

price/rent ratio	gross rental yield (%)	
5	20	Very undervalued
6.7	15	Very undervalued
8.3	12	Undervalued
10	10	Undervalued
12.5	8	Slightly undervalued
14.2	7	Fairly priced
16.7	6	Fairly priced
20	5	Slightly overvalued
25	4	Overvalued
33.3	3	Overvalued
40	2.5	Very overvalued
50	2	Very overvalued

Take an example of a property worth £100,000. If it currently has a gross rental yield of 5 per cent per annum then it will be generating £5,000 p.a. income. The price/rent ratio is 20. (£100,000 is 20 times £5,000). As the table indicates, this is just about acceptable.

Now let's suppose that the same property is being sold at £125,000. The gross rental yield is unchanged at £5,000. Now the yield as a percentage is reduced to 4 per cent. (Remember how to work out rental yield from Chapter 5?) The price/rent ratio is now 25 (£125,000 is 25 times £5,000) and the property starts to look expensive or 'overvalued'.

🍴 Food for thought

Low price/rent ratios push the housing market higher

If rental yield levels are high and the cost of borrowing to buy a house is low compared with the cost of renting:

- Potential buyers will pay less to borrow from the bank (in order to buy) than they pay when renting a house. Many will move from being renters to buyers.
- Buy to let investors will find it makes sense to buy and will become active in acquiring property to rent out.

Both these factors put upward pressure on house prices.

High price/rent ratios put downward pressure on house prices

If rental yield levels are low, this will tend to mean that the interest cost of buying a house is high, compared with the cost of renting a house:

- Potential buyers will find that to buy a house involves paying much more to the lender than it costs to rent. Buyers, especially first-time buyers, may have difficulty financing housing. Banks will be worried about over-lending at loan/income ratios, which means that a slight increase in interest rates will result in financial difficulty for the borrower.
- Investors will find that buying to let won't pay.

So high price/rent ratios tend to put downward pressure on house prices.

So if you know what rental yield a property is achieving (or could achieve) then this will be a great help in deciding on a fair price for the property. Obviously don't just take this in isolation, since there may be other factors that come into play, for example, when strong future growth in value is expected, such as land on an undiscovered but beautiful beach or properties in an area whose communications infrastructure is being upgraded. Here relatively low yields (earnings) can be acceptable. This is where you, as an investor, have to make a judgement.

Relative price comparison

This is the most popular way of checking whether the price of a property is high, low or about right. Gather as much evidence in the way of comparable properties as possible. If you can, take a look at the costs per square metre since this allows you to compare like for like.

We talked about tools which you can employ to compare property prices in Chapter 4, so to recap:

- Use data on similar properties in the area that have sold recently.
- If this is not widely available, use comparables of properties on the market, but be aware that the price at which a property is listed doesn't necessarily give you a true value of what it is worth. Ultimately, any property is worth only what someone is prepared to pay for it.

Affordability

The general affordability of housing in relation to the 'wealth' of a location is a useful yardstick. If house prices are so high that very few people can afford to buy them, then their value is likely to fall in the future. A reasonable measure of value is GDP per capita as a multiple of house prices per square metre.

Affordability: how many square metres of major housing does a country's per person GDP per capita buy?

Country	A City centre price per sq. metre (€)	B GDP per capita (€)	Affordability (B÷A)
Luxembourg	3,934	70,227	17.85
Belgium, Brussels	2,150	30,047	13.98
Norway, Oslo	5,117	58,402	11.41
Denmark, Copenhagen	3,784	41,615	11.00
Sweden, Stockholm	3,167	33,961	10.72
Austria, Vienna	3,000	31,524	10.51
Switzerland, Bern	3,967	41,609	10.49
Greece, Athens	1,833	18,358	10.01
Germany, Frankfurt	2,917	28,097	9.63
Finland, Helsinki	3,333	31,736	9.52
Switzerland, Geneva	4,417	41,609	9.42
Ireland, Dublin	5,000	43,669	8.73
Cyprus, Limassol	2,167	16,842	7.77
Switzerland, Zurich	5,934	41,609	7.01
Slovakia, Bratislava	1,292	8,638	6.69
Spain, Madrid	4,000	24,237	6.06
Poland, Warsaw	1,175	7,039	5.99
Portugal, Lisbon	2,517	14,735	5.85
Slovenia, Ljubljana	2,467	14,015	5.68
Malta, Valletta	1,967	11,152	5.67
Czech Republic, Prague	2,367	11,601	4.90
Netherlands, Amsterdam	6,667	32,668	4.90

Hungary, Budapest	1,792	8,338	4.65
UK, Central London	7,199	32,055	4.45
France, Paris	6,667	28,584	4.29
Italy – Rome (historical area)	6,083	25,270	4.15
Estonia, Tallinn	2,383	9,880	4.15
Bulgaria, Sofia	1,042	3,113	2.99
Latvia, Riga	3,020	7,696	2.55
Macedonia, Skopje	1,125	2,322	2.06
Romania, Bucharest	2,350	4,842	2.06
Lithuania, Vilnius	3,792	7,349	1.94
Turkey, Istanbul	2,467	4,138	1.68
Russia, Moscow	6,266	6,251	1.00
Moldova, Chisinau	917	705	0.77
Ukraine, Kiev	2,807	1,650	0.59

Source: Global Property Guide Research

In the table above, relative to GDP per capita levels:

- House prices in Luxembourg, Belgium, Norway, Denmark, Sweden and Austria seem cheap.
- House prices in the UK, France, Italy and the Netherlands seem comparatively expensive.

However, note that housing in poor countries always tends to be relatively highly priced relative to the local standard of living, so a substantial difference between countries at different income levels is unsurprising. This GDP per square metre yardstick is best used to compare countries with the same GDP.

Price to replacement cost

The final method of evaluating property prices is the price to replacement cost. Developers will tend to construct new buildings if house prices are much higher than new build construction costs. Over the long run that will tend to put pressure on prices, as new supply comes into the housing market. So when house prices are far greater than new build costs, it's a danger sign that there could be a correction in the market.

There is one obvious exception to this: in cases where regulations tend to restrict the construction of new buildings and, therefore, new build prices have less significance. The UK is replete with building codes, permits and quantitative restrictions which limit the amount of new housing supply. Such regulations tend to guarantee that house prices remain above new build costs.

Although fairly technical, these four methods should give you a range of solid benchmarks to use when evaluating the price of property and deciding whether or not it is a good time to buy. You can apply these rules not just to the UK property market, but also to overseas property markets.

Opportunity cost

If you are going to invest in property, you need to understand the concept of opportunity cost. Economists use this term to describe the cost to you of having to give up one thing in order to have another. If you decide to invest your hard-earned cash into property, you will have to give up the opportunity of investing that money in another venture, and so the opportunity cost to you is the value that you put on the opportunity foregone.

If you look at different forms of investment and compare their returns over a set period of time, then you can work out the opportunity cost.

Using a simple example, let's compare a hypothetical investment of £100 in different commodities over a 10-year period from 1997 to 2007. The relative performance of these assets is as below:

Commodity	Value in 1997	Value in 2007	Percentage change
Marbles	£100	£230	+130%
Wagon wheels	£100	£160	+60 %
Potatoes	£100	£107	+7%
Sunflower seeds	£100	£56	-44%

Note: all figures are for illustrative purposes only.

Had you invested in sunflower seeds, then you would have not only lost 44 per cent on your original investment of £100 but the *opportunity cost* is actually 174 per cent because you could have invested in marbles instead (130% + 44% = 174%).

When comparing different property markets or deals, there will always be an opportunity cost of backing one horse, because you have had to forego the other.

Negotiating the best deal

Now that you have a number of measures to allow you to establish what properties are worth, you will be able to make a judgement on an individual deal as to whether it is a fair price, cheap or expensive. On the basis that the property you are considering buying is priced fairly, then there are some useful 'tricks of the trade' that you can use to negotiate the best deal.

General ideas on buying property at the keenest price

- If you are negotiating on a property via an estate agent, remember that they actually work on behalf of the vendor and, although they may seem to be your best friend, their loyalties should lie with getting the best (highest) price for the property. Given that their remuneration is often a commission percentage of the actual agreed sales price of the property, any lowering of the price actually means the estate agent is doing him/herself out of money. You may want to offer the estate agent a bonus of some sort if they are able to get the property at the price that you want.

- Don't appear too keen, even if you really do want to buy the property. As an investor you should be taking off your 'emotional' hat and treating the purchase like a business transaction. Know what you are willing and prepared to pay and don't be afraid to walk away if you can't come to an agreement with the seller.

- If the price of the property is close to a Stamp Duty threshold, consider paying an amount for the property (which is what is declared on the title) and then negotiate a separate amount for fittings and furniture. This could save you paying the next level of Stamp Duty but clearly, you can do this only with a relatively modest proportion of the property value and the tax authorities are not stupid, so don't try a ridiculous figure. Items that are to be paid for separately will have to be fully documented. Details of current Stamp Duty thresholds are available on www.hmrc.gov.uk.

Example

The property you are buying is priced around the £250,000 level where stamp duty increases from 1 per cent to 3 per cent. If you buy the property at £249,950, the amount of Stamp Duty is £2,499. However, if you agree to pay £251,000, then the amount of Stamp Duty is increased to £7,530 – a difference of £5,031! So, if the vendor needs to achieve say £255,000 and assuming you are happy to pay this amount, you could agree on £250,000 for the property and then pay £5,000 as a separate transaction for fittings and furniture, so long as these are genuinely available for purchase.

- Offer a lower price on the basis that you can exchange contracts and/or complete quickly. Your ability to do this will depend on how you are financing the purchase (if you have to arrange a mortgage, this may take time to sort out) and the speed at which your solicitor can carry out the necessary checks. Make this offer only if you are genuinely able to fulfil it, otherwise you will annoy everybody and soon lose credibility with future contacts.
- Have a selection of comparable properties to hand to show the vendor. They may be unaware of current market conditions and that their property is over-priced. Remember people buy from people so be pleasant and polite in all your dealings. Many people want to sell their property – which could have been in their family for years – to someone who they like and they think will look after it.

Strategies for identifying bargains (below market value properties)

Armed with the information about what property values ought to be in a particular location, you should aim to buy properties that are 'below market value' (i.e. they are bargains). Understanding how to identify below market value properties and putting forward an offer on them that the vendor accepts is a key skill in becoming a successful property investor.

Property is a unique asset class. Unlike many things we buy which have a set price, the price we pay for property is reached through negotiation and all sorts of factors influence the price. The circumstances of the seller, how 'motivated' they are to sell at a particular time and their perception of the value of their property are just some of the factors which determine what price is eventually agreed.

If you know your onions, it is possible to find and buy below market value properties, even when the market is strong and it appears that other properties being sold are reaching their asking price.

Using estate agents and letting agents to find bargains

There are numerous estate agents that vendors could use to sell their houses for them, but most sellers aren't property investors and they won't do the same research that you would do in picking the best estate agent in their area to achieve the best possible price for them. Some agents are simply not as good as others – they have lower standards of professionalism and employ less helpful and qualified staff. These estate agents are often the ones that have shabby offices and out-of-date window displays. Paradoxically they could be good for finding properties that are below market value.

Look for properties that have been for sale with an estate agent for a while and seem to be sticking. The agent is probably fed up with having this property on the books and will be less inclined to fight hard to achieve a premium price from the vendor – they just want it sold. Any property which has been on the market for three months or more is worth exploring further, since the vendor may be doubting whether the property was listed at the right price in the first place and could be getting nervous about the fact that it hasn't sold, particularly if they are working to a particular timescale.

Watch for properties that are listed with multiple agents or that appear with new agents regularly. These are tell-tale signs that the seller is keen to sell the property and should therefore be motivated.

Quiz the agent on the circumstances surrounding the sale of the property and the level of interest it is receiving. If the agent comes with you on an accompanied viewing, this is an ideal time for a relaxed, informal information gathering exercise. Things to ask the agent include:

- Why is the property being sold? Is the vendor under pressure to complete the transaction within a specific timeframe?
- What is the vendor's situation? Are they working or retired, investor or developer?
- What interest has there been so far in the property? How many viewings has the agent done? How many second viewings have been carried out? This will give you a good idea of whether or not other people are interested in the property.
- Have any other offers been submitted? If so, what price was offered?
- What is the general 'mood' in the market? Is the agent busy at the moment? How many properties did they sell in the last month? Is this normal, above or below average? This will give you a feel for the local sales climate.
- What does the agent think the property will sell for? They might not answer you, but if they do you could discover that the agent is listing the property at the price that the vendor hopes to achieve, not the estate agent's opinion of what it is worth. There could be some correction of expectations to be had in the mind of the vendor, and you want to be around with your offer on the table when this happens!

Ask the agent about probate sales where properties are being sold after the owner has died. These can often be negotiated as the executors will want to realize the value of the estate as quickly as possible.

Consider making offers on property during traditionally quieter times for house sales. December and August are generally slower months in the industry. Vendors might be more inclined to take your offer then (even if it is lower than they had hoped) if the option is potentially to have to wait months for a possible sale.

Look at properties that are for sale with an estate agent, but are outside the agent's normal area. These are often anomalies and the agent may be less experienced at selling in this area and willing to put forward a lower offer to get the property 'off their books'.

Dealing directly with developers
In Chapter 6 we talked about the benefits of buying property 'off plan' from developers. This in itself can be a good way of

securing property at a keen price, by signing a purchase contract today and paying a deposit with a view to completing on the property, then paying the balance at a point in the future. However, there are also other ways that you can secure below market value properties from developers.

- Get in early in phase 1 of the development, even before the project is formally launched. The developer may be keen to strike a deal in order to secure a set number of pre-sales to demonstrate to their sources of borrowing that they have the ability to make sales. They may also need to make some early sales in order to secure the next tranche of funding.
- Alternatively, buy at the very end of the project when there are a few units remaining. These may not be the most desirable plots but if you can pick them up at below market value and the financial case still stacks up, it doesn't matter. After all, you're probably not going to be living in the property. The developer may be keen to tie up the last few units on a development so will be more ready to make a deal.
- If you are buying from a UK developer, find out when is the financial year end for the company. The developer may be more receptive to negotiation at the end of the trading year.
- Negotiate with the developer for multiple purchases. If you are buying more than one property, you might find that they are prepared to offer you a discount.
- If the developer can't knock anything off the purchase price, see if there are other incentives they can offer you such as free carpets and curtains or Stamp Duty paid in the UK, or if overseas, a free or discounted furniture pack.

Dealing directly with vendors

First, identify properties that you are interested in buying. Perhaps you already own property in an apartment block where you know the demand for rent is strong, it is a popular place to live and you would like to buy more properties there. If so, approach people who own property in this location by means of a leaflet drop or even calling door to door. They may not actually have their property on the market but are considering selling. Your approach may be just the thing to spur them into action. Remember that a vendor potentially stands to save several thousand pounds in estate agent fees if they can cut out the 'middle man' and deal directly with the purchaser. This is a saving that could be partly passed on to you.

The kinds of vendors who are most likely to be keen to sell and, therefore, receptive to a below market value offer are:

- people who need a quick, clean sale that doesn't involve getting into a chain
- people who are getting divorced and may need to sell the marital home quickly to settle matters
- people who have lived in the property for a long time; they often have low expectations of what the property is worth and don't have a mortgage on it which needs to be repaid
- people who are in debt and financially over-committed and who may sell quickly to release the burden
- people who are in a chain already and have been let down by their buyer and risk losing the property that they want to buy
- people who know the property has problems and they need to sell to an investor or developer who isn't going to be put off by these issues
- people who are emigrating and need to sell in a specified period of time and who have often already psychologically left the country; they just 'want out' and to start their new life abroad. Very often the property they are moving to in the other country will cost less than their UK home and so they have less need to achieve the maximum possible price
- landlords of properties which are not renting well – although you obviously need to understand why.

You could also consider placing an advertisement in the local press saying that you are a property investor looking to acquire property in a certain area. This may bring vendors to you who don't actually have their property on the market. However, you are also likely to receive interest from people wanting to sell but who aren't motivated enough to sell to you at below market value.

Another way of approaching vendors directly is to scour the local papers to find properties that are advertised as 'for sale by vendor'. This is becoming an increasingly popular way for people to sell, as home owners have recognized the power of the Internet for marketing properties and feel that they can list their home themselves. If this is the case, they may not be getting advice from professionals on what their property is worth and so could quite simply undervalue it. People who aren't 'into' property and have lived in their home for a long time often have very low expectations of the current value of their property.

If the 'for sale by vendor' listing contains phrases such as 'ONO' (or nearest offer), 'Vendor Emigrating' or 'priced for quick sale' then these are tell-tale signs that this is a motivated seller who wants to get their property sold.

Finally, if you have your eye on a property which you believe to be empty (at least most of the time), chances are the person who owns it has already 'moved on'. It may be a second home or simply a property that is surplus to requirements. In both these cases, it is probable that the vendor doesn't have a mortgage on the property and therefore doesn't have a minimum price level to sell. If you can track down the owner, either through neighbours, the council or the Land Registry, and make a direct approach to them to buy their property, they may be grateful for someone taking a problem off their hands.

How to structure the deal – making the offer

Once you have sifted through properties, identified those that you want to buy and have decided on what price you believe they are worth, then you need to make an offer to the vendor. If you have arrived at a sensible price, then offer it. Don't 'chance it' with a deliberately cheeky low offer. It will insult the vendor and you will lose credibility with the agent. It is better to do your research and make a judgement on what the property is worth to you. If you are aiming to secure the property at below market value, then once you have assessed the market and have an indication of what the property should be sold at, then offer somewhere in the region of 15 to 20 per cent below this.

While you may present your offer verbally to the estate agent listing the property, you should always confirm it in writing. Not only does this allow you to write in some caveats (see below) but it shows that you are a professional and there is no chance for anything in relation to the offer to be misinterpreted. In your offer letter, you might also want to:

• state a timescale for which the offer is valid. This not only indicates that you are a professional and have other deals to consider, but it also focuses the mind of the seller. It shows that you want to move things forwards and want to conclude the negotiations by a certain date.

- state any conditions that apply to the offer. These are things you may have discussed with the agent (or vendor if you are dealing directly with them) such as fixtures, fittings, furniture.

Minimizing deposits

It's traditional that on exchange of contracts you will be required to give a 10 per cent non-refundable deposit. However, this is not cast in stone. If a vendor chooses to do so, they could accept a 5 per cent, or even a 0 per cent deposit. You would obviously have to make up the full purchase price on completion but it could enable you to structure creative financing deals, such as the instant remortgage options that are covered elsewhere in this book.

Reducing the amount of your money that you need

A motivated vendor can be approached with all manner of purchase deals – all perfectly legal and which could make the difference between a sale proceeding and not. These include:

- gifted deposits – when the vendor agrees to pay your deposit for you
- staggered payment options – when you are given a period of time to pay your deposit in instalments, even after the sale has completed
- sell and rent back scheme – where the seller agrees to sell you the property and then immediately rent it back from you. This can help with obtaining a favourable buy to let mortgage.

Fees and disbursements

Average solicitor's/legal fees

There are no fixed amounts that a solicitor has to charge you for conveyancing a property purchase for you. There are guidelines and average 'going rates', but basically if you can negotiate a deal then go for it. Try to establish a good working relationship with your solicitor; they can be a major ally and are certainly part of your 'dream team' (which we cover in Chapter 9).

Remember, they too have to earn a living so negotiating too hard with them could be counterproductive.

Finance deals

If you are taking out a traditional mortgage, it may be that there are few fees associated with it – or that they can be added to the mortgage. Fixed rate, discounted or special offers will usually have higher arrangement fees. If you are looking at using more creative finance to complete your purchase – such as a bridging loan – then you should expect to pay arrangement fees of between 1 per cent and 2 per cent of the amount financed, plus high rates of ongoing interest.

Property finding fees

Property Finders will either charge a set fee for every deal they bring to you (around £2,000 to £5,000), or a percentage of the property price. If, however, they have located a particularly attractive deal, then these fees are worth it.

Home Information Packs (HIPs)

Unfortunately, as you may know, buying and selling property doesn't always go to plan. One in four sales collapses before contracts are exchanged even though the terms of the sale may have been agreed. More than two-fifths of these failures are the result of a survey or valuation inspection report highlighting faults with the property. Currently most of this important information emerges only after an offer has been made and often results in a buyer pulling out of the sale, which means money wasted on searches and legal fees. It's estimated that £1 million a day is lost through transactions failing at a late stage, not to mention the added stress and anxiety this can cause!

The delay in obtaining searches is one of the frequent causes of sales falling through, as buyers become disillusioned and look for another property.

Amid much controversy, HIPs were introduced at the start of August 2007. Initially property with four bedrooms or more was required to have a HIP, then homes with three or more bedrooms, and now all properties offered for sale require them.

The government has introduced HIPs in an attempt to make buying and selling clearer and more straightforward, as well as to encourage homes to be more energy efficient. The pack provides buyers with important information early on in the process and highlights any issues they need to be aware of before making an offer.

Estate agents marketing homes with HIPs are now required by law to be registered with the Ombudsman for Estate Agents (OEA). This means that whether you are a buyer or a seller, you should get a better standard of service, and if not, you can complain to this independent industry body if you are not satisfied with the service.

The responsibility for the HIP is with the seller. Buyers will not have to pay for a copy of a HIP, and so the scheme could help struggling first-time buyers and make it easier and cheaper for them to get their foot on the property ladder.

What information does the HIP contain?

The HIP (also known as a 'seller's pack'), is made up of 'required' and 'authorized' information about a property. The 'required' documents are mandatory, while the 'authorized' documents can be included if the seller thinks they may be important to buyers.

The **required** documents are:

- An **index** (i.e. a list of the documents included in the pack).
- A **sale statement** including name of seller and address of property being sold, whether the property is freehold or leasehold.
- **Evidence of title** – proof that the seller owns the property and, therefore, has the right to sell it, and whether the property is registered or unregistered.
- The **Property Register** and the **Title Plan** – official copies from the Land Registry. The Property Register provides a brief description of the property and whether the property is freehold or leasehold (including remaining years on the lease, legal rights and duties of the leaseholder and landlord). There should be details of the ground rent and service charges payable for the property.
- Local property **searches** which are usually provided by the relevant local authority. While every effort must be made to get hold of all the relevant information to complete a search,

if any questions can't be answered, an insurance policy should be included to protect the buyer in case of any problems arising at a later date.

- A standalone **Energy Performance Certificate** (or an optional Home Condition Report containing a separate Energy Performance Certificate). This tells buyers how energy efficient the home is on a scale of A to G. The most efficient homes, which should have the lowest running costs, are in band A. The certificate also tells you, on a scale of A to G, what impact the property has on the environment. The higher the rating, the fewer carbon dioxide emissions it should produce. The average UK property falls into bands D to E for both categories. Recommendations are included about how the energy efficiency can be improved to save money and help the environment.
- Where appropriate, **commonhold information** (commonhold is an alternative to the conventional method of owning flats and other interdependent properties under a lease and is a new form of freehold ownership) including a copy of the commonhold community statement.
- **Leasehold information** if appropriate (including a copy of the lease, information on service charges and insurance).
- Where appropriate, a **New Homes Warranty**.
- Where appropriate, a **report on a home that is not physically complete**.

If you are selling a leasehold flat you will also need to provide:

- A copy of the lease.
- Any landlord or management company regulations.
- The most recent service charge accounts and receipts.
- Details of your buildings insurance policy and payment receipts.
- Memorandum and articles of the landlord or management company.

The **authorized** documents that can also be included are:

- A Home Condition Report.
- Guarantees and warranties.
- Fixtures and fittings list, detailing what's included or excluded from the sale.
- Other searches.

Home Condition Reports

A seller can top up a pack voluntarily to include a full Home Condition Report. This report will contain an Energy Performance Certificate and information about the condition of each part of the home on a scale of 1 to 3 (where 1 is best) advising the seller and buyer of any repairs needed and, if so, whether or not they are serious. This is a reliable report as it is carried out by Home Inspectors who are qualified, accredited and insured.

You are more likely to speed up the sale of your property and reduce the likelihood of buyers pulling out if you offer a full Home Condition Report because you will be providing more information upfront, minimizing the chances of unwanted surprises coming to light. The government is working with HIP arrangers to encourage them to take up the full Home Condition Report.

How are HIPs arranged?

It is the responsibility of the person marketing the property, for example the estate agent, or the seller if the property is being sold privately, to arrange the HIP and this must be available on the first day the property is marketed. There are financial penalties if you market a home without a HIP. If estate agents breach their HIP responsibilities, this will be treated as an 'undesirable practice' under the Estate Agents Act and they will be reported to the Office of Fair Trading (OFT). An estate agent who deliberately flouts the HIP regulations will risk being banned by the OFT.

You can get a pack from a recognized 'pack provider'. Consider having your pack ready before signing up with an estate agent or other home selling arrangement. That way you'll have more flexibility in how to sell your property and get a competitively priced HIP.

How much does a HIP cost?

A HIP is likely to cost anything up to £600 if it includes a Home Condition Report, or half that amount if it does not.

You can find out more about Home Information Packs by visiting www.homeinformationpacks.gov.uk

Summary

In this chapter we have looked at:

- Various mechanisms for how property pricing works
  - The price/rent ratio
  - Relative price comparison
  - Affordability
  - Price to replacement costs.
- Tricks of the trade when negotiating the best price for property to buy.
- How to get the best deal as a seller.
- How to structure the best deal.
- What to expect to pay in fees and disbursements.
- Home Information Packs.

08

renovation projects ...

In this chapter you will learn about:
- the process behind a renovation project
- common mistakes and how to avoid them
- surveys and specialist reports
- major issues and how to deal with them
- budgeting effectively and sticking to it
- planning issues
- Building Regulations
- financing renovation projects
- where to spend the money
- eco-building

... the good, the bad and the ugly

One of the most alluring aspects of property investment is the strategy of buying properties that are in need of renovation and doing them up to sell on at a profit.

Most property investors will, at some stage, have been attracted to the idea of buying a property that is derelict or in need of modernization or renovation and it's easy to understand why – very often these properties can be purchased at below market value and, provided that you budget for the works effectively, there can be a good profit in it. It also can be a fun and extremely satisfying way of making money from property. However, it's not always as easy as it sounds and can be extremely hard work. To be successful with this kind of property investment, you will need to have good organizational skills, be able to negotiate with contractors and tradespeople, manage a team effectively, plan and execute a project successfully, juggle finances and have an eye for design and layout.

In this chapter we will look at the common mistakes that inexperienced developers often make, and suggest ways to avoid them. We'll also talk about the process of renovating and the steps that you can expect to have to take, including surveys and specialist reports and planning applications. Finally, there will be guidance about which aspects of the renovation are worth spending the money on and which are not.

However, bear in mind that the contents this chapter could form a book in their own right, so I can give you only an overview of the main issues. For more information, visit my website www.makingmoneyfromproperty.tv or read some of the numerous specialist books and other websites that are out there.

First and foremost, before you tackle a renovation project, it is important to be clear what your end outcome is going to be. Are you buying to renovate and then sell on, or do you want to buy and then eventually rent out? Different strategies require a different approach, so it's important that you have this in mind at the start. You also need carefully to consider your target market for either resale or rental, and tailor all aspects of your project to attracting this target market. If you are renovating a larger property that will serve as a family home, you'll want to emphasize the kitchen, lounge or living area and garden to appeal to this market. If, on the other hand, your end user is a professional couple, then they may be more interested in open plan, modern living and will place greater emphasis on the quality of fixtures and finishing and how well the property lends itself to entertaining.

Before you start down the route of renovating, there are a few key questions that you should ask yourself to determine whether this type of property development is for you:

1 What skills do you have to lend to a renovation project? If you have to 'buy in' skills from professionals such as painters and decorators, then this will need to be factored into your overall budget.

2 What time do you have available to apply to the project? If you are working full time and intend to fit the work into your spare time, be honest with yourself about whether you are realistically going to able to do this. What impact on the length of time from purchase to completion of the project will this have? (If you are doing a lot of the work yourself during evenings and weekends, it will clearly take you longer to complete than if you have professionals working on the project five days a week.)

3 What budget do you have to carry out the renovation works, and do you have a contingency plan if you overspend? There will always be hidden costs and extras that you haven't accounted for, and this will tip some developers over their budget, with no means of finding the extra money to pay for any additional costs.

4 Is the building structurally sound? Before starting with any renovation project, you must ensure that the fabric of the building is sound. Having a full structural survey at the outset is vital and could save you literally thousands of pounds in the long run.

5 Are you going to need to apply for planning permission before the renovation work can be done? If so, how confident are you that this will be granted? If you are new to the process of applying for planning permission, it can be a bit of a shock to the system and will definitely have an impact on the length of time the project takes. Whatever you do, don't commit to buying a property that you intend to make extensive alterations to without checking out the planning situation first. Planners will often give you an idea of whether or not planning will be granted 'in principle' over the telephone.

6 How good are you at managing your money? The financial side of any renovation project is the most critical and the capital you have available will underpin every element of the project. You will need to be able to manage your cashflow successfully, so if you know you're not good with money, sticking to a budget or negotiating for the best price, this type of development might not suit you.

The process behind a renovation project

So what is the process of renovating a property?

In some cases the process can be fairly straightforward, and successful property developers embarking on renovation projects will be able to predict each step, and have a good idea how long each element of the project will take to complete. One of the common mistakes made by inexperienced developers is that they don't consider all the steps in the process, and badly underestimate the length of time they may take to complete. This means the project overruns which can have drastic effects on the budget – if the money has been borrowed, delays mean more interest payments and you could 'miss the market' in terms of resale or let.

Essentially, a successful project involves various stages:

Research stage

General research

Carrying out research on the area, the type of property available and prices they are achieving – as well as planning considerations. You should also carry out research on your exit strategy: if you are buying to rent out then how many similar rental properties are there in the area? Does demand exceed supply? You certainly don't want to spend all your money and effort renovating a property to have it sit vacant on the market for months afterwards.

Property research

This is finding a suitable property to renovate. You should cast your net as wide as possible in order that you can consider as many projects as possible. See Chapter 3 on Where to find properties to buy.

Financial research

Make sure that you can secure the money not only for the purchase of the property, but for the works to be carried out and also for the eventual resale or let of the finished project and the associated costs. This may include buying furniture or 'dressing' the property when you put it back on the market. If you are planning to borrow money through a mortgage, then you need to be certain that you will be able to get one. Certain issues will mean you simply will not be able to find a lender willing to finance against the property.

Preparation stage

Surveys and reports

You will need to have a survey done on the property to evaluate the extent of works to be carried out. If you are applying for a mortgage to help purchase the property, then undoubtedly the lender will require a survey to be undertaken. Don't cut corners on this. The temptation is to go for just a basic valuation which is the minimum that the lender will require to evaluate whether the property is worth what you are paying for it. A full structural survey will pay dividends in the long run.

Planning and budgeting

Once a survey has been carried out, you will have a good idea of the extent of works that need to be done. Write down a comprehensive list of all the jobs that need to be undertaken. List all the jobs in the same order in which the work needs to be done. Some jobs will have to be completed before others can start, so careful consideration of this at the outset will give you a far better project plan. You also need to write down the time each part of the project is going to take. If you don't have this information you soon will, when you contact contractors and tradespeople and ask them to quote you for work. Once you've had quotes, you will also be able to allocate an indicative cost to all the jobs on your list and therefore work out a total budget.

In time you will be able to develop expertise to enable you to spot and avoid problem properties, but in the early stages of your property developing experience it's vital that you surround yourself with as much expert professional help as possible and spend your money carefully.

Finding contractors and tradespeople

This can be one of the most challenging aspects of a renovation project. Finding good, reliable tradespeople who are available to do your work when you need them isn't easy. Word of mouth and personal recommendation are by far the best way to source tradespeople. If you are buying in an area that you are unfamiliar with, ask the local estate agents and letting agents for their recommendations – most will have a number of contacts that you can call. There are also many professional bodies that tradespeople belong to, such as the Federation of Master Builders, where members adopt minimum standards.

Obtaining and finalizing quotes

Make sure you obtain at least three written quotes from different tradespeople for the work. Assess all aspects of what they will provide before making your final choice – the cheapest may not always be the best.

Professional advice

Employ the services of a qualified architect if you are making structural changes and talk over the project with professionals such as estate agents, letting agents and builders before you go too far down the planning route. They should all be able to guide you in terms of the viability of a project and how best to make a profit. Remember most people like offering advice and you could be surprised at how forthcoming the are.

Execution stage

Managing the project

This is where a well thought through budget and plan will pay dividends as it will be clear where in the project you are and how it is performing against the budget and timescales. Be honest with yourself on your ability to do this – you may decide that you are better off employing the services of a project manager to oversee the day-to-day running of things. If you can't afford this, consider at least seeking a second opinion from a trusted friend or relative to help you control your budget.

Exit

This is a very important aspect of the project. There is absolutely no point in going through the whole process of renovating a property only to watch it sit on the market for months on end when it is completed. This is demoralizing and costly. You should have a clear idea of your intended exit strategy, for example resale or let, at the beginning. Having more than one exit strategy also reduces your risk with the project. Spend time researching what demand is like in the area for the kind of property you aim to create, and speak to as many estate and letting agents as you can to get their professional opinions on realistic values at completion.

Profit and taxes

Hopefully, you will have made a good healthy profit on the project at completion. The final stage is to sort out the finances so that you know what your net profit actually is and what tax you are due to pay. Remember that any property that isn't your principal place of residence is liable to Capital Gains Tax on the profits that you make. If you are serious about becoming a full-time property developer, discuss with your accountant how best to set yourself up in business to minimize your tax bill. This could include forming a limited company.

Common mistakes and how to avoid them

Property development isn't easy and it takes a good head and experience to make it work. Very often, inexperienced property developers come unstuck and end up making very little or no money out of a project. Worse still, some find that they make a loss on a project, which clearly isn't the idea! Below are a few of the common mistakes that inexperienced property developers make and suggestions on how best to avoid them.

Getting only a basic valuation done rather than a proper survey

When you are working to a tight budget, spending several hundred pounds on instructing a full survey to be done seems tough, especially at this stage when you don't know if you are actually going to buy the property. However, getting a full survey done is imperative to the success of a renovation project. This is not an area to cut back on costs.

Paying too much for a property

When you become excited about a really interesting renovation or development project it is very easy to get carried away and pay too much for the property to begin with. These days, competition among other developers and buyers can be high, particularly if the property is unusual or has lots of potential.

Do your price research thoroughly and agree the maximum price that you are willing to pay once you have costed out all the renovation works. Then **stick** to this maximum price.

Falling out with contractors and tradespeople

It is important to develop good working relationships with your contractors, builders and tradespeople. There should be mutual respect on both sides with each party addressing problems or concerns in a professional manner. Conduct yourself with professionalism at the outset. Be authoritative but not argumentative and listen to their views – they may have suggestions and ideas which you hadn't considered. Use only reputable builders and, if possible, employ people who have been personally recommended to you. At the very least, check out the credentials of your team before employing them, and take up references or view examples of previously completed work before deciding on who to take on.

Building costs go over budget

Once you have engaged the services of a builder and work is underway it's a tricky situation to then discover that building costs are running above budget. There may be legitimate reasons for this, for example there has been some unexpected expense that you hadn't factored into your plan. But strict, careful budget planning at the start of the project should eliminate this happening in most cases. Always add in a contingency of 15 per cent for this eventuality. Make sure you have well written, legally binding contracts in place with builders and contractors that you employ which you can call on if the work takes longer than expected or costs more than originally quoted.

Finishings costs go over budget

You will need to be disciplined and businesslike when choosing your fixtures, fittings and furniture. Stick to the budget that you have allocated because it is easy to let your heart rule your head and to buy expensive pieces just because you like them.

Once finished, property stays vacant on the market for too long

This problem can be avoided by thinking through your exit strategy very carefully at the beginning. If you have purchased and renovated a project that is suitable for the target market that you are aiming at, then there should be plenty of people wanting to view on completion, provided that you are asking a realistic price. Once again, research and having an understanding of what the market will support are key. If you do your sums and find that you have to market the property for more than comparable properties in order to give you the profit that you want, then it may not be the property to go for (or you need to rethink your budget). Developers who have put their heart and soul into a renovation project which has been a long labour of love sometimes have unrealistic expectations of the eventual resale or lettable value of that property.

£ Martin's tip

Guidelines for a successful project

We've looked at some of the common mistakes that inexperienced (and sometimes experienced!) developers make. The following is a list of general guidelines for making the project a success:

- Don't get personal. Don't be tempted to spend money on things just because you like them if they don't fit with your target market or create an overspend on your budget. What you think is fabulous might not be to everyone else's taste.

- Get a full structural survey done. Know what you're letting yourself in for. Don't ever start renovation without knowing everything about the property – warts and all. Having a survey carried out early on in the process will let you work out what the whole project will involve and whether it's something you want and have the ability to take on.

- Be professional. Conduct yourself in a professional manner when dealing with estate agents, surveyors and tradespeople. They will respect you for being open, honest and fair. Don't cut corners in your project. Always do things properly. If you let your standards slip then you set a precedent in the mindset of your contractors that you don't mind if things aren't done correctly – this can mean that the whole project becomes shoddy.

- Keep abreast of legislation. As with any profession, it is important that you keep up to date with rules and regulations that affect the work you do. In particular, make sure you (or at the very least, your project manager) is aware of current Building Regulations. If you are developing to rent the property out, make sure you are aware of your obligations as a landlord, in particular if the property falls within HMO regulation.

- Get organized. If you're not good with administration either delegate this responsibility to someone else close to you, or get yourself into a mindset of being organized. You need to have an efficient system for filing of all paperwork, records and receipts including quotes for work and contracts. This will prove to be invaluable should the project run into difficulty or you have a disagreement with a contractor. Make notes during or immediately after your conversations with anyone involved in the project – don't rely on your memory.
- Be proactive. Nip any potential difficulties in the bud before they develop, and try to plan ahead with the project.

Surveys and specialist reports

One of the most important steps in your research and planning stage is getting a survey done. This will give you an accurate idea of the extent of work that needs to be carried out and is not an area to scrimp on. The minimum that a mortgage lender will require will be a 'basic valuation' to assess that the property is worth what you are proposing to pay for it, but if you are buying an older property or something in need of renovation (which in this case you are) it is better to get a proper survey done.

There are three main types of survey:

Basic valuation

This is carried out on behalf of the mortgage lender to make sure that the property is worth at least what you are going to be borrowing. It will look at the structure of the property and report on any issues that could affect the value of the property and, therefore, the security of the loan. The surveyor will place a value on the property and the mortgage lender will base their mortgage offer on this valuation. You, as the borrower, will usually be expected to pay for this valuation, but the level of fee will be made clear to you at the outset. Be aware that this kind of valuation is not a proper survey and if there are defects with the house that are not a concern of the lender, then they won't be reported to you. Although the surveyor should comment on all parts of the property that are readily accessible, they won't lift carpets or do a more in-depth inspection. You have no legal recourse if the valuation turns out to be inaccurate or you buy the property and then subsequently discover defects that weren't covered in the valuation. The report is really for the benefit of the lender only.

Homebuyer's survey

A homebuyer's survey and valuation report (HSV) is for the benefit of the buyer and is much more detailed than the basic valuation. It will report on the property's general condition, defects in accessible parts of the property and urgent works that should be addressed before exchanging contracts. If there has been any testing of walls for damp, the results will be included in the report as well as general comments on damage to timbers, condition of any damp proofing, insulation and drainage. The report will also give you an indication of the value of the property on the open market and the recommended reinstatement cost for insurance purposes. While the HSV is far more detailed than a basic valuation report, a surveyor will report only on things that they can see and they won't necessarily lift floorboards or scrabble around in the roof space. Since this report is carried out for the benefit of you, the buyer, rather than the lender, you do have a certain amount of recourse if the report is inaccurate.

Full structural survey

This is an in-depth and comprehensive inspection of the property that has to be carried out by a fully qualified chartered surveyor. Because it is much more in-depth, a full structural survey (sometimes called a building survey) is more expensive than a homebuyer's report. However, it will report on all faults however minor, suggest implications of any defects and give an indication of costs to put it right, comment on the existence and condition of damp proofing, insulation and drainage as well as including results of tests on walls and timbers for signs of damp, woodworm and rot. It will also include technical information on the age and style of construction of the property and the materials used. It is recommended that a full structural survey is carried out on older properties, listed buildings, unusual properties that have perhaps been constructed in an unconventional way and properties that have already been altered extensively from their original design.

So what happens if the survey reveals a few gremlins in the property? The reality is that virtually any defect can be sorted out. You just need to be confident that it makes financial sense to do it and that you are ready to cope with the extra work and time involved.

---

⑪ Food for thought

Share your Experiences

You can share your property development experiences with others on the website that accompanies this book www.makingmoneyfromproperty.tv. Offer or ask advice – and even upload videos and pictures of your property projects. Share your triumphs and disasters, and learn from others, or help them to avoid the mistakes you made.

Major issues and how to deal with them

The following section gives an overview of the some of the major problems you may encounter during a renovation project, including:

- damp
- mould and rot
- infestation
- subsidence.

Again, each of these subjects could easily fill a chapter in its own right, so please view the following as an overview and seek professional advice on all these issues if you are at all new to the property renovation game.

Damp and how to deal with it

Damp is one of the most common problems you will encounter while renovating property. It can cause literally thousands of pounds of damage and untold problems if not treated quickly and effectively. Never has the expression 'a stitch in time saves nine' had such relevance.

By spotting and remedying the cause of damp, you can significantly speed up the property renovation process. There are different types of damp:

- Rising damp
- Penetrating damp
- Accidental damp.

Learning about all three is an important part of being a property renovator. In the meantime, there are specialist companies who will survey and suggest remedies for property where there is a problem with damp.

Rising damp

As the name suggests, this is damp that rises from a water source below where it is visible. The most common cause will be a breakdown of the damp-proof course, or the fact that the property is of older construction, when damp proofing was not installed. However, older properties were designed with this in mind and if the house is functioning as it should, there should be no issues. Natural ventilation is key in these kinds of properties, and if you allow the house to 'breathe' normally, it will look after itself. Blocked up chimneys or air blocks, hermetically sealed windows or older houses with double glazing and tight-fitting doors stopping airflow are likely to cause problems. Before you know it you will be saying 'hello' to nasty black mould all over the place and a fusty smell. (For a compendium of different varieties of mould see the pictures in the centre of the book.)

 Martin's tip

Top tips for spotting and avoiding rising damp

1 Don't block natural ventilation – especially in older houses.
2 Ensure that drains are kept clear and free flowing – saturated soil will result in water seeping back into the house.
3 Make sure there are no large trees within 20 metres of the property – roots will damage drains and footings.
4 Consider a drainage survey in older homes. This may reveal cracked or leaking drains which could lead to future damp problems.
5 Make sure all rainwater goods, such as gutterings and downpipes, are free and not blocked.

---

6 Make sure you inspect the cellar if there is one. Check the condition of the underside of the joists and floorboards. Be suspicious if areas of the cellar ceiling or walls have recently been decorated – it could be concealing damp problems.

7 A long horizontal line of small holes drilled into an exterior wall could be an indication that someone has installed a chemical injection damp-proof course. These can be effective and usually come with a guarantee. This is often transferable to a new owner, so make sure you get the guarantee certificate from the vendor.

8 Plants and weeds growing around drains and manhole covers can be an indication of problems below.

Penetrating damp

This is damp which comes in through the walls and around windows either horizontally or from above. The most frequent cause of this will be a leaking roof or rainwater goods such as gutters and downpipes. The irritating thing is that the area where the damp appears may be some distance away from where the water is coming in. Water may travel down beams, through natural gullies, down electric cables and along joists before it finally makes an appearance on the wall. The result will generally be the same though: mould, leading on to rot, leading on to a huge hole in your restoration budget! I've seen properties where water has continually seeped from a tiny hole in a gutter for a long period of time. An issue that would have cost less than £10 to fix has caused tens of thousands of pounds worth of damage as mould turned to rot, then to dry rot, turning joists and floorboards to dust.

🖹 Martin's tip

Top tips for spotting and avoiding penetrating damp

1 Check all rainwater goods regularly. Look for external damp patches soon after rain, where most of the water has dried out but a damp patch is left.

2 Feel the walls with your hand. Do they feel damp? Have they been freshly painted? This is sometimes done by unscrupulous sellers in an attempt to conceal obvious signs of damp.

3 Pay particular attention to ceilings and in and around windows, especially dormer windows and roof lights. These are classic places for penetrating damp.

4 Make sure you inspect the loft area and check the condition of the underfelt (if there is any). Turn the lights off when you are up there. Can you see daylight coming through the roof anywhere? This will show places where water could come in.

5 Visiting a property when it is raining can be an obvious but very useful way to see if any water is coming in.

6 Use a pair of binoculars to check the condition of the roof. Pay particular attention to the ridge tiles and the area around the base of the chimney stack. Look at the condition of the cement securing the ridge tiles and any lead flashing.

7 Look for any signs of algae or mould on exterior walls. This can be an indication of recurring dampness and could lead to associated problems on corresponding interior walls.

8 If you plan to purchase a lot of property, consider investing in a damp-proof meter. These can be bought for around £100.

Accidental damp

This is the term I use to describe the damp that's been caused by accidental leakage, such as from a leaking water pipe or tap. Older pipework is particularly susceptible to leakage from joints, and as pipework is hidden this can be very difficult to spot. A good plumber should be able to tell you if hidden pipework is leaking. Another common area for problems to occur is around poorly fitted sanitary ware, shower cubicles and baths.

 Martin's tip

Top tips for spotting and avoiding accidental damp

1 Always turn off the main water stopcock when a property is left vacant for any period of time.

2 Drain the water and central heating systems of any property that is vacant – especially over cold periods. Frozen pipes are expensive to repair and the damage caused by them even more so.

3 Thoroughly check around all areas where water is used, such as the kitchen sink, bathroom fittings, shower units, central heating boilers, etc. Look for signs of leakage – long or short term.

4 Ask a qualified plumber along to give you an informal assessment of the state of the water and central heating systems. They may spot things you won't.

Mould and rot and how to deal with it

Left unchecked, all varieties of damp will lead to mould and potentially on to rot. This is one of the most common types of problem that I see in the properties that I visit for *Homes Under the Hammer*. Your job as a property investor is to know how to differentiate between the mould and rot that's 'nothing to worry about', and that which should have you scurrying away to look at alternative property.

No mould or rot problem is impossible to sort out, but the amount of money it will cost to do so can vary massively. Discovering you have dry rot in a property to which you have allocated £2,000 for renovation will blow your budget quicker than you can say 'Oh deary me, that's somewhat inconvenient'.

The good news is that fairly harmless mould still looks pretty horrible and it can put inexperienced investors off. You can suck through your teeth, feign horror at the prospect of the work involved and negotiate a hefty chunk off the asking price.

So the trick is to know your moulds. I've spent the last six months photographing all the mould and rot I've come across in the hundreds of properties I've visited in that time. They are proudly presented for your delight and delectation in the 'Compendium of Mould and Rot' in the middle colour pages of this book and also on the accompanying website: www.making moneyfromproperty.tv.

£ Martin's tip

Top tips for spotting and avoiding mould and rot

1 Eliminate the cause of damp that is allowing the formation of mould and rot.

2 Investigate all obvious potentially damp areas such as cellars and around chimney breasts.

3 If possible, lift floorboards and check underneath. Pay particular attention to the point where the floor joists go into the wall.

4 Dry rot is everyone's worst fear. Familiarize yourself with what it looks like from the photos in the 'Compendium of Mould and Rot' in the colour section of this book or on the website www.makingmoneyfromproperty.tv.

5 Use your sense of smell as well as your eyes. Damp, mouldy houses smell musty.

6 If woodwork is crumbling or turning to dust, this is a good indication that something is not right.

Infestation and how to deal with it

Infestation broadly breaks down into two categories: animals and insects.

Animals

The most likely animals to occupy your property are rodents. Mice and rats love unoccupied buildings and will have a field day chewing through cables, rampaging through your rafters and burrowing through your floorboards. Your local authority can provide advice on how to eradicate rodents or there are numerous private firms that can also do so. Other possible unwelcome guests (or welcome depending on your viewpoint) are bats. Be aware that bats are protected and that to kill them, or to disturb a bat or its roost, is a criminal offence.

Insects

Woodworm

Woodworm will cause considerable damage to all wood in your property. Joists will be reduced to powder and elegant floorboards will be pock-marked beyond repair. By the time you see a woodworm hole the woodworm has gone. You need to prevent woodworm by ensuring that all vulnerable timber has been suitably treated with specialist chemicals. The time to do this is early on in the restoration process, since floorboards will have to be lifted to give access to the underlying timbers.

plate 1 Aaaahhhh.... the joys of filming Homes Under The Hammer! I used to present the travel show Wish You Were Here...? Now it's Derby, not Dubrovnik!

Some potential problems

plate 2 Roots from nearby trees will cause potential damage to drains and foundations

plate 3 Dormer windows can be problematic but can create useful extra space

plate 4 Flat roofs are notorious for leaks. Try and inspect them from above

plate 5 Blocked up fireplaces are potential sources of damp. Make sure there is adequate ventilation

plate 6   Old gas fires need to be inspected by a specialist. They are potentially lethal

plate 7   Check planning permission exists for any extensions. This one only has a single skin of brick, leading to damp problems

plate 8   Check the loft. Here there is no wall between adjoining properties, creating a serious fire hazard

plate 9 'Non standard Construction' – such as houses made from concrete block like this one – will be difficult to raise finance on

plate 10 Have electrics checked by a professional – otherwise the consequences could be devastating

plate 11 Leaking or damaged drains will cause huge potential problems. Look for subsidence around them

plate 12   This house has a 'flying freehold' over the alleyway. Your solicitor should check the title deeds of a property like this very carefully

plate 13   Old boilers and badly installed water and central heating systems should be thoroughly checked or replaced

plate 14 Don't underestimate the cost of clearing a garden, such as the one on the right. It could be thousands of pounds

plate 15 Damaged guttering is not expensive to fix, but left unchecked will lead to huge damp problems

plate 16 Pay particular attention to leaks from blocked or cracked hoppers like this one

plate 17   An idyllic setting, but this house is positioned on a protected loch which will lead to major planning restrictions

plate 18   This house is surrounded by commercial units, which could give problems with obtaining a mortgage and resale

plate 19   A classic. Looks great in the catalogue...until you see where it is located...At least you won't have noisy neighbours!

plate 20 An attractive barn for conversion – however, a right of way and footpath over the land will restrict development

plate 21 Idyllic, tranquil, rural farmhouse...errr...or not

plate 22 On the plus side – this unassuming bungalow has a huge garden with easy access and probably easy planning permission. Gold in your garden

plate 24   Check the quality of any remedial work. This has been done well

plate 23   Cracks like this indicate serious subsidence

plate 25   Take care looking around houses – the floor in this one has collapsed

plate 26   Windows are a good place to spot subsidence

plate 27   Look at the roof line – it's bowed! Tiles are missing and guttering is shoddy. New roof required!

plate 28 Lintels above windows are another good place to spot subsidence

plate 29 As are doors, both outside...

plate 30 ...and inside. Look at the angle at the top

plate 31   You could see through this crack in to the neighbouring property

plate 32   The arch is collapsing

plate 33   Talk about 'papering over the cracks'!!

plate 34   Notice the leaning chimney stack...

plate 35   ...somebody has taken out the chimney breast and not put back any support

plate 36 Top left: Nothing serious, but find and fix the source of the damp
Top right: Beautiful but deadly. This is dry rot
Middle left: 'Blown' plaster and paint will need hacking off and replacing
Middle right: Tell tale signs of dry rot
Bottom left: More dry rot – spreading through wood, brick and plaster
Bottom right: If possible check under floor boards and the ceiling void

plate 37   A selection of kitchens and bathrooms in need of attention. Don't be too quick to remove period features, but effort and money spent on improving these rooms will pay huge dividends

plate 38   Churches make fabulous conversion projects but may also have planning restrictions and structural complications

plate 39   Old utilities buildings, telephone exchanges and civil offices have great potential but obtaining permission for 'change of use' may be difficult

plate 40   Commercial property provides good
diversification in your portfolio and potentially
high rental yields

plate 41   When you've got to go...! Two of the most amusing loos I've seen whilst filming Homes Under The Hammer

Ants and wasps

These can often be an indication of other problems. Wasps may be entering via a hole in the roof or facia boards and ants may be coming through gaps around windows. Neither are a significant problem but the problems they are highlighting may be.

Subsidence – the tell-tale signs and what to do about it

Subsidence is the downward movement of the ground supporting a building. A property with subsidence may have large cracks in the walls as the foundations of the property have become unstable; however, not all cracks in a property are due to subsidence, so you need to know what you are looking for. Subsidence can be caused by:

- **certain soils** – Clay soils are particularly vulnerable since they shrink and swell depending on their moisture content.
- **vegetation** – Trees and shrubs take moisture from the soil causing it to shrink, especially during long periods of dry weather as roots extend in search of water
- **leaking drains** – Damaged drains can soften or wash away the ground beneath the foundations.

Although less common, you can get subsidence if a property has been built over, or close to, mine workings so if you are considering buying in an area which you know to have a mining history, a mining survey and a keen eye are invaluable.

Other types of ground movement, which although less common, can still result in cracking and structural damage, are:

- **heave** – The upward movement of the ground supporting the building, the reverse of subsidence, which arises when the soil absorbs more water and therefore expands.
- **landslip** – Movement of ground down a slope caused by a variety of soil related issues, including clay creep, deep-seated soil slip and shallow slop.

What are the tell-tale signs of subsidence?

We're now entering the realm of a specialist structural survey and as I've said before you should think about commissioning one before purchasing a property. The information given here is not a substitute for the experienced attentions of a specialist surveyor.

The most obvious sign of subsidence is the appearance of cracks. However, not all cracks indicate that there is a problem – most buildings experience cracking at some time. Cracks are not uncommon in new properties and newly built extensions. They are likely to be the result of the building settling under its own weight. These are generally nothing to worry about, nor are fine cracks which often appear in newly plastered walls as the water content dries out. Buildings shrink and swell naturally due to changes in temperature and humidity, which can lead to minor cracks where walls and ceilings meet. These too should not normally be anything to worry about.

£ Martin's tip

Tell-tale signs of subsidence

Look out for small, usually diagonal, cracks around doors and windows. The cracks will normally be quite substantial and usually wider at the top than the bottom. Doors and windows may also 'stick' due to the distortion of the building. Take a look at the property from a distance. Do the windows and door frames look 'true' and are the roof ridge line and walls straight?

Once again, if you are considering buying a property and you believe it may have subsidence you must get it checked out by a structural engineer or specialist surveyor to assess the extent of the problem.

How do you deal with subsidence?

Subsidence is usually remedied by having the building underpinned. But before you start to tackle the problem, you need to identify the cause. A chartered engineer experienced in such matters will obtain the necessary information about the soil and match it with the cracking patterns in your walls. Having formed an initial opinion about the probable causes, they will then arrange tests of the soils and building structure. The tests will help the engineer to see if underpinning is needed and, if so, how deep and how great an area of underpinning is required. If subsidence seems to be caused by a leaking drain, the drain should be repaired but underpinning may still be needed, to ensure the subsidence doesn't continue.

Budgeting effectively and sticking to it

Planning your budget and sticking to it is probably the singularly most important aspect of any renovation or development project. If projects fail, it is often because the developer has been unrealistic about the costs involved or hasn't kept on top of the finances, and the budget is left to run out of control.

To be able to plan your budget successfully, you must be aware of all the costs involved at the outset. A sensible investment of time at this stage, researching, sourcing realistic costs and getting quotes for work to be done, will help you to manage your project successfully and generate the profit that you intended. Once you have calculated all the costs involved, you need to add on a contingency of around 15 per cent to cover eventualities which had not been planned. You do not want to be in a position where you run out of money because of unexpected expenses – particularly if you don't have a back-up plan.

There are three main areas of cost:

The property acquisition

Aside from the cost of the property itself, there are a number of fees and expenses involved in acquiring the property:

- Solicitor's or conveyancing fees – payable for the legal work involved in buying the property.
- Survey fees – will depend on the type of survey you have carried out, for example, a homebuyer's survey or a full structural survey.
- Stamp Duty – 1 per cent of the purchase price from £125,001 to £250,000 increasing to 3 per cent for properties from £250,001 to £500,000 and 4 per cent for properties over £500,000. Properties priced up to £125,000 do not attract Stamp Duty and if the property is in a designated 'disadvantaged' area, then any property up to £150,000 is at the 0 per cent rate.
- Mortgage broker fee or arrangement fee – Most mortgage companies charge an administration or arrangement fee and if you have used a mortgage broker, they too may charge you a fee for their work.
- Re-inspection fee – Some mortgage companies will withhold part of the loan until you carry out some of the work on the property. If this is the case, they will charge a re-inspection fee

to visit the property to see if the work has actually been done before they release the rest of the money.

- If you are buying abroad, there may also be other purchase costs. See Chapter 13 for more information about buying overseas.

Renovation/refurbishment costs

This is the part which is easy to overspend on, so be realistic with your budget and disciplined during the course of the project. You will need to account for:

Labour

Depending on the amount of work you are undertaking yourself, obtain written quotations from several builders and tradespeople and ensure that your contract with them makes provision for extra work and/or costs that may occur.

Building materials

Itemize all the materials you require and obtain quotations from local suppliers. Again, it pays to shop around and research several different sources including builders' merchants, trade discount stores, the Internet and local suppliers. Remember to budget for delivery. If you are using a builder, check what materials are included in their quotation and what materials they are expecting you to provide.

Plant hire

You may need to pay for scaffolding, skips and other plant hire. These may be surprisingly expensive. Again, check with your builder what is included in the quotation. The costs of clearing a site of old materials and preparing it for renovation shouldn't be overlooked.

Tools and equipment

If you are intending to do work yourself, you will need to have the right tools and equipment. Sometimes, it is just as cost effective to buy – particularly if you imagine doing other projects in the future – than to hire. You don't need to cost right down to the last screw, but do think carefully about what tools you have available to you and what you are going to need.

Internal materials

These include paint, wallpaper and tiles, and so on. It can be more cost effective to go for a simple, neutral colour scheme throughout the property.

Fixtures and fittings

All the little things like light switches, taps, shelving or handles add to the costs so try to work out what fixtures and fittings you are going to need. Imagine moving into the property to live and you'll see exactly what is needed to make the place habitable aside from furniture. This is an area where it is really easy to get carried away and blow the budget. Be strict with yourself and keep the end user in mind. Spending thousands on an Italian designer tap set is unlikely to add the equivalent price to the property value. Again the Internet can be a good source of discounted fixtures and fittings.

Furniture

You may want to 'stage' your finished project for resale or let, in which case you will need to source suitable furniture. This can help prospective tenants/buyers to visualize how they might live in the property. If you are buying furniture for this purpose, you will need to consider storing it or negotiating for it to be included in the price of the property when you sell, or rent 'furnished'.

Insurance

You should keep your insurance company informed of any building work that is being carried out on the property.

Planning permission

There are also costs associated with obtaining planning permission.

Running costs

Mortgage payments

If you have taken out a mortgage to buy the property, you need to factor in the monthly repayments for the duration of your project until you finally sell or rent. If you are renovating to sell (and therefore repaying the mortgage after a short period of time) ensure you take out a suitable mortgage that has no early repayment charges.

Transport

Your personal trips to and from the property and general running around are running costs. If you don't live near to the property, these can add up. Also consider delivery charges or transport of materials to the site.

Cleaning and maintenance

At the end of the project you will need a professional 'builder's clean' to remove all debris from the building process. If you are keeping the property to let then you will require a full clean between lets. You are better off employing the services of a specialist cleaning company for this. Similarly, regular maintenance of any properties that you are keeping to let is vital to keep your property in good order.

Property management and letting

If you are serious about building a portfolio then you are likely to engage a property management and lettings company to take care of matters to do with your tenants. This means that they look after things on your behalf but will refer to you for any major expense. They will often have their own team of plumbers, electricians, and so on, who they can call on to remedy any faults that occur, otherwise you will be expected to get them sorted out yourself.

Accounts

You need to keep accurate accounts in respect of the project. You can either do this yourself if you feel you have the necessary skills, or employ a book-keeper to keep these records for you.

Utilities

You will need to pay for gas, electricity and water during the project, up until you resell or let the property. Depending on the nature of the project, there may also be connection charges. Splitting one supply into several, if you are converting one house into, say, several flats can cost thousands of pounds.

Council tax

Again, you will be responsible for this up until the time you resell or let out the property.

Having planned and put together your budget, you need to keep to it! The easiest way to do this is to refer to it often throughout the project. There is no point having a great spreadsheet at the beginning that then just gets ignored once the work starts. Setting your budget at the beginning will also help with some of the numerous decisions you will have to make along the way. It may also help stop your heart from ruling your head. If you save money on one particular element of the project, don't just think that you've got more to spend elsewhere. Instead, add it to your contingency fund, and if you complete the project under budget – then use it to splash out and celebrate!

Planning issues

It is quite probable that you will have to obtain planning permission before your refurbishment work can be undertaken, although some home improvements do not require planning permission. It's worth chatting to your local planning office before you start any renovation works to be sure that you are clear.

Chances are, you'll need to apply for planning permission if you:

- want to add an extension to the property, and
  - the extension would be closer to a highway than any part of the original house (unless there would be at least 20 metres between the highway and your extension);
  - the extension would be greater than half the area of land surrounding the house;
  - the extension would be higher than the highest part of the roof of your original house;
  - the extension would be more than 4 metres high and within 2 metres of the boundary of your property;
  - the house is terraced and the extension would increase the volume by 10 per cent or more or 50 cubic metres, whichever is the greater;
  - the extension would be to any roof slope that faces a highway;
  - the extension would increase the height of the existing roof.
- want to build a separate building in the garden, and
  - the new building would be closer to a highway than any part of the original house (unless there is more than 20 metres between the highway and the building);
  - more than half of the area of land surrounding your house is taken up with the new building
  - the height of the roof is more than 3 metres or 4 metres if ridged.
- want to build a porch onto your house, and
  - the porch would be greater than 3 square metres;
  - the porch would be higher than 3 metres above ground level;
  - there is less than 2 metres between the porch and a highway.

You may also need planning permission if you want to:

- divide off part of the property to make a separate self-contained flat or bedroom;
- build a parking space for a commercial vehicle and/or divide the property into separate work or living accommodation;
- change the designated use of a commercial property or change from residential to commercial use.

You should take particular care if your property is a listed building, since special planning conditions apply. Your local planning office will be able to offer advice.

It's important to be clear on whether or not planning permission is required before you start. Beginning works without seeking the appropriate consent could result in you being served with an enforcement order from the local planning office, insisting that you cease works, apply for the relevant permissions then comply with the requirements. This could mean having to pull down or rebuild work already completed.

If you are employing the services of an architect, they will generally apply for Planning Permission on your behalf. If not, you will have to go through the process yourself.

The process of applying for planning permission

1 Obtain a planning application form from the local council.
2 Employ the services of an architect to draw up scale drawings of the existing dwelling and proposed work (so, a before and after picture).These drawings need to be accurate and to an approved scale.
3 Submit the plans to the council along with the completed application form and appropriate fee.
4 The council will acknowledge receipt of the application and then write to the owners/occupiers of properties that are located in the immediate vicinity to inform them of your application. Usually you will also be sent a notice which briefly states the proposed changes, which you display somewhere on your property. If anyone has any issue with the proposed changes, they have 21 days within which to lodge an objection.
5 If there are more than two objections to your proposed changes, the council will automatically submit your application to a committee for a decision on whether or not the works can be carried out.

6 The council will either grant you planning permission or refuse it and you will be notified of this decision. If planning permission is granted you must stick strictly to the plans in your application and any conditions imposed by the council. Any changes will require you to submit an amendment and this will be reviewed by a planning officer. If the changes are significant, you may have to apply for full planning permission again.

7 You have a set period of time within which you must start the work proposed. If no work is undertaken before the expiry of the planning permission (usually five years) then the planning permission will lapse and you will have to re-apply if you decide to do the work at a later date.

8 Even if your application is turned down, you still have the option to appeal and persistence can sometimes bring results.

Building Regulations

What are Building Regulations?

Building Regulations set standards for the design and construction of buildings to ensure the safety and health of people living or working in or around those buildings. They also include requirements for fuel and power conservation facilities and for those with disabilities.

Building Regulations approval is a separate issue to obtaining planning permission. A project may require planning permission as well as Building Regulations compliance.

Difference between planning permission and building regulations

In a nutshell, Building Regulations are rules governing the actual construction specifications of buildings. They apply to individual properties. Planning seeks to guide the way our towns, cities and countryside develop. This includes the use of land and buildings, the appearance of buildings, landscaping considerations, highway access and the impact that the development will have on the general environment.

For many types of building work, separate permission under both regimes will be required. For other building work, such as internal alterations, Buildings Regulations approval will probably be needed, but planning permission may not be. If you are in any doubt you should contact your Local Planning Authority or Building Control body.

It is important to understand how Building Regulations apply to your project as you are responsible for making sure that the work complies. If you are employing a builder, the responsibility will usually be theirs, but you should confirm this at the very beginning. You should also bear in mind that if you are the owner of the building, it is ultimately you who may be served with an enforcement notice if the work does not comply with the regulations.

To help you achieve compliance with the regulations, you are required to use one of two types of Building Control service:

• your local authority Building Control service; or
• an approved inspector's Building Control service.

However, if your building work specifically consists only of the installation of certain types of services or fittings (e.g. some types of drain, fuel burning appliances, replacement windows, WCs and showers) and you employ an installer registered with a relevant scheme designated in the Building Regulations (a *competent person*), that installer may be able to self-certify the work. Therefore, you will not need to involve a Building Control Service.

Contraventions

If the building work you have carried out does not comply with the requirements contained in the Building Regulations you will be deemed to have contravened them and you can expect a visit from the Buildings Inspector. They can use enforcement powers to require alteration to the work and impose fines.

Conservation areas and listed buildings

Conservation areas

A conservation area is one that has been identified as an area of special architectural or historic importance, the character of which it is desirable to preserve or enhance.

If you buy a property in a conservation area, then it will be subject to extra planning controls. This preserves the character of the property and the area. Conservation areas vary in both size and character, ranging from small groups of buildings to town squares or even open spaces.

Planning considerations in conservation areas

Conservation areas have extra planning controls. Anything which is likely to have an impact on the general façade of a building (such as placement of satellite dishes) will definitely be subject to these rules, the most notable of which is a reduction in the size of extensions that can be built without planning permission. Similarly, the demolition of any buildings within conservation areas will also be restricted. Many trees within a conservation area are also protected.

☺ **Did you know?**

Tree Preservation Orders

Many trees in conservation areas and elsewhere are protected and it is a criminal offence to damage or fell them. Individual trees will have a Tree Preservation Order on them, and their location and species will be held on record by the relevant regulating authorities. You can find out more by visiting www.communities.gov.uk

---

Listed buildings

Certain buildings are listed to ensure that their architectural and historic interest is carefully considered before any alterations, either outside or inside, are agreed. Once a building has been listed, it is a criminal offence to demolish or alter it (including the interior of the building) without the consent from the relevant authorities.

Don't confuse planning permission with listed building consent – the two are separate, albeit closely linked, and each is governed by different legislation. If you are planning on making any changes to the interior, exterior or grounds of a listed building, you will need to check out whether listed building consent is needed or not. Although certain works and alterations to listed buildings are acceptable, clearly very high standards need to be met and you may need to consult with a specialist company for their advice on what to do.

Listed buildings are graded to show their relative architectural or historic interest:

- Grade I buildings are of exceptional interest.
- Grade II* are particularly important buildings of more than special interest.
- Grade II are of special interest, warranting every effort to preserve them.

There is also an additional category relating to ancient monuments, for example Stonehenge, where you are unlikely to get approval for a conservatory!

Listing currently protects 500,000 or so buildings in the UK, of which the majority – more than 90 per cent – are Grade II. Grade I and II* buildings may be eligible for English Heritage grants for urgent major repairs.

Financing renovation projects

In Chapter 14 there is a more in-depth look at raising finance for all sorts of property investment opportunities. Here we are going to deal solely with the subject of raising finance for renovation projects.

If the property is mortgageable, then you may decide to borrow money to finance your renovation project. This can be worthwhile even if you have the cash to purchase the property and pay for the works to be done from your own means, since there may be unexpected expenses that you would not have the money to pay for. There are a number of routes that you can go down to obtain finance for a renovation project and it is worth considering different alternatives. Even if you decide to take out a mortgage for the majority of the purchase price, you will still need to raise the deposit and pay for works to be done. Creative financing and 'thinking outside the box' could offer up financial solutions which hadn't initially been apparent.

Here are a number of ways in which you can raise the finance for a renovation project:

1 **Taking out a mortgage or loan from a bank, building society or specialist mortgage company.** The institution lending you the money will need to satisfy itself that you are able to make the payments and so, depending on the level of borrowing that you are seeking, you will have to provide a certain amount of personal financial information.

2 **Borrowing money from an individual or investor in the form of a loan.** You will need to budget for the interest payments back to this financial backer. They may also want to take a personal guarantee against your other assets.

3 **Joint venture with an individual or investor.** Another person could contribute towards the project by means of a capital injection in return for a share in the profits at eventual resale. You may come to some agreement whereby you do the work but they put up the money. If this is the case, the investor will want to see your budget, project plan and cashflow forecast to satisfy him/herself that there is going to be an acceptable return.

In all cases, it is likely that you are going to have to put some of your own money into the project, either by way of a deposit or a contribution towards the renovation costs. Once again, there are several sources of potential finance:

1 **Credit cards and loans.** Borrowing money on an unsecured basis isn't the cheapest way to raise finance, but it is readily available provided that you have a reasonable credit rating. You should be able to raise money this way quickly. I know of property investors who started out by also getting close family members to take out money on credit cards to help them. Clearly, this is a high-risk strategy but if you have relatives or friends prepared to do this, you may be surprised by how much cash you can raise.

2 **Second mortgages or charges.** If you own property already, you may be able to find a lender who will take out a second charge against this property and loan you the money. You will need to consider whether you are happy to put up your own home for this kind of security since it will be at risk if things go wrong.

3 **Loans against endowments or pension policies.** If you can prove that you are a high net worth individual, there are specialist lenders who will take other financial assets as security for a loan. These may include bonds and savings plans as well. It means that you don't actually have to cash in these policies to benefit from their value.

Finally, it is also worth checking out whether or not there is any financial assistance available from the government or local authority. If you are buying a run-down property to renovate in an area of regeneration, then there may be grants available to help you with this.

I should reiterate at this point that I am not qualified to give specialist financial advice, and you should seek the guidance of a suitably qualified and regulated financial adviser and solicitor before undertaking any financial commitment. Your main home may be at risk if you borrow against it and are unable to keep up the repayments.

☺ **Did you know?**

Non-standard construction

This is the term applied to any property which is built not using what are considered 'normal materials' (brick, breeze block, etc). The most common form of non-standard construction is concrete. This was used extensively in houses that were built just after the Second World War when large numbers of properties had to be built quickly to house those people who had lost their homes. Intrinsically, there is often nothing wrong with these properties, and will probably last for many years without a problem. The issue is that some are susceptible to construction defects in the concrete (such as 'concrete cancer') and as such many mortgage companies do not lend money against them. You will, therefore, have to find other means of purchasing a property such as this and, if you were to find out, say, after an auction, when you were intending to get a mortgage, you would be in trouble. A proper survey or the experience to spot this kind of construction will avoid problems.

Where to spend the money

There are certain parts of any property that are worth concentrating on. Even if your refurbishment project is just a cosmetic overhaul, then paying particular attention to kitchens, bathrooms and the outside of the property can pay dividends. Here are a few useful tips to consider:

Kitchens and bathrooms

Kitchens

If you renovate only one room in a house, the kitchen should be it. Overnight you will transform the saleability of the property and add considerable value. This is also one room where you can spend a fortune or relatively little and achieve a similar result. By choosing your replacement units and design carefully, you can create the 'wow' factor you are hoping for in your house without the corresponding 'ouch' factor in your budget. Try not to be personal in your choice of design and pick one that will appeal to the widest cross-section.

There are many specialist kitchen design companies that will help you and also superb bespoke kitchen makers who will create something that really sets your renovation apart from the norm.

£ Martin's tip

Improving kitchens

- The bigger, the better. Consider knocking through walls and into cupboards to generate a feeling of space.
- Positioning within the house is very important. Plan to move the kitchen early on in the restoration process, if required. People like views from the kitchen window, and ventilation is an important consideration.
- You can save literally thousands of pounds by shopping around for kitchen units and fittings. Check out display models in local DIY stores, and look on Internet auction sites such as eBay.
- Don't scrimp on fixtures and fittings. Cheap taps and appliances will lower the overall impression. On the other hand, over-expensive items will not return their value.
- Think carefully about kitchen design as it relates to the end user. If you're refurbishing a family home, you will need to adopt a different approach from if you were refurbishing a student let.
- Remember electricity and gas supplies early on in the process. These will need to be installed by a qualified engineer.
- Lighting will make a huge difference to the overall feel of the finished kitchen. Plan it early and try to strike a balance between practicalities and atmosphere.

Bathrooms

The reason I'm sitting in a bath full of money on the front cover of this book is that, like kitchens, refurbished bathrooms can add considerable value to a property. Like kitchens, it is possible to spend a fortune on them, but it can sometimes be worth it.

Positioning of the bathroom is vital, but moving it can be an expensive undertaking that should be embarked on only if there are significant financial advantages of doing so. Generally, the more bathrooms, the better.

£ Martin's tip

Improving bathrooms

- Nothing beats plain white sanitary ware such as the loo, hand basin and bath. It's timeless and of universal appeal.
- Don't rush to remove old sanitary ware if it is still in reasonable condition. Clearly a 1980s avocado bathroom suite should be first on your list of things to remove, but a 1930s pedestal basin could add an individual feel to your restoration. A fairly recent suite can also be effectively updated by replacing the surrounding tiles and flooring.
- Moving the location of the bathroom can dramatically alter the saleability of a property. Houses where the bathroom is upstairs will always be more popular than others that have bathrooms only downstairs. However, think carefully about creating an upstairs bathroom at the expense of a bedroom. This may have a detrimental effect on the value.
- You will need to consider carefully the location of the soil pipe. Moving it can be a costly undertaking.
- The price of bathroom suites, fixtures and fittings varies enormously, so shop around. Don't overspend on expensive fancy choices unless you're embarking on a really high-end restoration, as you will not recoup your outlay.
- Baths come in all shapes and sizes these days, allowing creative use of even small spaces. Alternatively, consider a shower unit.
- Ensuite bathrooms can often be easy to create and yet they give an upmarket feel to any renovation project.

Extensions and loft conversions

A carefully planned extension can add many more times its cost to the value of a house. However, badly planned extensions can have the opposite effect. Before embarking on a major project you need to be certain that there is not a ceiling on property prices for similar properties, with or without extensions, in the area where your property is located. For instance, it's not financially sensible to build a £50,000 extension on a mid-terrace house that cost you £100,000 to buy, where the maximum price will only ever be £120,000. Similarly, a £50,000 extension that will add £100,000 to the value of a £500,000 house makes sense.

A clever architect will be able to create an extension that provides extra space, and also enhances the look of the existing building. In my experience, it's always better to build an extension that is slightly larger than you think it needs to be, as when it's finished, you will be thankful for the extra space.

Loft conversions

Converting a loft into a habitable space is a good way to increase the accommodation in a property, and doesn't have to cost as much as alternative extensions. However, some of the work requires specialist skills that you may not have. Adding a dormer window, for instance, is a fairly involved project. There are many Building Regulations to consider when converting a loft, such as fire escapes, width of stairs, sound proofing and strength of floor joists. A good builder or architect will advise you on these. However, a well-thought-out and constructed loft conversion will add considerable value and appeal to a property.

Cellars

Rather than going up or out, another renovation option is to go down. Digging out or converting a cellar can be a fantastic way to add extra space to a property. Many houses already have cellars that are crying out to be utilzed – and they may not require a lot of work to make them habitable.

The biggest issue with cellars will be damp. Eradicating it is a complicated task and you may want to call on the expertise of a specialist firm to help you. Walls will need to be waterproofed (or 'tanked'), floors will probably need to have a damp-proof membrane installed – or specialist conversion techniques will be employed.

If you are converting the cellar under a flat, you will have to check the conditions of the lease and freehold, and then probably seek the approval of all the other flat owners. In addition, you should not embark on the project without having your plans checked by a structural engineer. Damage the foundations of the house, or inadvertently knock down a supporting wall and it could turn into a very, very bad day in property renovator city.

🏦 Martin's tip

Converting cellars

- It is vital that you check for the location of services such as drains and utilities. Accidentally digging into a main sewer would be bad news!

- Adequate ventilation is key to keeping cellars dry. Also install heating to help the process.

- Check out how easy it will be to remove waste and bring in materials for the project. Labour intensive construction as opposed to machinery can often be the only option – and this will be expensive.

- Be creative with lighting to create a dramatic and useful space that will add considerable value to your property.

External features – gardens and outbuildings

The external appearance of a property is crucial to creating the right first impression and 'kerb appeal', so it is worth allocating some of your time and budget to ensuring that it looks good from the outside. It may not be necessary to employ a landscape gardener and do a complete overhaul of the garden or plot surrounding the property, but it is worth making sure that the garden is neat, hedges are trimmed, fence panels are complete and flower borders are not full of weeds. Even if you're not very green fingered, make sure you cut back trees and shrubs so that they aren't dominating, and in particular make sure that they do not obscure parts of the house (i.e. windows). If you are going to dress your property for resale or let, then make sure that driveways and pathways are weed-free and in good order. You can create a splash of colour with a few simple tubs planted with bright flowers, even if the rest of the garden is fairly lifeless.

☺ Did you know?

Party wall agreements

If you intend to carry out work on a property that shares any walls with a neighbouring property, it's important to understand the significance of party walls. They are walls which properties share, and before you can start any work on your part, you have to get the approval of the other party. This can be a costly and time-consuming process – and approval is in no way guaranteed. For more information visit www.communities.gov.uk

Garages and outbuildings are valuable extra features of a property but they can also detract from its appeal. Outbuildings often block views and garages are often ramshackle. Consider demolishing both if the exterior areas would benefit as a result. However, large outbuildings that have potential for conversion to habitable space should be photographed or inspected by the planning authorities first so you can prove a building has existed on the site.

☺ **Did you know?**

Asbestos garages

Many older garages are made from asbestos sheet and should be demolished and disposed of only by a specialist disposal firm. Doing it without the necessary safety and health procedures can be potentially lethal. For more information visit the Health and Safety Executive website at www.hse.gov.uk/asbestos.

Eco-building

In recent years, eco-building has become increasingly acknowledged. We are more environmentally conscious than ever before, and techniques for building property that minimizes the impact on the environment are growing in popularity. Often employing these techniques will mean a larger outlay at the beginning (i.e. when these features are being put into a property) but the saving in fuel bills and utilities over time should readily compensate for these additional costs. The social responsibility issues cannot be undervalued.

A few eco-friendly measures you could consider are:

1 **Solar panels** – Using solar panels to provide heating and hot water.
2 **Geothermal exchange heating** – A series of pipes sunk deep into the earth is connected to a heat pump. This wonderful, simple idea, developed in Sweden, works like a fridge in reverse, and converts low-grade heat from the ground into high-grade heat for radiators and hot water. You cut your carbon dioxide emissions massively and with soaring fuel prices, you could see a quick return on your investment.

3 **Sun pipes** – A way to pipe natural daylight from your rooftop into your home to brighten areas which daylight from windows cannot reach. Sun pipes are super-reflective tubes which have an internal mirror finish that intensifies and reflects natural daylight, delivering free outdoor light to a room or area below.

Summary

In this chapter we have looked at:

- The process behind a renovation project.
- Common mistakes and how to avoid them
  - Guidelines for a successful project.
- Surveys and specialist reports.
- Major issues and how to deal with them
  - Damp, and how to deal with it
  - Mould and rot, and how to deal with it
  - Infestation, and how to deal with it
  - Subsidence, and how to deal with it.
- Budgeting effectively and sticking to it.
- Planning issues
  - Conservation areas and listed buildings.
- Building Regulations
  - The difference between planning permission and Building Regulations.
- Financing renovation projects.
- Where to spend the money
  - Kitchens and bathrooms
  - Extensions
  - Cellar and loft conversions
  - External features.
- Eco-building.

09

project management ...

In this chapter you will learn:
- how to put together the dream team
- how to deal with each element effectively
- how to spot rogue contractors
- building contracts and what to include in them

... putting together the dream team

Successful property investing combines a huge range of disciplines and experience – some of which you are unlikely to have – so it is important to surround yourself with people who are experts in their own field and who can support you in your property activities.

Buying, renovating, developing or renting property is rarely a one-person job. The successful property investor works with a team of professionals at each stage of the process. However, if you are new to property investment and this is your first experience of 'hiring and firing' and managing a team of people, this aspect of property developing can be quite daunting. This chapter aims to help you identify and build the 'power base' of contacts and partners to help make a success of every project. It also looks at how to spot rogue contractors or tradespeople and your responsibilities to the people you employ, as well as some pointers on what you should include in your contracts with tradespeople.

First, it is important that you always conduct yourself in a professional manner during all your dealings and negotiations with the people whose services you will employ. You need to be authoritative, but you also need to be approachable and encourage an open dialogue so that your workers will feel able to come to you with problems or suggestions. While you need to drive the project, you also want to encourage your team to put forward their views and opinions – especially if they have more property development experience than you. Treat everyone in your team with respect and integrity. Pay on time and at good rates and you will build up great loyalty among your 'employees' so that they put your work and job first. Over time, you will build up a list of people, covering all aspects of a typical project, whom you can call on at short notice if you need to, and who will make your projects their priority.

Estate agents and/or property finders

If you have chosen to invest in property in a particular area then you need to build up a circle of contacts who can help you find and buy the right kind of property. You should register your interest with as many estate agents as you can, and make sure you brief them fully on your requirements. The more information that you can give to an estate agent, the more likely it is that they will be successful in identifying and presenting you with property opportunities that are going to appeal. Let them know what sort of properties you are in the market to buy and what your financial position is, so that they know to call you when they see a deal that may suit. You want to be the first person an agent rings when a really juicy property lands on their desk, and if you work at nurturing this relationshi then, in time, this will happen. If so, remember to reward the agent for thinking of you. A proper 'thank you' will go a long way (even if you aren't successful in buying the property the fact is that the agent thought to give you a first bite at the cherry) and will mean that they will be more inclined to call you first next time. Bundles of used £10 notes usually go down a treat. Only kidding! But a bottle of wine would probably be a good investment for the future!

You'll probably find that, in time, if you are buying property regularly, you will build up a rapport with a few key estate agents with whom you will work closely. Treat these people as you would business partners – because in effect, this is what they are! If you are buying, don't over-promise your ability to exchange or complete if it is going to leave them having to explain delays to the vendor. This puts them in a bad light with the seller of the property and will create bad feeling between you and the estate agent. Remember that the estate agent works on behalf of the seller, so their priority will be to look after the seller's interests, not yours as a buyer.

Sooner or later, though you will also be a vendor and in this case you need to find an estate agent that you are happy to market your property for sale. This is clearly a very important step in the process for you since what you actually achieve as a sale price will determine the actual profit you get in the deal!

Choose an agent that is a member of one of the recognized organizations, for example:

NAEA – the National Association of Estate Agents
ARLA – the Association of Residential Letting Agents
RICS – the Royal Institute of Chartered Surveyors

Many estate agents belong to national firms (i.e. they are divisions of building societies or financial services companies), while others are independent companies (often owner-managed) who tend to exist only in a particular area. There are pros and cons of each type:

National firms

- These will share property details among their offices, so your property could be advertised throughout a whole network right across the country. This gives your property maximum exposure.
- Sales negotiators working for national firms tend to be salaried salespeople (perhaps with a small commission on sales). This could make them less 'aggressive' in their approach.
- You may find that a national firm can be a one-stop shop, providing furniture removal, letting and legal services all under the same umbrella. This may save you money over engaging these services individually.

Independent firms

- These are sometimes just one-office practices – or there may be a small handful of offices located in the same area.
- Salespeople working for independent firms may be commission only or have a greater reliance on commission on sales. This means they are arguably more proactive and motivated to sell your property or strike a deal.
- Very often, independent firms are part of larger collaborations of estate agents, so your property can achieve national exposure across the network.

Clearly, the advent of the Internet has meant that any estate agent, wherever they are based and whatever their status, can advertise properties on a national (and worldwide) basis. In your research regarding which estate agent to engage, finding out what Internet presence your property will have is a vital ingredient in the marketing plan. In today's market, buyers will almost certainly search the Internet looking for properties.

Apart from their Internet policy, also ask the estate agent to show you:

- **examples of other forms of advertising** they will do (i.e. local press, etc.). Ask them how they will be advertising your property. How regularly will it be advertised and what sort of advert it will have? The amount of advertising is crucial to the level of exposure your property will achieve.
- **examples of property particulars** that they will produce on your property. Ask to see details of properties that are similar to yours. This will give you an idea of how your property will be presented to prospective buyers. Consider how well the

property has been described. Does it sound appealing to you? Also take a look at the photographs that are included. Are they taken in sunlight or on a bright day so they look attractive? Are the photographs colour and do they show off the property? As the saying goes, a picture paints a thousand words and the photos of your property will be the most important element of the listing.

- **examples of properties advertised on the Internet.** Ask if the estate agent will be including photos of your property on various websites. Prospective buyers browsing online are far more likely to seek further information if they can see good photos of the property. Some agents now also offer 'virtual tours' online. This involves filming the interior of the property and having this on the website listing. This is really powerful since it allows buyers to view your property from the comfort of their own home.

- **their terms and conditions,** especially if you are entering into a sole agency agreement with them. You should negotiate to have your property listed with a sole agent for a limited specified period of time, for example six weeks. During this initial period, the agent will be the most motivated to sell and will be able to tap into their database of buyers to match suitable people with your property. If they are unable to sell your property during these first crucial weeks, you'll find that viewings and interest will tail off as the agent is then reliant on new buyers coming to them. You also want to be able to get out of an agreement with any agent fairly swiftly if you aren't happy with the level of service that they are providing but also offer the agent the chance to do a good job for you – so 4 to 6 weeks' sole agency seems to be a good balance.

£ Martin's tip

Multiple or sole agency?

Choosing whether to list your property for sale with just one agent (sole agency) or many agents (multiple agency) is an important decision. Generally, you will be able to negotiate a more competitive commission rate if you list with just one, but you may have more chance of a sale if you list it with many. I recommend sole agency, but with a short time limit – say, six weeks – after which time you can either switch to another agent or list with multiple.

159 project management 09

Other tips to consider when you are choosing an estate agent

Make sure you ask at least three estate agents to view your property and give you a market appraisal. Choose agents who appear to be most active in the area: 'For Sale' and 'Sold' boards outside properties in the immediate vicinity are a good sign. Look through the local newspapers to see which ones are advertising, and take a critical view of the advert itself. If you were looking to buy a property, which ads are you drawn to? Also check out the website of the agents you are considering, since your potential buyers will undoubtedly be looking online too. The site should be easy to navigate and give concise, clear information about the properties.

Don't be pressurized into entering into a sole agency agreement that lasts any longer than six weeks. This is the period of time when the agent will be most proactive and fresh to your property. If you aren't happy with their efforts and approach during this time then you can switch to another agent. However, don't go with more than two consecutive sole agency arrangements with different firms. Prospective buyers will pick up on the fact that the same property is being advertised with different agents and this could make them think that there is something wrong with the property. It is better to do your research upfront, find the right agent and stick with them at least for a while.

Try not to get too 'hung up' on the rate of commission charged by an agent. If the agent that you most like charges a higher rate than others in your area, then it is worth negotiating with them to see if they are prepared to lower it. They may take a view that if you are an active seller you may be bringing plenty more properties their way and so offer you a reduction. Don't over-negotiate though. If you drive such a hard bargain that the agent feels undervalued, then they will be less motivated to sell your property.

Don't necessarily choose the agent who gives you the highest valuation on your property. In my experience less reputable agents sometimes give a high market appraisal just so they can get your business and then suggest to you that you should consider a price reduction quite soon after.

Make sure the agent is prepared to undertake all viewings of the property themselves. You are paying the agent to sell the property for you and carrying out viewings with prospective buyers is a fundamental part of this service. From the buyers' point of view, they will feel more comfortable being shown around by a third party and are more likely to make open comments about their impression of the property than if they are being shown around by the vendor. A good agent will pick up on what viewers are saying and feed this back to you – however negative!

Make sure you spend time reviewing the property particulars that an agent draws up for you. You know the property better than anyone else and can hone in on the best features (e.g. proximity to services and transport links, etc). However, let the agent use their own words in actually putting the description together – they probably have far more experience at this than you and will know what words and phrases draw the attention of buyers.

Agree a time each week when you speak to your agent to get feedback on any viewings. If they know that they have to call you at a certain time they will plan for this and get the relevant information ready. Take on board negative comments in a professional manner and if the same issues keep coming up, discuss with the agent how you can overcome them or consider fixing the problem.

Finally, you may decide to engage the services of a property finder to source properties for you. This saves you the trouble of scouring local press, Internet, estate agents, and so on to find suitable properties. A property finder will take your brief and find properties to meet the requirements that you have laid out. Property finders will charge you either a flat fee for their services or a percentage of the purchase price.

Mortgage/finance broker

Your mortgage broker and their ability to find the right finance deals for you could in some instances be the difference between you successfully buying a property and not. They need to have their finger on the pulse of what is happening in the mortgage market, which lenders are offering good deals and which can give you an offer on a property quickly. The UK mortgage market is now a very complex place to be, with literally thousands of mortgage deals out there. A good broker will know:

- which lenders are in the market to lend money at a given time
- what the underwriting requirements are (i.e. how much background information and evidence are you going to have to produce to be offered the loan)
- what the service levels are like; ideally, you want to be dealing only with mortgage lenders who can move fast and make you an offer in better than average time
- what early redemption penalties apply to a mortgage product. This is particularly relevant if you are buying below market value properties that are in 'distressed' state with a view to modernizing and then reselling quickly, since you are unlikely to be keeping the mortgage deal for very long.

Don't lie to your broker about your circumstances. They can often work around issues that you may think are a problem, but if undisclosed information crops up later on in the process – and it probably will – they will be in a much weaker position to fight your corner.

For details of mortgage brokers, refer to 'Taking it further' or visit www.makingmoneyfromproperty.tv.

Solicitor/lawyer

If you are going to be buying hot property opportunities, you may need to be able to move quickly to secure a certain deal, so building up a good relationship with your solicitor could prove to be a very valuable investment of time. Be sympathetic though to the fact that the solicitor will need to carry out certain checks on the property, and this can be a slow process irrespective of how quickly your solicitor is willing and able to work. Remember that they are professionals and have a lot to lose if things go wrong, so you should respect this and allow them sufficient time to do their job properly.

Once again, you need to find a solicitor with whom you are entirely happy, and work to build up a close working relationship with them. Early on in the relationship it is worth considering paying a sum of money into the solicitor's client account, pending future work that they may do for you. This indicates that you are serious and sends out the message that you are professional. It's unlikely that any of the solicitor's other clients will pay up front for work yet to be done, so you'll stand out in their mind. That way when you want them to pull out all the stops so that you can exchange or complete on a deal in double-quick time, they will feel much more inclined to go the extra mile for you. It's just common relationship-building sense.

Finding a solicitor/lawyer

It's not necessary for your solicitor to be located in the same geographical region as the property that you are buying. Since they are not going to actually visit the property, your solicitor could be based anywhere in the country. Having a solicitor located close to where you live will help when it comes to signing paperwork. The estate agents that you deal with will probably have solicitors who they know and can refer you to, but asking around friends and family and other property investors for their recommendations is a good way to go.

Be aware that if you are taking out a mortgage on the property, the lender will also use a solicitor and it may be beneficial for you to employ the same one in order to keep costs down. At the very least, if you need to find a solicitor, your lender is likely to be able to provide you with a list to choose from. Alternatively, you can find details of solicitors from the Law Society – www.lawsociety.org.uk or see 'Taking it further'.

When you first contact a solicitor to see about engaging their services, you need to make sure you fully understand what their fees and charges are going to be before asking them to do any work for you. You should also ask the solicitor how they usually communicate with their clients and make sure that you are happy with their chosen method.

A solicitor will then issue you a client care letter which will detail their charges, levels of service and responsibilities.

Builder, project manager and tradespeople

The project manager, builder and tradespeople are other critical appointments within your dream team. You need to select people who will create a high standard of finish, operate ethically and professionally, treat other team members with respect, charge reasonable rates for the work they do and ultimately do a good job and who can be trusted, and will not 'rip you off'. In an ideal world you also want people who aren't

£ Martin's tip

Finding and working with contractors

- If possible, use only people who have been referred to you by others – either other property investors or your friends and family. A word-of-mouth recommendation is by far the best way to be introduced to someone.

- Take up references with other satisfied customers and, if possible, ask the contractor if they can refer you to other people in the area who have had similar work to what you are proposing carried out. This will give you a good idea of this person's ability and standards of work.

- Be aware of people who 'cold call'. Good reliable contractors are kept busy without the need to knock on doors to drum up work.

- If you are unable to source a particular type of contractor by personal recommendation, try contacting the relevant trade bodies for a list of people who are in your area.

- Brief the contractor thoroughly on the job that you want them to carry out. If you are employing the services of someone to carry out more than one task, write down a list of all the jobs you want doing and be as detailed as you can. Make sure that the contractor fully understands what your requirements are before they quote.

- Make sure you get a written quotation or estimate for the work. You need to seek three separate quotes before making any decisions on who to give the work to. Keep all quotations received, as well as your briefing notes, on file. This way you have a back-up of what was said and agreed and at what cost, at the outset of the project.

- Whenever possible, get the contractor to quote for work on a 'fixed price' basis – so you don't get penalized if the job takes longer than they anticipated.

- If the contractor shows that they are part of a trade organization, check this out. Make sure that their membership is still valid.

- Make sure that the contractors have their own public liability insurance and ask to see a copy of the policy schedule, if required.

- Discuss whether or not there are any guarantees or warranties on the work that they do.

in a rush to be anywhere else or do other things, and who may be available at short notice and during emergencies. In the case of renovation projects, even if you are doing much of the work yourself, it is likely that you will still need to call on the services of tradespeople for some of the time.

How to spot rogue contractors

It's every property developer's nightmare: having cowboys undertake work on the project who deliver overpriced, shoddy work that looks poor and brings down the standard of the property, or worse still, is dangerous. When employing contactors, keep your head and be cynical. Don't be afraid to quiz them about other work they have completed and definitely take up references.

Here are a few other things that should make the alarm bells ring:

- The contractor has knocked on your door looking for work just because they happen to be 'in the area'.
- They want payment in cash or offer their services heavily discounted for cash. If the work is poor and needs sorting out, it's much harder to seek legal redress from the contractor.
- They seem reluctant to provide you with references of other satisfied customers – chances are if they are cowboys, then there won't be any!
- They come up with excuses as to why they can't provide a written quotation. Engaging the services of any contractor, however professional they may appear at the outset, who won't provide a written estimate is leaving yourself vulnerable.
- They can't commit to a timescale of when they will finish the work. Cowboys will very often drag out the work unnecessarily so that they can charge you more.
- They want to start the work immediately. If they are able to do so, question them to find out why, because most reputable tradespeople and contractors are booked up weeks in advance.
- They want a large deposit before they actually start the work. This would indicate they have no cashflow, whereas professional, reputable builders will have the means to source materials themselves.

- They seem to use unnecessary complicated jargon and technical phrases – probably intended to blind you with science.
- They are quick to criticize other builders' work or 'knock' the competition.
- They are difficult to contact and perhaps have only a mobile phone as means of reaching them.

Finding a builder

If you are looking for a professional builder, the Federation of Master Builders is a good place to start. As the building industry's largest trade organization, representing more than 13,000 small and medium-sized companies throughout the UK, the FMB promotes standards of excellence and helps its members continually to improve levels of business performance and customer service. Members are vetted before they are allowed to join, and are required to adhere to a strict Code of Practice. Check out their website www.findabuilder.co.uk where you can search to find a builder in your area.

Building contracts and what to include in them

When you engage the services of any builder or tradesperson it is important that there is a common understanding between you and them of the extent of the work to be done to avoid misunderstanding. You need to write down exactly what you require them to do. Don't worry if you don't know the technical terms but it should be a comprehensive description of the work as you see it.

For building works, you should then draw up a building contract which will mean that both parties know and understand what is expected, how much it will cost and what happens if the scope of the work needs to be changed. Essentially, the contract should cover:

- price and payment terms
- working hours
- what happens in the event that extra work is needed or the project takes longer than expected
- how to solve disputes
- insurance information
- information about any guarantees or warranties.

Once again the Federation of Master Builders has a useful website – www.fmb.org.uk. The consumer section has a free downloadable Plain English building contract which you can use.

Rental and property management company

If you want to concentrate on developing and renovating property, you may find that the additional workload of actually managing your properties and looking after tenants is something that you can do without. If this is the case, then you can employ the services of a property management company and/or rental/lettings company. There is no shortage of companies offering to take a percentage of your monthly rent to do this job for you. How much of the rent you will have to pay depends on the degree of involvement of the rental or management company. Types of service available include:

- A tenant introduction or finding service where the letting agent simply advertises, finds and vets a tenant for you. They will be responsible for collecting appropriate references from the tenant and arranging the tenancy agreement. Some agents will charge a flat fee for this, while others will charge a percentage of the monthly income.
- A full lettings service where the agent not only finds the tenant and sorts out the tenancy agreement, but they will also be responsible for collecting the rent on your behalf. They will then take their fee (typically around 12–13 per cent of the monthly income) and forward the balance directly to you.
- A full management service where the agent, in addition to finding you a tenant and collecting the rent on your behalf, will also actively manage the property – sorting out any repairs and ensuring everything is in working order and paying regular (or random) visits. Charges for this type of service are usually around 15 per cent of the rent.

As with choosing an estate agent, it is a valuable investment of time researching which letting agents in your area are most successful handling the type of property that you have. Some agents specialize in smaller flats, student accommodation or larger family homes, so again take a look in the local paper to see which letting agencies are advertising properties similar to yours. You should aim to visit three local lettings companies to talk over your requirements and during this visit try to establish how many tenants they have on their books and how they generally advertise available properties for rent. Ask them for a full list of the services they provide so you are clear on exactly what is included in your fee. They will also assess your property for it's rental worth and this is why it is better to have more than one opinion. If you are letting your property either fully or partly furnished, it is the responsibility of the letting agent also to draw up an inventory of items included at the outset and to take at least one month's deposit from any incoming tenant to cover breakages and damage.

Accountant/tax adviser

You will need to have an experienced fully qualified accountant onboard to look after your tax affairs and help you with your tax return. All monies you spend on genuine business expenses will be allowable against any profit you make.

If you diversify into overseas markets then you may also need to employ the services of a specialist tax adviser to ensure that you purchase property in the most tax efficient manner. You will need to know whether it is best to buy properties in your own name, jointly with your spouse, in your children's names, in the name of a UK or offshore company or through a trust. This could be a complex matter, particularly if you end up with a portfolio of properties across the world, and it is imperative that you get it right from the start. Buying through the wrong entity can be very costly so time and money spent early on could literally save you thousands in future tax bills.

For details of qualified accountants, visit www.icaewfirms.co.uk and see 'Taking it further'.

Architect/surveyor

If you intend to renovate property then you also need to find a good architect with whom you can discuss your plans and proposals. They may become a good sounding board for ideas and a 'sense check' on what is viable. Your architect will be responsible for drawing up detailed plans of any changes you make to the property which you will require if you need to apply for planning permission.

For more information on qualified architects visit the website of the Royal Institute of British Architects on www.ribafind.org.

Summary

In this chapter, we have looked at:

- How to put together the dream team
  - Estate agents and/or property finders
  - Mortgage/finance broker
  - Solicitor/lawyer
  - Builder, project manager and tradespeople
  - Rental and property management company
  - Accountant/tax adviser
  - Architect/surveyor.
- How to deal with each element effectively.
- How to spot rogue contractors.
- Building contracts and what to include in them.

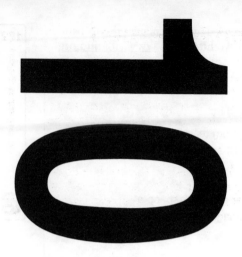

10 buying at auction ...

In this chapter you will learn about:
- the case for buying at auction
- the auction process
- what kind of properties are sold at auction
- pre- and post-auction opportunities
- finding auctions
- where to buy in the UK
- raising finance
- selling property at auction
- buying 'blind'
- top tips for buying at auction

... top tips from the expert

Buying property at auction is something any property investor should consider – particularly if your strategy includes an element of renovation or conversion. It can be an extremely exciting and financially shrewd way of buying property and is becoming increasingly popular. It may also be a strategy that you might wish to employ to sell your properties, but first I'm going to look at the process of **buying** property at auction.

With over 5 years and 350 episodes of *Homes Under the Hammer*, it goes without saying that I've visited more auction properties than I've had hot dinners, so I've seen people do it the right way – and also get it horribly wrong.

The case for buying at auction

One of the main reasons that property developers go to auctions is that you can get some great deals – and even though they are becoming harder to find, you can still potentially save a great deal of money by buying at auction. One analysis suggested that 90 per cent of 'cheap' properties are sold at auction – so if you are looking for bargains, you should definitely be scouring the auction catalogues. Mortgage lenders often put up their repossessed properties for sale at auction, usually at deliberately reduced 'reserve' prices to ensure they sell quickly. It is also usual to find probate properties, and local authorities and housing associations also tend to sell their housing stock at auctions for similar reasons – they all want a quick sale. The good news about the latter is that government departments and housing associations have a lot of flats/houses 'on their books' and probably don't value them as much as you might. They basically just want to get rid of them and recoup money as fast as possible.

The other good news is that if you are successful at bidding at an auction, you know the property is yours as soon as the hammer falls and that you won't have to wait any longer than 28 days in order to be able to complete and pick up the keys. On the fall of the hammer, you are legally committed to the purchase and, in effect, that final winning bid acceptance becomes the 'exchange of contracts' and you cannot pull out of the completion. It also, of course, means you cannot be gazumped, nor can the vendor pull out at the last minute.

Another benefit of buying at auction is that you can buy your property more quickly because auction properties aren't part of a slow-moving chain.

In general, the kind of properties put up for auction will be those with development potential, that are difficult to sell or are unusual. However many 'normal' properties end up in the auction rooms too, and if you can spot the gems, there are killings to be made. In my time presenting *Homes Under the Hammer* I have covered a wide variety of properties that have been sold at auction – everything from Martello towers, windmills, churches, barns, lock-up garages and even public conveniences! So if you are looking for property to develop, auctions are likely to be good hunting grounds for you.

The auction process

Once a seller has decided to sell their property at auction, the estate agent or auction company will prepare the details as with a conventional sale. The seller's solicitor will also obtain the title deeds and carry out the usual local authority and Land Registry searches and prepare any special conditions of sale required by the auctioneer. These will be included in the auction pack, which you can obtain before the auction or, at the very least, read on the day. Properties sold at auction need to have a HIP (see Chapter 7), but much of the information will have been included in the auction pack.

The auctioneer will then feature the property in their catalogue for the next auction and distribute this to people on the mailing list.

Prior to the auction

Once you have identified property that you would like to bid on by looking through the auction catalogue or viewing lots online, you should check it out legally. The vendor's solicitors will have prepared legal packs containing (where applicable) special conditions of sale, title deeds, leases and searches. These will help you make an informed decision about the lot. If you need further legal information you should contact the vendor's solicitor, the details of which are usually provided in the catalogue or on the auctioneer's website.

Check what methods of payment the auctioneer will accept for the deposit on the property. If you are the successful purchaser, you will usually be required to pay a 10 per cent deposit subject to a minimum specified in the catalogue immediately after the sale and you should, therefore, have sufficient funds to cover this. It may be necessary, for example, to make arrangements for a banker's draft prior to the sale.

The auctioneer acts as an agent for each seller. They prepare the catalogue from information supplied by or on behalf of each seller. This will usually include a photograph of the property, a brief description and a guide price. You should not assume that the catalogue details are accurate or that the picture is a realistic representation of the property.

Most properties are subject to a reserve price, below which the auctioneer cannot sell the property at the auction. It will be made clear whether the property is being sold subject to a reserve in the catalogue or conditions of the sale, although the reserve price will not usually be disclosed. What will be listed is a 'guide price': this may be set deliberately low in order to attract interest among potential buyers. It is likely that the guide price will be exceeded quite substantially on auction day, sometimes as much as 100 per cent or more.

If you want to put in an offer prior to the auction, you can usually do this in writing, (by letter, fax or by email) at any time up to the date of the auction, but if your offer is accepted you will have to be in a position to exchange contracts and pay your deposit immediately, as if you had bought at the auction. It can be a risky strategy, as I have met many people who have bought a property at the auction for considerably less than the price offered prior to the auction.

If you are intending to bid by telephone or proxy, you will need to make arrangements for this with the auction house prior to the event. Usually the auction catalogue will contain instructions on what to do if you want to bid but can't actually attend the event in person. You will need to complete a registration form and a cheque to cover your deposit relevant to your maximum bid will need to be provided to the auctioneer in the event that you are successful. This does rather 'show your hand' somewhat, as you have revealed your maximum bid, and in my experience there is no substitute for attending the auction in person.

On the day itself

If possible, arrive early and familiarize yourself with the empty auction room. On arrival, you will need to register with the auction house. In order to bid you will be given a unique bidder number prior to the start of the auction. Obtain a copy of any addendum sheet. These are distributed around the auction room and contain late information or alterations. Don't assume that all the properties included in the catalogue will be offered on the day of the auction. Some may be withdrawn or sold prior to the auction.

If you haven't already done so prior to the auction, check out the legal pack in respect of any properties that you intend to bid on. This is another good reason to arrive early: sometimes the legal pack can take quite a bit of time to read through and, depending on the level of interest in the property, could be in great demand on the day. Some people deliberately hold on to the legal pack at the auction to prevent other interested parties who may be 'competition' reviewing it. This might sound uncharitable, but this is business, and clearly the fewer people interested in the property, the less the property is going to fetch.

If you have any queries on the day of the sale ask the auctioneer or the staff. They are approachable and knowledgeable about the properties they sell.

Take a seat or stand somewhere in the room where the auctioneer will able to see you bidding clearly. More of the reasons for this later. Listen carefully to the opening remarks of the auctioneer. Amendments may be announced which directly affect the property in which you are interested.

It is a popular myth that auctioneers mistake any casual movement such as a nose scratch for a bid. Don't worry – auctioneers are able to distinguish between someone scratching their head and bidding, but make sure you gesture clearly at the auctioneer. Subtle twitches and winks will not be picked up. Either raise your hand or nod/shake your head clearly. The auctioneer will warn the room when a sale is concluding and will invite anyone still wanting to bid to make themselves known. If for some reason a mistake is made, tell the auctioneer straight away; do not wait until the end of the sale.

The auctioneer may give an indication when the property has reached its reserve price. Phrases like 'It's in the room to sell ...' or 'This one's selling today' are clues that the reserve price has been reached and the property will be sold to the highest bidder from that point.

Once the bidding slows down, the auctioneer will say 'Going once ... going twice ...' This is the point at which some people choose to join the bidding, which is why it's important that the auctioneer can see you as decisions happen very quickly, so the bidding will recommence. Eventually, the auctioneer will say 'Going for a third and final time ...' and if there are no more bids they will either bring down the gavel and say 'sold' or say 'I'm sorry, that property didn't reach its reserve price'.

If a property fails to reach its reserve price, don't give up! The vendor may decide to accept your bid immediately following the auction. So if the property you were interested in wasn't sold, leave your details with the auctioneer since you may be able to come to a private arrangement with the vendor. This could be immediately or some days after the sale.

You will need to take two forms of identification with you, such as a driving licence or passport and a bank statement or utility bill as proof of address. You will also need your cheque book or debit card, details of your solicitor and all your banking details. If your bid is successful you are legally bound to buy the property and will need to put a downpayment deposit there and then of 10 per cent of the property's price. You will also be required to sign the purchase contract in the sale room. The seller is legally bound to complete on the specified day (usually within the next 28 days). You would then pay them the rest of the purchase price (i.e. 90 per cent).

Don't forget that the property becomes the buyer's insurable risk as soon as the hammer falls. If any damage is done to the property between exchange and completion it is your responsibility and loss.

The auction terms and conditions assume that the buyer has acted like a prudent buyer. If you choose to buy a lot without taking these normal precautions you do so at your own risk. The expression 'Buyer Beware' cannot be overemphasized.

I have seen people make huge mistakes because they didn't do their research, bought 'blind' or sometimes on a whim because a property 'seemed cheap'.

> **☺ Did you know?**
>
> Until the bidding reaches the reserve price, the auctioneer may take bids 'off the wall'. This is the crafty (but entirely legal) practice of the auctioneer pretending that someone has bid when they haven't. This is used to entice would-be bidders to join in the bidding and can help kick-start the bidding on a property if it is slow to begin.

What kinds of properties are sold at auction?

Every and all kinds of property are for sale through auction houses, but generally speaking the type of properties that are sold at auction are just the ones that you should be looking for if you want to buy at below market value. They are sometimes unusual or quirky properties that will not normally sell through estate agents and really need to attract property investors, cash buyers or people looking for special deals. However, there are also perfectly standard properties that are being sold via this route, and you'll find a large proportion of mid-terrace and first-time buyer development projects in the pages of the auction catalogues. What makes auctions so interesting is that there is a great breadth of property and land deals:

- Properties that are requiring renovation: derelict properties and properties that are in poor decorative state
- Properties needing complete modernization
- Properties with structural problems
- Properties that have tenants already in-situ
- Leasehold properties on very short leases
- Properties which are subject to restrictions or covenants
- Properties which are unmortgageable (or at least it will require specialist financing to get a mortgage secured on them)
- Properties owned by local authorities, mortgage companies and other public bodies such as water boards
- Properties which are going to require 'change of use' planning permission to be turned into housing such as ambulance stations, public lavatories and railway buildings
- Lock-up garages and other 'storage' dwellings

- Smaller plots of land suitable for individuals to buy (some of which may have outline planning permission for development, others may have full planning in place).

However, the certainty and convenience of auction is attracting more and more vendors to use this route to sell – and standard bungalows, flats, houses and land development opportunities are all regularly available.

Pre- and post-auction opportunities

If you are interested in an auction property, carry out extensive research before you decide to bid or make an offer on it. Auction properties sometimes have defects or unusual restrictions or covenants in place. Assess the property properly for any defects and, as with all renovation projects, have an accurate estimate in mind of what it will cost to put right. Visiting the property will unveil some of the more obvious structural problems, but you should consider having a full survey carried out to identify any less glaring issues. Your solicitor should also check the legal status carefully.

Pre-auction offers

On the basis that you do want to buy the property, you may want to see if the vendor will accept a pre-auction offer. Many vendors will not want to, preferring instead to wait and see what happens on the day – and who can blame them. If there is more than one person interested in the property, there is the chance of the property being subject to a bidding war and achieving a far higher price than the guide price. Of course, it could go the other way and you could end up paying more than you would if you attended the auction. There is no way of knowing. It's a gamble.

Whether or not a vendor will accept a pre-auction offer depends very much on their situation and circumstances. Local authorities, housing associations, mortgage lenders and other government bodies won't accept pre-auction offers. Neither will pre-auction offers be accepted on properties that are being sold on behalf of individuals or businesses by receivers or trustees. They are usually bound to demonstrate that they are aiming to achieve the highest possible price in a fair and open way, and taking the property to auction allows them to do this.

You are more likely to have a pre-auction offer accepted if the vendor is a private individual, a small- to medium-sized landlord or a small developer.

Post-auction offers

If a property does not sell at the auction, it is worth approaching the auctioneer directly afterwards to make an offer. If the seller is an individual in the room and the property failed to reach the reserve price, the vendor will have had their expectations of the property's value readjusted. They may now be more open to accept a lower offer. Alternatively, if there are properties that do not sell that you haven't particularly researched, you could ask for a list of unsold lots from the auctioneer and then carry out the necessary checks and put in an offer a few days later. Once again, the vendor will be in a weaker position following the auction and may be more receptive to your approach.

Finding auctions

It isn't always easy to find out about auctions taking place and the areas covered by auction houses are also not necessarily local to them. An auction house in Northern England may well be selling property in London or vice versa.

One method of finding auctions is to take note of any 'For Sale' signs which mention that the sale will be by auction. Phone the number on the board. It will either be an estate agent or the auctioneers themselves. If it's an estate agent ask them who the auctioneers are. Phone the auctioneers and ask them to put you on their mailing list. There maybe a charge for this.

Even if you simply want the catalogue – showing what's for sale in the forthcoming auction – you may well have to order it via a premium rate phone number, with associated cost.

The Internet is another good source of information about auctions taking place, but if you are serious about buying property this way, then it may be worth subscribing to some of the 'membership sites' that will give you the inside information about forthcoming events and auction properties.

My own website www.makingmoneyfromproperty.tv has details of auctions from the main UK auction houses and forthcoming auctions and properties for sale, as well as auction hints and tips and stories from my time presenting *Homes Under The Hammer*.

Time is precious. On average you've only got three or four weeks to play with, so you need to know what's coming on at auction as soon as possible, and to get a head start over your competition you need to be one of the first to get the catalogue. It's no use getting it a day before the auction takes place!

Where to buy in the UK

The property market in the UK is in a constant state of flux, with areas that are on the up, down and going nowhere changing on a month-by-month basis. If I wrote that a particular place was 'hot' right now that might be out of date by the time you're reading this. What I've tried to do in this book is give you the skills to enable you to pick out the areas and types of property that are likely to perform well for your own set of criteria. That said, the auctions in Derby, Stoke, Plymouth, Harrogate, Lincoln, London and Manchester still seem to be producing some very interesting investment opportunities. At the end of the day, there are potential bargains to be had at every property auction. It all depends on who is there on the day and what they are prepared to pay.

Raising finance

I can't emphasize strongly enough the importance of sorting out your mortgage or finance early in the process if you are buying a property at auction. If you are the winning bidder, you will be required to pay the 10 per cent deposit there and then, and complete on the purchase in 28 days – so if you haven't secured your mortgage or finance upfront you could be in for a stressful month!

It is possible to get a mortgage agreed 'in principle' before you go to the auction. This could be on a specific property, or in general, based on your income and personal circumstances.

If you are intending to buy a property at auction that is a renovation project, and that you believe to be undervalued, then you may choose to use a bridging loan.

Bridging loans

A bridging loan is a loan that is usually taken out to solve a temporary cash shortfall that may arise when buying a property, or perhaps paying for a renovation, for instance, when you want to buy a second property but haven't yet sold your first. You may also need one if you're buying property at auction.

Bridging loans are more expensive than a traditional mortgage and should be used only for short-term financing. But they can enable you to complete on a purchase of a 'below market value' property and then immediately remortgage at the true market value. This can result in 'no money down' deals.

For details of companies offering bridging loan finance, see 'Taking it further'.

Selling property at auction

If you are considering selling your property at auction, you must be able to give vacant possession on a fixed date. Unless the sale is subject to tenancies, this is usually four weeks after the date of the auction. You should be ready to move out at this time.

In order to arrange a sale:

1 Consult a qualified property auctioneer who will advise you whether your property is suitable to sell at auction.

2 If the auctioneer considers the property suitable, discuss the procedure, possible sale date, whether it will be included in the sale of other properties and viewing arrangements.

3 Always obtain a copy of the auctioneer's terms of business and read them carefully.

4 The auctioneer will discuss with you the likely sale price and reserve, the price below which you do not wish the auctioneer to sell your property at auction. You don't have to set this until the date of the auction and you can vary it depending on the amount of interest that has been shown.

5 At this stage you should also discuss the cost of the sale and the rate of commission charged by the auctioneer. You may be required to pay for special advertising or the printing of a brochure. If your property fails to sell, you may be required to pay certain costs incurred and this should be clarified before the sale.

6 Instruct a solicitor who will obtain the title deeds and prepare the special conditions of sale required by the auctioneer. Local authority and Land Registry searches may be put in for the use of prospective purchasers and for completing the legal pack.

7 Close to the date of the sale the auctioneer will discuss with you whether the reserve price should be adjusted, either way, to reflect current market conditions for your property and the level of interest shown by viewings.

8 If the bidding exceeds this figure, your decision to sell at auction has been justified. If the reserve is not reached, the property may still be sold privately; sometimes immediately after the sale to someone who has expressed an interest at the auction.

9 If your property is sold at auction the auctioneer will sign the contract on your behalf in the saleroom and collect a deposit from the purchaser. This is usually 10 per cent, depending on the terms of the contract. The remaining 90 per cent of the price required to complete the purchase will usually be paid within 28 days of the sale.

10 The account from the auctioneer for commission and auction expenses will usually be received by your solicitor who will pay it, subject to your approval. After paying off other outstanding charges such as your mortgage and solicitor's fees, your solicitor will send you the balance of the payment to you or transfer this into your bank account.

Buying 'blind'

Buying 'blind' is the term used to describe the process of buying a property that you have not visited.

It still amazes me how many people do this, and I'm not talking about cheaper properties that you could 'take a punt' on, but houses costing hundreds of thousands of pounds. I interviewed one person for the show who had spent £450,000 on a property that he hadn't visited and that he decided to buy 'on a whim' at the auction because it 'seemed cheap'. I believe this is the approach of the foolhardy investor, and unless you are completely familiar with a particular area, or such a significant investor that you can afford to make a few mistakes – don't do it! There are many reasons for this:

- The auction catalogue will give only the briefest details of the property. You need to see it for yourself to assess its potential or otherwise.
- Only by visiting will you be able to see the area in which the property is situated.
- You will also discover any nasty surprises such as a major road located directly outside or a municipal rubbish dump next door.
- You will be able to get a much better feel for how much it is going to cost to bring the property up to standard.
- You will be able to see any major structural defects or issues, such as dry rot and woodworm.

Occasionally, people are successful with properties they buy blind, but more often than not they end up with problems on their hands. I have talked to people who have bought property thinking it was in a different place, a bungalow when it was a house, a residential property when it was a shop, derelict beyond belief when they though they could move straight in, and a bargain when it was totally overpriced. See the photos in the centre of the book for examples of properties that were not as they first appeared.

 Martin's tip

Top ten tips for buying at auction

Buying at auction, while a potential way of picking up bargains, isn't in itself your ticket to huge profits. You need to do your research and pick the right property as if you were buying a property through an estate agent. Here are my top tips for getting the most out of buying at auction:

1 If you are relying on the sale of another property in order to buy, don't bid on a property before you've sold yours (i.e. before the completion has happened). You could find yourself having to complete on your auction purchase without the proceeds of your sale. You would then have to take out bridging finance to assist you until your first property is sold, with the associated costs.

2 Always set yourself a maximum price limit on the property and stick to it. It is very easy to get carried away at the auction and so it is important that you discipline yourself to bid only up to your maximum. To calculate your maximum,

work backwards from the end value, having factored in renovation costs, finance and legal costs and a payment for your time.

3 Always make sure that you get a valuation or survey carried out before you decide to go to the auction and bid. At the very least visit the property with someone who knows what they are doing and can spot potential problems. This way you'll know what issues the property might have and can factor this into your calculations for renovation costs.

4 If you are new to buying at auction, attend a few as an observer so that you can get a feel for them and the way they work. This way when you actually go along to bid it won't seem so daunting.

5 Always read the legal pack in advance, if there is one, and discuss the contents of this with your solicitor. Make sure your solicitor has checked the title deeds and any special conditions of sale.

6 Always view the auction property thoroughly before placing a bid. Buying blind is a risky strategy.

7 If you really are nervous about the auction process you could get someone else to do the bidding for you. You can either attend the auction with them or, if you prefer, stay at home and wait for the phone to ring with the news. Either way, you need to give your bidder clear instructions on your maximum price.

8 Pick auctions at unpopular times of the year, such as approaching Christmas or during the summer holidays. There are likely to be fewer people attending, which could lead to lower prices.

9 Bid with confidence up to your limit. It's like a game of poker and you can't let the other side know how strong your hand is.

10 Don't worry if you aren't successful. There are plenty of auctions and plenty of properties out there.

Summary

In this chapter, we have looked at:

- The benefits of buying properties at auction.
- What the auction process involves in the lead up to the auction and on the day.
- Some examples of the kind of properties that are sold at auction.
- How to submit offers pre- and post-auction, and when it is likely to be worthwhile.
- Where to find out about auctions taking place in the UK.
- Where to buy in the UK.
- How to raise finance for property bought at auction.
- Selling property at auction.
- Buying 'blind'.
- Top tips for buying at auction.

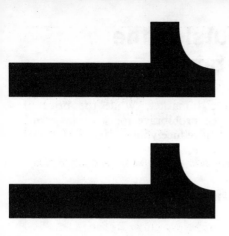

1

buying commercial property ...

In this chapter you will learn about:
- the case for buying commercial property
- drawbacks of investing in commercial property
- ways of investing in commercial property
- types of commercial property
- what to look for in commercial property
- how to value commercial property
- the 'entry level' commercial property choices
- raising finance for commercial property

... thinking outside the 'Residential' box

Another field of property investment that should not be overlooked is the commercial market. While the price of property in this sector can be prohibitive for some investors, there are ways to buy that can reduce your capital outlay, and the returns can be very attractive.

The case for buying commercial property

Although generally more expensive to acquire, commercial property is also a very attractive investment strategy. You've only got to look at the fact that historically institutional investors – life and general insurance funds, pension funds, property unit trusts and investment trusts – have invested heavily in commercial property, to understand that it offers a very high performing, yet low-risk investment choice. More than half of the commercial property in the UK is owned by investors (with the remainder being owner-occupied) and this percentage is rising.

The volatility of stockmarkets and the highly publicized 'pension crisis' have also fuelled an interest in commercial property by private investors. Since it is a more specialist area than buying residential property and requires larger sums of capital, there have been a growing number of financial institutions and other product providers that have devised investment products targeted at 'sophisticated investors' and high net worth individuals (i.e. with more that £25,000 to invest) to make it easier for them to buy commercial property. There are therefore a number of tax efficient vehicles allowing you to invest in commercial property such as Self Invested Personal Pensions (SIPPs), Real Estate Investment Trusts (REITs), Unit Trusts and Investment Trusts. So, if it is an area of property investment that appeals, it has never been easier to get involved. We cover more on ways of investing in property indirectly in Chapter 15.

Benefits of commercial property

There are reasons why institutions have favoured commercial property over the years. These can be summarized as below:

- **Stable cashflow** – Commercial property income is relatively secure as a result of the length of the lease and a low level of default among commercial property tenants. In the event that a tenant does go into liquidation, the liquidator may continue paying the rent in order to stop the lease being forfeited.
- **Strong performance** – Commercial property has generally outperformed equities, gilts and cash deposits, with the average annualized return over the past 30 years being in excess of 12 per cent per annum. This is far better than more 'conventional' forms of investment like stocks, shares and gilts. Similarly, rental yields have averaged over 7 per cent which is more than the yield offered by equities and even residential property. It is also less volatile than other asset classes, including residential property.
- **Diversification** – Commercial property offers a great opportunity to diversify if you have a portfolio of investment property. If you are fortunate enough to have the means to make several investments then anyone will tell you that it is better to spread your risk and choose different types of assets. Even if you are heavily committed to property as an investment choice, it is better to vary the type and location of properties that you hold.
- **Tangible** – As we've already discussed, one of the most compelling reasons for investing in property over other types of asset is that it is tangible. So for institutional investors, investment in a commercial property has a 'physical value', in that it can be seen, touched, photographed, walked around or driven past.
- **Longer leases** – Commercial property generally has longer leases than residential property, so once you have a tenant in place, providing that they are a good tenant, you won't have to search for a new one for several years.

Commercial versus residential

Commercial property investment is quite different from residential property investment in several key ways:

- **Leases for commercial property will generally be longer than for residential** – with periods in excess of 10 years not being uncommon and in some cases stretching beyond 20 years.

This is somewhat different from the relatively short tenancy arrangements with residential property. This means that you don't have to incur the expense and risk of looking for new tenants every year, and there is a lower level of risk.

- The fact that your 'tenant' is also a business means they offer a **stronger covenant and your rent is more guaranteed than with a private individual.** This does, of course, depend on the nature of the business: a large, well-established PLC looking for new business premises is a more attractive proposition than a small start-up operation. Similarly, there are certain industry sectors that are generally safer than others; for example, accountants, solicitors and surveyors tend to come with a solid trading history, as opposed to a business within an industry sector that is more volatile.

- Tenants of commercial property are typically **liable for repairing the property** but landlords of residential property usually remain responsible for repairs. Similarly, if the property needs to be altered internally to suit the nature of the business, this is the responsibility of the tenant. Premises may be updated, modernized and improved at no cost to the landlord.

- Returns on residential property are usually measured by increases in capital value, whereas a significant component of a **commercial property's value arises from the level of income** it can generate.

- Rents for commercial property are frequently paid on a **quarterly basis in advance,** while rents for residential property are generally paid monthly.

- In the event of a problem tenant or a falling out between the tenant and the landlord, **contract law in relation to commercial property is more in favour of the landlord.** This is in contrast to law governing residential property, where the tenant has legal rights, even if they have defaulted on the rent, making eviction much more difficult.

- Once a tenant has been found for a commercial property and they have moved into the property, you **don't require the ongoing services of a management company** as with residential property. The tenant is responsible for the upkeep of the property and so the ongoing management effort is much lower for commercial property.

- A company leasing a commercial property may at some point decide to **sublet all or part of the building** providing that the lease contract allows for this. This gives the tenant company more choice on how to use the property.

Drawbacks of commercial property

However, there are some drawbacks of investing directly into commercial property, and these should be taken into consideration when deciding if this type of property is right for you.

Capital requirements

The main downside is the fact that if you want to invest directly into commercial property, prices are often considerably larger than residential, so more capital is needed. Investment in a single commercial property can run into millions, so there can be significant exposure to the quality and performance of that one holding. This exposure can be mitigated if you are investing with others via a fund large enough to hold a broad spread of property types and locations.

Low liquidity

By its nature, commercial property is a less liquid asset – in other words, you can't buy and sell it as quickly. This is in part due to the length of typical leases, but also because the market for commercial property is more limited. The value could be seriously affected in the event of the need to sell in a short timescale. This is a specialist investment sector and, although supported by solid levels of income, can nevertheless be volatile in adverse market conditions.

Finance

Commercial property mortgages are less common than residential mortgages and so you have fewer options and deals. Typically, the lending institution will lend only a maximum of 75 per cent of the value of the property and so you will require a deposit of 25 per cent or more. When this is on a higher value property, it's easy to see that you are going to tie up far more capital than with residential purchases. Also the interest rate will generally be higher than residential loans (typically 2 per cent above base) and you may be able to secure only a capital repayment mortgage, or at best, interest only for only a couple of years at the start of the loan. Finally, the term of the loan will often be tied into the length of time remaining on the lease, reflecting the lender's view that there is no guarantee that the property will be relet once the existing lease expires. This could make your mortgage costs high.

Valuations

Unlike shares and bonds, where 'pure' market forces of supply and demand determine valuations through daily dealings, commercial property price valuations are largely determined by independent experts and are a matter of their expert opinion. It can, therefore, sometimes be difficult to get an accurate valuation of the property. Only the actual sale of a property can be relied upon as an unequivocal means of valuation.

Failure to renew

There is a risk of the loss of income from a property if the tenant chooses not to renew the lease at its end. The property may stand vacant for a long period of time before another tenant is found.

Tenant default

One of the advantages of commercial property is that a large proportion of the return is fixed in the form of contracted rental income. There is always a risk, however, that tenants can default on payments. While the income stream can be reinstated by reletting, this may take time and will affect the income yield.

Scarcity

Commercial property simply just doesn't come up for sale as often as residential property and is therefore more scarce.

Economic influence

Commercial property is also more influenced by the general state of the economy, the demand being linked to business and industry rather that the need for people to have somewhere to live. Successful investment in commercial property requires an assessment of the current and future condition of the economy and its potential impact on the tenant company or property being considered, and an understanding of the risks involved. For example, if a sharp rise in short-term interest rates is expected, this may dampen consumer spending and reduce the investment appeal of shops and other retail property.

With all that said, for both institutions and private investors, commercial property is now an investment category that cannot be ignored.

Ways of investing in commercial property

While direct investment into commercial property is possible for large institutions and wealthy investors, as a private individual, the more likely way of gaining exposure to commercial property is through a 'pooled' investment vehicle. Here you invest alongside other people, by means of a unit trust or investment trust fund. It's less 'hands on' than owning property directly, but does enable you to invest in this market without needing lots of money.

There are various ways that an individual can indirectly invest in commercial property:

- **Property unit trusts** – An authorized property unit trust is one that invests up to 80 per cent of its assets in property directly or in property securities.
- **Life and pension funds** – Unit-linked pension funds are typically part of a range of funds on offer to investors in occupational or personal pension schemes. Unit-linked life funds are accessible to individuals through either lump sum ('investment bonds') or regular savings products.
- **Investment trusts** – A UK investment trust is an investment company listed on the Stock Exchange that is approved as such by HM Revenue & Customs. Approval means that the investment trust enjoys exemption from tax on capital gains.
- **Property companies** – There are a number of companies listed in the real estate section of the FTSE All-Share Index. Property company shares offer investors a more 'liquid' investment than direct property, but the shares are also usually more volatile than the underlying investments.

Since most of these vehicles are regulated and fall under the remit of the Financial Services Authority (FSA), you will need to speak to an appropriately qualified accountant or financial adviser about investing in these products.

Types of commercial property

The commercial property investment market is made up of three principal sectors:

1 **Retail** (shopping centres, retail warehouses, standard shops, supermarkets and department stores) – Retail property has been the better performer over recent years, helped by buoyant consumer spending. More than 28 per cent of UK retail investment property by value is concentrated in London and the South East.

2 **Offices** (standard offices and business parks) – Office property has grown in popularity and office space has been subject to the changing technology demands of tenants, for example for communications and computer cabling. Predictably, London dominates the office investment property market, alone accounting for 50 per cent of the UK total.

3 **Industrial** (standard industrial estates and distribution warehousing) – This is the smallest category by value. Again, the South East has the largest concentration by value of industrial property, with the North and Scotland coming second.

In addition, there are a number of smaller sectors such as leisure (leisure parks, restaurants, pubs and hotels). The predictable income streams from some of these have been the focus of some innovative financing schemes in recent years.

Planning classifications and usage

Commercial premises are given a classification by the local planning authority as to the type of trade or use to which the property may be put.

A1 – Retail Shops. Basically any property that is used for the retailing of goods other than hot food. This will include post offices, travel/ticket agents, hairdressers, funeral directors, dry cleaners and sandwich bars as well as more conventional shops where goods for sale will be on display. Change of classification is rarely permitted.

A2 – Professional and Financial Services. To include banks, building societies, insurance brokers, solicitors, estate/ employment agents and any other financial and professional services. Change of classification to A1 may be granted (where a ground-floor display window exists).

A3 – Restaurants and Cafés. Covers restaurants, snack bars and cafés. Change of classification to A1 or A2 is permitted.

A4 – Drinking Establishments. Covers pubs and bars. Change of classification to A1, A2 or A3 is permitted.

A5 – Hot Food Takeaways. Covers food takeaways. Change of classification to A1, A2 or A3 is permitted.

B1 – Business. Includes offices other than those in class A2.

B2 – General Industrial. Covers industrial processes such as manufacturing and repairing which do not come under B1 or the special industrial classes B3–B7.

B3–B7 – Special Industrial Classes which have potential for environmental harm.

B8 – Storage and Distribution, warehousing, etc.

Change of use involves getting planning permission from the local authority. The change is more likely to be successful if it can be shown that the new type of business will serve a need not already being provided in the area. Factors to be taken into account might be:

- the need for that type of business in the area
- trading hours
- other similar businesses already present and their number
- traffic flows and parking requirements
- any likely causes of nuisance connected with the business: noise, smells, traffic and environmental hazards
- the requirements of nearby residential occupiers – housing, flats above shops
- objections from other occupiers.

Some use classes, particularly A3, can be difficult to obtain, but this will usually be reflected in increased rental values for these types of premises.

What to look for in commercial property

Location

As with all property investments, location is the single most important factor in determining how well a commercial property investment will perform.

It is one of the reasons why office space in London costs so much more to rent or buy than office space at the other end of the M4 in Swansea. The importance of location also explains why London and the South East are so dominant in the commercial property arena. Location is a factor that can vary over time. Improved transport links can boost the value of property by making it more accessible to potential tenants and users. Not all improvements, however, are necessarily beneficial. For example, a new shopping centre may enhance an area, but it could also depress the values of existing high-street shops nearby.

For the commercial property investor, the ideal location is one that is improving but has so far not attracted other investors' attention. This sounds all very well in principle but is less easy to achieve in practice. As with any kind of property investment, it is essential to keep a constant eye on any changes that might affect a particular location's attractiveness to potential commercial tenants.

Lease

If you are buying into a commercial property that has an existing lease in place, then this will be an important aspect to consider when assessing how attractive the property deal is. A lease is a contract between a landlord and a tenant that sets out the terms under which a tenant occupies a property. Once agreed the terms of a lease cannot be changed unless there is mutual consent between both parties. Sometimes there are provisions within the lease itself for it to be altered and, if this is the case, you need to have this checked out. Historically, UK leases for commercial properties had terms of 25 years, but for a variety of reasons the average length has been falling and is currently less than 15 years.

Most UK leases include provisions under which the rent is reviewed, usually every five years. The revised rent is negotiated between the landlord and tenant, taking into account recent rent review agreements on comparable properties and general market forces. If the two parties cannot agree on a new rent, it is referred to arbitration, which is binding on both sides.

Something to look out for in the lease is if it has an 'upward only' review basis. This means that at review the rent cannot fall below the current level. Obviously this is an attractive condition and the presence of this in commercial leases is one reason why this type of property is considered to have a very stable income.

When a lease reaches the end of its term, the tenant has the option to negotiate its renewal or walk away, leaving the landlord to relet the property. If the tenant decides to move elsewhere, they will usually be required under the terms of the lease to reinstate the property to the condition in which it was originally let. The tenants may either complete the work themselves or make a 'dilapidations' payment to the landlord. In practice there are often a number of reasons why tenants renew their leases, including the cost and disruption of relocating to new premises.

Tenant

The financial strength of the tenant is a key factor in considering investment in a particular property. Upwards only rent reviews are of no use if the tenant defaults. The tenant's ability to pay the rent – the tenant's covenant – is taken into account when acquiring, valuing and letting a property.

Tenants who are the least likely to stop paying rent – such as government departments – are favoured for obvious reasons. Also the stability of the particular industry or sector that the business is in. If a tenant defaults, other fundamentals such as location, age, condition and specification are all the more important. Well-located properties with modern specifications should relet more quickly than poorly located, unrefurbished properties.

Specification

The property needs to be suitable for the use to which it is put. This may sound obvious, but history shows that a building's usefulness can change markedly over time. The most obvious example of this is office space built in the 1960s and 1970s. This became unsuitable for many potential tenants because of its lack of air conditioning and ventilation. Some of this redundant office space has since been converted into city centre residential accommodation.

A building with a good specification gives the tenant the ability to adapt to changes that occur over the lease period, which can be as long as 25 years. The flipside is that a poorly specified building may fail to find new tenants when the existing lease expires – and not all redundant commercial property lends itself to residential conversion.

How to value commercial property

Residential property has a value which is irrespective of the rental return it can achieve. The value of residential property is therefore based on how much someone is prepared to pay for it on the basis that they want to live there. Commercial property, however, is valued differently. Far more emphasis is placed on the investment yield that it can return. It is much more difficult, therefore, to make an amateur 'guess' at what the value of a particular commercial property is, based on similar properties in the same area – you will need an expert opinion.

A valuation of a commercial property will assess its location, condition, size and facilities. But it will also take into consideration its usage classification and versatility to be put to different uses. Finally, the rental income return gives a rough yardstick to the value of the property. This multiplier varies, as property prices do, and can be anything from 10 to 30 times the annual rent. So, if the rental income from a property is £20,000 per annum, and the multiplier in that area at that time is 20, then the rough 'yardstick' valuation would be:

$$20 \times £20,000 = £400,000.$$

The 'entry level' commercial property choices

Buying commercial property for own use

If you like the idea of commercial property and want to expand your residential portfolio, where do you start? Many investors buy commercial property not only as an investment, but also as business premises for themselves. Indeed, the government has encouraged businesses to acquire their own premises and has given them tax incentives to do this, by way of allowing commercial property to be held within certain types of pension plans (SIPPs and SSASs).

Buying a commercial property for your business through a SIPP

If you are a business owner and want to purchase the shop, office or factory that you operate from, then you can do so by setting up a Self Invested Personal Pension (SIPP). In this instance, the property is purchased by the pension fund. Any rent payable on the property (by your company or partnership) to the pension fund can be offset against earnings. In addition, because the property is held in a pension, no tax on rental income or Capital Gains Tax on any profit generated by a sale will be paid. Any income that you draw from your pension while retired is taxed.

I should stress that this is a specialist topic, and if you want to find out more about buying commercial property through a pension plan, then you should consult an appropriately qualified Independent Financial Adviser or SIPP specialist. See 'Taking it further' for details.

Buying commercial property as a 'buy to let'

If you're not interested in buying commercial property for your business to use, then you are likely to be investing in a property that you will then rent out to another company on a commercial 'buy to let' basis. Buying a commercial property to rent out to a business is one of the fastest growing forms of investment in the UK, following on from the rapid rise in residential buy to let ventures and the capital growth potential of commercial property. The types of properties lenders generally consider suitable for investment purposes as buy to lets include offices, retail premises and restaurants.

Offices

One of the attractions of buying office space is that if you buy the right property in the right location, there will always be plenty of tenants. Offices offer a great deal of versatility and a whole cross-section of businesses can rent from you. You might want to consider investing in serviced or managed office space that provides the tenant with furniture, equipment, telephone lines and infrastructure already in place, and leases can be more flexible, so this kind of arrangement can be ideal for many businesses. Remember also that your business tenant may also sublet some or all of the space, and by allowing this, you as a landlord are removing one obstacle to a company renting from you.

Many town and city centre offices are above retail premises, and income can be gained from buying the building and letting out the office above and shop below your property on a separate basis.

Retail premises

The ability to find shops or retail outlets to invest in is relatively easy compared with other types of commercial property, but if you are buying a building with an established business in situ, you will need to assess the business itself and its ability to generate a steady income.

You will need to look at the net operating profit. This must take into account all ongoing running expenses such as staff costs, utilities and telephone charges, tax and the cost of buying stock. Obviously, profits will change from year to year, but you will want to see that there is enough 'comfort margin' for the business owner so that paying the rent to you is not a struggle.

Restaurants

The growth in popularity of eating out and the explosion of restaurants has seen many commercial mortgage lenders become more willing to lend on restaurant premises. The main factors to consider when looking at restaurant/café are:

- Location – This is especially important since restaurants rely heavily on passing trade.
- Local demographics – Are there plenty of potential customers with sufficient spending power likely to be attracted to eat at the establishment?
- Is the building a standalone property, or part of a complex?
- The value of the property itself, rather than the existing goodwill, which may or may not last.

If buying a restaurant that is a going concern, you will also need to check out the experience and credentials of the operator – not just their ability to cook but their ability to run a profitable business.

You will also need to survey the fabric of the building and consider environmental issues such as whether there is any asbestos on site. Any potential health issues should be rigorously checked as local council environmental officers will enforce if the property does not meet specifications once the business is trading, and could even threaten to close it down.

Raising finance for commercial property

When buying commercial property to let out, typically most lenders will want to make sure the rent will cover the mortgage by 130 per cent. All lenders will have their own criteria, but typically they will lend up to 75 per cent of the market value of the property.

When making an application for a commercial buy to let mortgage, the lender will usually require details of income and liabilities, copies of at least three months' bank statements (sometimes as many as six months' may be needed) and full details of all leases on the property.

Mortgages are structured in several different ways but the two important aspects to consider are the interest rate and the repayment schedule for the mortgage.

The two interest rate options are:

Commercial fixed rate

You have a set interest rate for a fixed period of time. Once this period has ended the mortgage will revert to the normal variable rate. Arrangement fees are normal when taking out this type of mortgage.

With a commercial fixed rate you may incur an early redemption charge (ERC), which may extend beyond the fixed rate term. For example, the fixed rate may apply for only three years but the penalty period may be an extra five years, during which time you must pay the variable rate of the lender.

Commercial variable interest rate

The variable interest rate mirrors and changes with the Bank of England's base rate. The current market rate and a set premium that remains unchanged throughout the mortgage, constitute the interest rate for each period, i.e. 2% above base. You can often initially get a lower interest rate on a variable interest rate than on a fixed rate mortgage.

The advantage of a variable interest rate mortgage is that you save money when the market rate decreases. The flip side to this is that you are not covered from an increase in the market rate. This simply means the interest rate you pay will increase with the market rate.

For more detailed advice on commercial mortgages contact a suitably qualified and regulated financial services intermediary or mortgage broker. See 'Taking it further' for details or visit www.makingmoneyfromproperty.tv.

Summary

Commercial property can offer the benefits of regular income and potential capital growth, together with healthy diversification. In this chapter, we have looked at:

- The case for buying commercial property
  - Benefits of commercial property
  - Commercial versus residential.
- Drawbacks of investing in commercial property.
- Ways of investing in commercial property.
- Types of commercial property
  - Planning classifications and usage.
- What to look for in commercial property.
- How to value commercial property.
- The 'entry level' commercial property choices
  - Buying a commercial property for your business through a SIPP
  - Buying commercial property as a 'buy to let'.
- Raising finance for commercial property.

12

buying land ...

In this chapter you will learn:
- about buying land
- things to be aware of when investing in land

... they don't make it anymore

As the American hero Will Rogers famously once said, 'Buy land – they ain't making it any more'.

If you are the type of investor who wants to make money without being too involved, then buying land may be a good choice for you, and it is definitely a viable investment strategy that can offer fantastic returns. Buy land in a sought-after location, or one that is likely to get planning permission granted for change of use and subsequent development, and you could make considerable sums. While this process can take many years, the point at which planning permission is granted will see the value of land increase substantially. Returns of over 400 per cent as soon as land gets the required permissions for development are not uncommon, and that's without having even put a spade in the ground!

Investing in land has really taken off in the past few years. A recent review showed that demand for farmland has increased by 42 per cent over the same period in the previous 12 months and according to the Royal Institute of Chartered Surveyors (RICS) the share of the land market being sold to non-farmers is 46 per cent. Rich City investors wanting to become 'lifestyle farmers' are largely driving the market and RICS predict that the value of the land will continue to increase as demand continues to increase.

If you look beyond our shores, there is great potential in buying land in emerging countries. Many people have dipped their toe into foreign markets by buying land and holding on to it for its value to increase. This is called 'land banking'.

The case for investing in land

There is a finite and limited supply of land
While buildings themselves can come and go, the land on which property can be built is in limited supply.

Land can increase in value in more than one way
Land can increase in value just as any other property asset can, as demand outstrips supply. In the UK, land prices have risen sharply over the last 20 years, which has been caused mainly by the much publicized shortage of housing to meet the needs of a growing and changing population within the UK. According to

a report from the Joseph Rowntree Foundation, the UK is heading for a property shortage of more than 1 million homes by 2022 unless house building is dramatically increased from its current rate. While the pundits are happy to report regularly on the increase in house prices, land itself gets less of the limelight – yet over the past two decades, land prices have increased by a staggering eight fold!

Land can also increase in value when it is granted planning permission for change of use and/or development and clearly this is where the real big returns can be made. For example, a £15,000 plot of land in the South East which gains planning permission to build a four-bedroomed detached house could immediately be worth in the region of £200,000 to a builder wanting to erect a £600,000 house on the land. £15,000 to £200,000 is a 1,300 per cent increase!

⍾▷ Food for thought

The pot of gold at the end of your garden

The shortage of suitable building land has pushed land in popular residential areas through the roof. Some people with large gardens have realized that they can portion off part of their land and sell it. The trick is to obtain planning permission for a dwelling, but if this can be done the potential returns are astronomical. For the show I've visited people who have sold off a part of their garden vegetable plot – previously used for growing potatoes and carrots, for which they'd then successfully obtained residential planning permission – and walked away with £300,000. They still have their house and a slightly smaller garden, but 300 grand buys a lot of potatoes!

Finally, land can also increase in value by the development of infrastructure on and around it, whether it is developed or not. The building of new transport links, shops or other public services will put pounds onto the value of any land in the vicinity, be it just a field or something which has already been developed.

Proven concept

The idea of purchasing agricultural, forestry or land in green belt areas is not new. Large developers and institutions have been doing it for decades. They tend to stockpile land into their own 'land banks' which they hold onto for many years. They choose their acquisitions by carefully studying each area for the likelihood of future planning permission being granted. It has only been in relatively recent years that the smaller, private investor can enjoy the same returns previously reserved for the large, wealthy corporate developers.

Low entry level

Another great 'plus' for buying land is that you can secure plots for a relatively modest investment. It is possible to buy a house-sized plot of land without planning permission for around £10,000. Alternatively, you can invest in a 'pooled' scheme where you don't directly buy a plot of land, but invest your money into a company that does. The amount of money required to invest via a pooled investment vehicle can be as little as a couple of thousand pounds.

Any nationality can buy land

You don't have to be a UK national to own a 'piece of England' and this is appealing. Indeed, the presence of overseas buyers wanting to secure land within the UK has contributed to strong demand and, therefore, increases in prices. Equally, there are many opportunities to own land in overseas destinations.

Tax advantages

Investing in agricultural land and forestry has many tax advantages. Owners of agricultural land and forestry pay no inheritance tax, provided the land has been held for at least two years prior to death. There are also ways of mitigating the Capital Gains Tax liability on sale of agricultural land. A tax adviser or accountant will be able to guide you further.

Easy to buy

The process of actually buying a piece of land is far more straightforward than buying a house. Quite simply, there is less to consider. All you are doing is transferring the title from one owner to another, and the complications usually associated with buying a property (such as covenants and defects with the building itself) aren't so prevalent. In fact, it is possible to buy a piece of land and have your name registered on the deeds with the Land Registry, within a month. Rarely is a property purchase concluded in this amount of time.

The land to property journey

If you decide to buy land, you are getting in, literally, at grass roots level of a development project. It doesn't get much rawer than buying the land itself. What is interesting is that at any stage after this initial acquisition, right up to when completed properties are being sold, you can decide to get out (or sell). The value of your investment will increase over time even if you do nothing with the land, but if you do decide to apply for planning permission and then ultimately develop the plot, the value will rise further on the achievement of each of the key steps in the process.

There are six main steps in the journey from pure land to finished property:

1 **Raw land** – You can buy and sell the land alone, undeveloped and in its rawest state. The value of this plot will largely be determined by external factors such as the supply and demand for land in the area as opposed to the status of your individual plot.

2 **Land with outline planning** – If you take the first step towards developing and apply for outline planning permission on the land and this is achieved, you will see a marked step up in the value of the plot. Even with just outline planning, the land will be worth far more than the raw land with no planning permission at all.

3 **Detailed planning** – The next step towards developing is the granting of detailed or full planning permission. Here things really start to get interesting as the plot of land now has a very real development opportunity, and anyone interested in buying your land will know what can be built on it. Getting detailed planning permission can see the value of your raw land rocket.

4 **Provision of services and utilities** – Moving forwards in the journey again, the next step is to have services put onto the land. This will include provision of road access, electricity and water supply and the associated pipe and cabling work. Whilst no actual building of property has yet taken place, the land is now prepared for this and has therefore reached another key milestone. Selling at this point would result in a higher value being achieved than in stage 3.

5 **Off plan and partial construction** – Once the building work commences, the value of the land will step up again. Something very real is now happening to it.

6 **Finished properties** – The final step in the journey is the sale of the land (and property) once the building work has been completed.

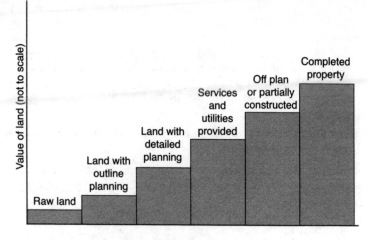

figure 12.1 the land to property journey

🍴 Food for thought

Rights of way

When buying land you should be particularly mindful of rights of way and public footpaths. It is a complicated and time-consuming process to get these changed – with no guarantee that it will ever happen. Careful checking of the deeds and large-scale ordinance survey maps will indicate any such issues.

Strategies for investing in land

There are a couple of different strategies employed by large property developers when it comes to investing in land:

1 **'Land banking'** – Companies buy land at today's prices and then 'bank' the land by holding it, unused, with a view to selling it or developing it at some point in the future. This is a good, solid strategy even during periods when the property market is flat or falling. However, you should take a long-term view because the timescale for when it is right to sell or develop the land may be several years.

2 **Speculation** – Here you invest in land purely on the basis that you anticipate it being 'rezoned' and then you can sell or develop at a greater profit.

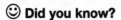

☺ **Did you know?**

'Hope' value

Sometimes a thing called 'hope value' will be included in any land valuation. This is an arbitrary amount to reflect the 'hope' that the land can be developed or its planning designation changed. The amount you pay for hope value will be subject to discussions between buyer and seller.

Zoning

Zoning outlines the use of land for residential, office, industrial, agricultural and other uses and defines the type of property and density of what can be built. If you buy land that is zoned for agricultural use, then it can't be used for anything other than grazing or growing crops. But if it is rezoned for residential use, then the land can be developed – and this is where the real 'big bucks' can be made. Of course, rezoning is by no means guaranteed, and if you are buying land in the hope that it gets rezoned in your favour, you should be aware that this is a speculative investment.

Valuing land

While it is comparatively easy to value a building such as a house, arriving at a valuation for plots of land for sale you are considering purchasing requires an assessment that takes account of a wider variety of different factors.

Many of the factors used to help value plots of land for sale are the same as those used to value houses, but plots of land are often valued in isolation, rather than by comparison with other plots. Often houses are valued by means of comparison with other similar houses in the same area, but land is valued by way of the expected return or yield that could be achieved.

Factors determining the value of land

Area

The value of the land for sale is directly related to the local housing market. Hence the land for sale in London, for example, will cost far more than a plot of similar size in say,

Liverpool. In general terms, a city centre location is more valuable than a residential suburb and this is more valuable than agricultural land. However, there are exceptions, for example residentially zoned land in a beautiful rural location may have a higher value than commercial land in a rundown town.

Transport links

Land located within close proximity to major transport links will usually be valued at a far higher price than an equivalent plot which is accessible only by little winding roads in the middle of nowhere.

Planning permission

The price of plots of land for sale is obviously massively affected by whether any type of planning permission has been granted for that piece of land. Property investors can make handsome profits by identifying and purchasing land that does not yet have the necessary planning permission, but which they believe will gain it shortly. Basically, the greater the planning rights, the higher the price. Each stage of the planning process takes time, so owners of land can raise its value by simply moving it along on the process to development and selling it on:

- **Not zoned.** The land is within a master plan but has not been allocated to any particular type of development.
- **Zoned.** The land has been zoned for agricultural, industrial/commercial or residential use.
- **Outline planning.** The general layout and density of building has been agreed, but not the full architectural plans.
- **Detailed planning.** An exact layout and design of the buildings has been passed by the authorities and development can start right away.

The location of the land, its proximity to new and existing housing developments and the house building targets imposed on the local authority by central government will all have an influence on how the land will be zoned and the probabilities of getting planning permission approved. An investor moving the plot along the 'land to property' journey can see the value increase exponentially once planning permission is granted.

For example: A plot of land, surrounded by existing housing, might be offered for sale at £30,000 if the vendor has not yet applied for planning permission. If the vendor applied and obtained planning permission the plot of land for sale might be priced in the region of £200,000.

> ☺ **Did you know?**
>
> **Overage or 'uplift' clauses**
>
> An 'overage' or 'uplift clause' in a contract on a plot of land entitles the existing owner to a proportion of the increase in value of the land if planning permission is granted within a specified period of time following its sale. It can also apply to existing dwellings when the same would apply if planning is granted to extend the property or build new dwellings within the grounds. If you are buying a plot of land, you must get your solicitor to check this out because, in effect, if you are successful in gaining planning permission, you could legally have to part with, say, one-third of the uplift in value to the previous owner.

Gaining planning permission can be tricky and unpredictable. It is far better to take a medium- to long-term view and set your mind on having to wait. Local planning officers and authorities have many competing priorities so what seems like a straightforward application might turn out to be anything but, especially when local politics gets involved. However, if this is a route you want to follow, then you may want to consider using a local planning consultant to represent your case, as they can increase your chances of gaining approval. Plots of land for sale in the deepest countryside or in an Area of Outstanding Natural Beauty are unlikely to gain permission to be built upon, especially if they are located far from other residential buildings and miles away from local amenities. Conversely, plots of land for sale close to existing residential housing, and in an area with good transport access and significant housing needs, will have a far higher chance of gaining permission.

Once planning has been granted other factors come into play, such as the floor to area ratio. The FAR is the ratio between total floor area allowed to be built and the size of the plot, and it dictates the density of building allowed. The density of development permitted will have a knock-on effect on the potential sales revenue.

The plot Itself

The above factors affect the value of land for sale in the local area. The value of a particular plot is also dependent on other factors, relating to the plot itself:

- What can be built on the land? If it is a house, how big a house, how many bedrooms, what style of house, etc?
- What are the costs of building the property? Will it require expensive foundations on an 'infill' site if it is on a hill? If the location is remote, will the services be expensive to connect?
- What value will the finished property have? Researching in local estate agents and the Internet will show what sale price you should expect from the finished property. Remember that new houses and flats generally sell at a premium.

Developers often use a rule of thumb method of valuing a plot by working out the percentage of the value of the completed project compared with the cost of the plot. If the completed house or block of flats is to have an expected market value of £200,000 and the vendors are asking £60,000 for the plot then the plot value is around 30 per cent.

Plot values vary depending on the market and location, but 30 per cent is considered to be the 'norm' for a developer. Although in some parts of the UK, this has risen to 40 per cent or more. If the price ticket for a piece of land is looking to be substantially more than one-third of the market value of the eventual property, then it is starting to look expensive. Similarly, if the land is going for much less than 30 per cent of the final resale price, then it looks like a bargain. Issues such as density of possible flats or houses also have to be considered.

Perceived risk in developing

Finally, the perceived risk to the investor in developing the land will affect its desirability. This is a bit of a 'catch all' and will be affected by all the other factors already mentioned. Essentially, a plot of land where a developer is confident of gaining planning permission, has existing transport links and infrastructure close to hand, has an established resale market for the finished properties and is in an area where there is a demand for housing will have a much lower perceived risk than a plot of land in an emerging destination. The latter may ultimately offer a greater return, but comes with a higher degree of risk.

🍴 Food for thought

Land for self-build

More and more people are buying plots of land on which to develop and build their own homes. 'Self-build' is a rapidly expanding area of the property market and there is much specialist information available on it. It does give you the chance to find your dream plot of land and then build exactly the house you need on it (subject to planning permission).

Things to be aware of

Buying land overseas

You may be tempted to invest in land overseas. In which case, you should use the same sense check and research criteria as if you were buying land in the UK. You should be aware that in some countries a lot of land is owned by private individuals and there are small plots that have been handed down through the family. In Bulgaria, for example, locals were given plots of land as a government 'hand-out' many years ago, and these plots have remained within the family legacy. To acquire a large plot, you may have to negotiate with several different vendors (some of whom could quite feasibly be elder members of a family) and this can be complicated. This is why in some countries, securing a plot size large enough for any substantial development can take lots of patience and plenty of negotiation!

Government policy

It's fair to say that the apparent value of land and its potential for increase is as much determined by government policy as it is by supply and demand dynamics. This is because the real money is made when land is approved for change of use and development, and the chances of this happening will be dictated by national and local policy on the change of use of land for property development.

☺ **Did you know?**

The difference between greenfield, green belt, green wedges and brownfield sites

- **Greenfield site** – Greenfield land is, simply, any undeveloped land. However, it includes land which used to have a development built on it but where little of the development remains; land where the development on it is limited by a planning condition which requires the land to be restored to its original pre-development condition when its useful life ends (this could be the case with a quarry); and land where the development has been for forestry or agriculture and development is no longer needed for forestry or agriculture.

- **Green belt** – Green belt is land which has been specifically designated for long-term protection from development. It has national importance and the protection of green belts is fiercely upheld by environmentalists and campaigners against development.

- **Green wedges** – Green wedges are areas of largely undeveloped land identified by local planning authorities to be protected from development because they are locally important. They are designated for the life of the local or regional development plan (usually about 10 years) and their designation will be seriously considered and justified each time a new plan is produced.

- **Brownfield site** – This is an existing commercial or industrial site, now abandoned or sparingly utilized.

Broadly speaking, a brownfield site will have a greater chance of a successful planning application than a site which is greenfield. This is because there is a precedent set and the land has previously been used in some commercial, residential or industrial capacity. If you want to develop houses on a brownfield site, you will find that the local government will encourage this as it puts redundant sites back into use – which is far better than developing a greenfield site. However, land contamination as a result of the previous use of the site could be a problem. Cleaning land that has chemical or other contamination is a costly and time-consuming process. Any brownfield site should have a full environmental assessment and contamination survey by a specialist before you purchase.

🍴 Food for thought

Claims and guarantees

Beware of claims made by companies selling land where planning permission is 'guaranteed'. It rarely is, and any investor choosing to invest in land in the hope of a substantial increase in the value because planning permission for change of use or development has been granted, should take the view that this is not guaranteed and can take many years to materialize.

Martin's tip

Investing in land

- Make sure you understand the various levels of planning that could apply to your land. This is particularly relevant if you are buying land overseas. Normally, countries have master national plans, regional plans and local restrictions.
- Get a professional opinion from a surveyor that the price you are paying is what the land is worth and that the size of the plot is clearly defined.
- Get professional opinions on the planning rights themselves and be clear on what you can and can't do.
- Check out what services, if any, are in place such as electricity and water supply. Understand what would be involved in getting these connections, for example how far away is the nearest connection point? Provision of services to a plot can be a major expense.
- Similarly, check access to the land. Can the existing access cope with a road being built? Is there an existing road or would you have to build one? If so, how much will this cost? Will you require approval from the highways authority and is this likely to be granted?
- If you are buying land in an undeveloped location, check out the status of neighbouring plots. Consider the implications if these were developed. What impact could this have on your land?
- Be prepared to negotiate with several different vendors if you are buying several plots. Do these form a coherent whole?
- Be wary of any land previously used for industrial or commercial purposes. There could be issues of contamination which will be expensive and time-consuming to resolve.

- If you are buying a large plot, say for residential development, visit the site every hour over a 24-hour period. There may be disturbances at certain times of day – such as factory deliveries in the early hours – that would affect the value of the property you are thinking about building.
- Look for the existence of public footpaths and rights of way.
- Make sure you check what access other people have over the land, for instance to get to their property.

Summary

In this chapter we have looked at:

- The case for buying land.
- Strategies for investing in land.
- How land appreciates in value.
- Valuing land.
- Things to be aware of when investing in land.

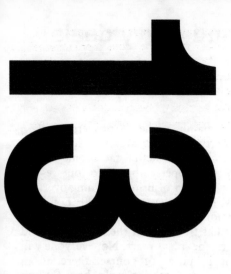

13

buying overseas property ...

In this chapter you will learn:
- the case for buying overseas property
- the risks of buying overseas property
- where to buy – factors to consider
- about new build, off plan and second-hand property
- the buying process
- how to raise finance for overseas purchases
- common mistakes when buying overseas

... sun, sea and savvy deals

Nowadays there is a wide choice of overseas property investment opportunities available to the UK property investor. In fact, the market has mushroomed in recent years and the level of choice is quite baffling.

So far we have concentrated mainly on the UK property market, but more and more property investors are now looking to foreign shores for their purchases. In actual fact, some 40 per cent of all Britons plan to buy property abroad for one reason or another. Estimates of the number of Britons owning overseas property vary significantly, from as few as 300,000 (Lombard Street Research) to 3.5 million (Halifax), but it is agreed across the board that the number has trebled over the last decade and is expected to double over the next few years. Not everyone will be buying for investment purposes of course, there are a multitude of factors influencing why people buy foreign property, but if property investment is your game, then the overseas market offers some very interesting and appealing opportunities, and certainly overseas property should form part of a balanced investment portfolio.

The case for buying overseas property

People are motivated by all sorts of factors when buying abroad, and although not all of them may apply to you now as someone who just wants to buy property to make money, these drivers are relevant to your eventual exit strategy or resale market.

Holidays and travel

Lots of people buy a second home abroad as a holiday home. The thought of having a 'home from home' abroad is really appealing – especially to people who have holidayed in a particular area for many years. Owning your own holiday home means that you know exactly what your accommodation is going to be like and you can personalize it to suit your own needs and requirements. The other great thing about having a holiday home is that you can leave your own personal belongings in the property and so a visit there may involve only as much as packing a small bag of clothes! This is very convenient, especially to parents with children. The availability of frequent low-cost flights to popular tourist spots from regional airports also means that actually getting to the property can be no more hassle than negotiating the UK motorway network.

Retirement

A huge part of the overseas property market is driven by people retiring abroad. Since the cost of living is so much less in some other European countries, people on a fixed income in retirement will find that their pension quite simply goes further. Couple this with warmer climates and a saving on heating bills, and the case for retirement abroad on financial terms alone looks compelling.

Lifestyle

Let's face it, few people enjoy the long dark nights of the UK winter months. Having a bolt-hole abroad, even if it is just to escape the depressing winter period, is really appealing. Sunny climates offer numerous health and lifestyle benefits, not least because they allow people to spend more time outdoors in the fresh air. Also the local diet – certainly in southern Europe – is far healthier and the general attitude to life is less stressful. People may be driven to living either permanently or semi-permanently abroad purely for the lifestyle benefits.

Affordability

In the UK, we have some of the most expensive house prices in the world. As prices have increased so strongly over the years, they are now disproportionate to average earnings. Many people can't afford to buy property in the UK, or even if they are fortunate enough to be on the housing ladder, they may not be able to afford the size or type of house that they desire. Property prices in foreign countries are often much cheaper. When you consider that in somewhere like Turkey, you could buy a very nice four-bedroom detached house with a pool and still get change out of £150,000, then it's easy to see how someone can buy more property for their money by going abroad. In the first-time buyer market, young people are looking at buying property in other European cities – where you can get onto the housing ladder for say, £35,000 – because they quite simply find the UK market out of their reach. Buying abroad gives them all the benefits of property investment over the long-term, even if they don't actually live in the property.

Financial stability

People looking to downsize are often able to sell up in the UK and buy an equivalent property in another country for a much lower price. Assuming their UK mortgage is paid off or at least reduced to a small amount, this exercise leaves them with a sizeable chunk of capital which they can live on.

Investment diversification

Anyone involved in property investment will know the benefits of having a spread of property in their portfolio. Diversification reduces risk, and if you diversify to other countries, then this diversification is even greater. If you own a spread of properties in say five or six different countries then it doesn't matter to you so much what happens to the UK housing market. In fact, a property slump in any of these countries will not have such a dramatic effect on your overall portfolio value.

Investment performance

There are many countries which are experiencing far faster economic growth than the UK. Central and Eastern European countries such as Bulgaria, Hungary, Romania and Poland are now playing 'catch up' with their Western European neighbours, as they are now part of the EU and benefiting from the grants and foreign investment that is being injected as a result. Other developing economies such as China, India and Brazil are now experiencing their own industrial revolutions. This all makes for strong GDP growth and that, in turn, impacts on the value of property. So, investors wanting to see the capital value of their properties rise quite rapidly may consider overseas investments to achieve this aim.

Figure 13.1 shows that while property in the UK has outperformed shares quite comfortably over the years, property in Bratislava and Buenos Aires has done even better.

UK market slowing

All markets move in cycles and the UK property market has experienced a long period of strong growth. It is now widely believed that while we probably won't experience a property crash (there remains too much demand for property to suggest this), we are entering a period where UK house price rises may slow, or even fall sightly. This period of contraction is perfectly

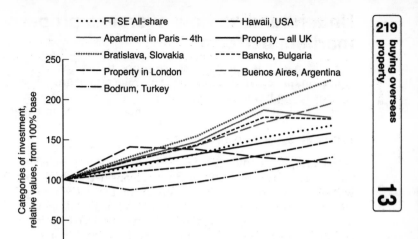

figure 13.1 property versus stocks – growth **and** income

normal, and canny investors will actually see a shrinking of the market as a buying opportunity, given that in the long-term prices will begin to rise again. However, anyone taking a shorter term view may prefer to invest in markets that are still at the early stages of the growth curve, where they will see positive returns quickly.

'Jet to let'

This is a term used to describe the exercise of buying property abroad which is then let out. In Chapter 5, we looked at the different types of letting strategy, but suffice to say that owning a property abroad that is then let out to help pay for the running costs is a very sensible thing to do. With rental yields falling in the UK residential market, investors may be able to achieve higher returns by buying in a popular residential area of another country and renting out to a local. The other aspect of 'jet to let' is buying property in a tourist destination that you then let out on a short-term basis to holidaymakers. This means that you can still make use of the property yourself and, to all intents and purposes, have free holidays!

Understanding how overseas property markets perform

The UK market is a mature, stable property market. Over the long term, prices will increase – the average rate of growth since records began has been around 10 per cent per year. When you start to look at overseas markets, you may be buying in a place which is still on the brink of land and property being of any significant value whatsoever.

For example, a plot of land right on the beach in an undiscovered tourist location may be considered pretty much worthless. Unless the land is capable of being used to grow crops or graze livestock, it might not be valued at all. However, if an airport opens up nearby and tourists start to trickle in, then the land starts to look more interesting. Early pioneering investors may be optimistic enough about the future draw of the area to buy this land. Later on, as the location gets press coverage and the tourist market becomes established, this beachfront plot of land becomes valuable to someone wanting to build a hotel or apartment complex there. At this point, the property market takes off. This typical growth pattern can be illustrated as shown in Figure 13.2.

In the very early years, values do not increase very much at all. Around years 8 or 9, values start to climb ... but it is still very early days and people who are buying there should expect the process to be a fairly rocky road. Most investors will aim to enter the market somewhere between 13 and 20 years into the cycle – when great growth can be expected but they are not so pioneering. From year 20 onwards, the market settles into maturity, when steady, but not as spectacular growth can be expected.

The risks of buying overseas property

Entering the overseas property market requires as much careful consideration as buying elsewhere. You should conduct your research fully as if you were buying a UK property and I always say to people when they start to look abroad 'Don't leave your brain at the airport when you get on the plane!' I hear some horror stories that are almost unbelievable – about people losing their money when buying abroad – but often these situations could have been avoided by simple measures, and by not doing things you wouldn't do if you were buying at home. The other

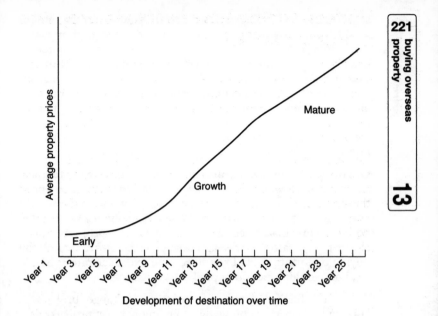

figure 13.2 growth pattern of a typical destination

vital thing is to get good independent advice, such as offered by my company, PropertyQC (www.propertyqc.com).

There are some risks or downsides of buying overseas which you should bear in mind:

Currency fluctuations

This is particularly relevant if you are buying a property off plan and your earnings or the capital being used to buy the property are based in sterling. Take a simple example where you negotiate a property price of €150,000 when the euro:sterling exchange rate is €1.50:£1.00. This means that the property will cost you £100,000 equivalent. By the time you complete on the property (which could be up to two years later), the exchange has shifted to €1.45:£1.00. In effect, where £1 previously bought you €1.50, it now only buys you €1.45. Your property at €150,000 now costs you in sterling terms nearly £103,450 – or 3.45 per cent more. People often forget this when they buy abroad and so for this reason I would recommend the use of a specialist foreign exchange broker. They are able to buy the foreign currency at more competitive rates than the UK high street banks and will also be able to fix your exchange rate for you. If you know that you are going to need a sum of money at some point in the future (say to pay the balance of the purchase price to a developer on an off plan purchase), a currency exchange broker will also be able to 'forward' buy for you. This means that for a small deposit (perhaps 10 per cent of the total amount of money) they can buy currency for you at today's rates. This is a great way to 'hedge' against the pound weakening against the other currency and simply means you know how much that currency is going to cost you.

Of course, the reverse can also apply. At the time of writing, the US dollar:sterling exchange rate is at a 26-year high in favour of the pound. So while not too long ago, £1 would have bought approximately $1.50, you can now get around $2.00 to the pound. This makes commodities including property much cheaper in relative terms and therefore creates a wonderful buying opportunity. Had you fixed your exchange rate at $1.50: £1, you wouldn't be too happy!

There are further details of currency exchange brokers in 'Taking it further', or on www.makingmoneyfromproperty.tv.

A word of warning on currency fluctuations: I advise people to *consider* it but not to let the 'currency tail wag the investment dog'. Don't buy a property just on the basis of the currency exchange position unless you consider yourself to be a speculator. Currency exchange rates can vary substantially and as the US dollar example has demonstrated, can be very volatile. The case for an overseas investment should stack up on all other levels, the currency exchange being just one aspect of this.

Economic instability

Many foreign destinations have a more unstable political and economic climate than the UK. A market which looks attractive one day may be on the brink of revolution or political unrest the next. In your research, you should look at wider macro-economic factors as well.

Transaction costs

The costs associated with buying and selling property abroad are often far higher than in the UK. Some countries have the equivalent of VAT on property – with rates ranging as high as 20 per cent. Couple this with higher legal costs, land registry fees and other taxes, and you may be in for a nasty surprise if you haven't considered the total cost of purchase. It is vitally important that you ask the agent or your solicitor to explain to you the total acquisition costs since this will have a big impact on your budget. It's not uncommon to have to add on an additional 15 per cent to the purchase price of the property to account for transaction costs. Similarly, if you want to sell a property abroad, it is not uncommon for estate agents to expect up to 6 per cent as their fee.

Running costs

Chances are that if you are buying a property abroad as an investment or holiday home and you don't intend to live in it, then you will have to pay an agent to look after it and manage it for you. Property management fees can be as high as 40 per cent in foreign destinations, depending on the type of service that you have. You will also need to take into consideration local taxes and charges on the property itself – although often cheaper than council tax, don't assume that because the property is in a foreign country there aren't ongoing costs to pay.

Legal title

The property market in some countries is extremely immature. In the UK, every property transaction is registered with the Land Registry and so it is easy to find out who is the legal owner of any property or piece of land. Not so in some other jurisdictions. Public records on land ownership can be best difficult to find and complicated to understand, and at worse, non existent. This means if you want to buy a property, you might have to go to great lengths to find out if the person who is selling it to you actually has the right to do so! If they are not the legal owner of the property, you could part with your money to someone who is not the registered owner. In a worse-case scenario, the actual real owner could turn up years later and demand the property back from you.

Also, a fact which often goes undetected by people buying abroad, is that in many countries mortgages or debts on a property go with the property itself, not the individual. This means that an unsuspecting person could buy a property and not realize that it has a mortgage on it. The liability for this mortgage would then be inherited with the property. For these reasons and many others, it is imperative that you appoint a fully qualified lawyer specializing in property transactions in the country where you are buying. They will be able to checkout the legal title of the property for you and advise if it has any loans or encumbrances on it.

Details of UK based lawyers who specialize in international property law are provided in 'Taking it further', and on www.makingmoneyfromproperty.tv.

Restrictions on ownership

While some countries actively encourage foreigners to buy property, others make it more difficult. These that are countries that essentially want to preserve home ownership for their own nationals and don't want foreigners to push property prices beyond what locals can afford. There are other reasons why some governments place restrictions on ownership by UK investors. For example, currently it is illegal for foreigners to own land in Bulgaria (so although you can buy the equivalent of a leasehold property, you cannot buy freehold). In other countries, you have to set up a company in the country of the property and a local resident has to have shares in this company. Many of the restrictions are not insurmountable but you might have to take additional measures and incur additional costs to overcome them.

Once you are the owner of a property, you may find that there are fewer tax concessions – for the same reasons; the government wants to limit the number of foreigners buying property. Also if you rent out the property or sell it, you may have a proportion of your money withheld by the government in order to ensure that you pay any tax due. All of these things need to be considered when you are doing your sums.

Availability of mortgages

In the UK, we have one of the most sophisticated mortgage markets in the world. We have literally thousands of different products, each with their own particular features. The mortgage market in other countries is usually more immature and at times non-existent, which means that your ability to leverage your purchase is more limited. You may have to effectively pay cash for the property and not have any borrowing at all (unless you borrow money secured against a UK property from a UK lender). The criteria and amount that you can borrow is also often much more restrictive – even in quite mature property markets. Forget the concept of 'self-certification'. You have to remember, that you may be an 'unknown' to the banks or lending institutions and so they will need to carry out checks to satisfy themselves that you are going to pay the mortgage. You may find that your usual income must cover not only your UK outgoings, but the mortgage interest on the foreign property as well – irrespective of the fact that you might be letting it out.

Unregulated market

The overseas property world is unregulated in the UK. In effect, any Tom, Dick or Harry can set themselves up as an overseas property agent and tell you whatever they think you want to hear about a property. They do not have to pass any exams or be a member of any regulatory body in order to operate. Couple this with the fact that the overseas property industry has mushroomed of late and high levels of commission are available for agents, and it means that the industry has its fair share of 'sharks'. Clearly, this is a risk to the unwary investor and adds even more importance to you doing your own research and due diligence.

☺ **Did you know?**

There is now a self-regulating body called the Association of International Property Professionals (AIPP) who have made a start towards trying to bring regulation into the overseas property world. Members have to be approved by an independent board and comply with a code of conduct. The objective of the AIPP is to bring greater standards of professionalism and integrity to the industry and provide more consumer protection. Look out for the AIPP logo on the marketing materials of agents and developers you deal with or log on to www.aipp.org.uk for more information.

Where to buy – factors to consider

The answer to the question, 'Where to buy?' is 'Anywhere in the world!' One thing's for certain, the world is becoming a smaller place and access to previously unheard-of destinations has opened up the property market there. Turn the clock back 10 years or so, and who would have heard of the Cape Verde Islands? If you were to have stopped people in the street, how many could have honestly pointed to where Dubai is on the map? Yet both these destinations are now boasting healthy property markets and many people from the UK are buying there.

The 'traditional' markets were Spain, France, Portugal and Florida, probably because a great many of us would have been there on holiday and had a certain familiarity with the place. However, the 'easyJet' effect and the opening up of the EU means that nowadays the choice for the overseas property investor is quite baffling. Attend any of the big overseas property trade shows and you will see a plethora of property developers and agents promoting properties across the board in places such as Bulgaria, Canada, Croatia, Cyprus, Greece, Hungary, Morocco, Poland, Romania and Turkey. Add to this the new Eastern European set including Czech Republic, Estonia, Latvia, Lithuania, Slovakia and Slovenia and also the more long haul emerging destinations such as Argentina, Brazil, China, India, Malaysia, South Africa and Thailand and you have a massive amount of choice.

However, all this choice makes for a potentially confused investor and so it is even more important to sit down and analyse why you are buying and your own objectives:

1 Is this going to be a pure investment for you or do you want to make use of the property yourself for holidays? What is your investment strategy?

2 What financial returns are you expecting? Do you need a minimum return to make it viable for you compared with other investment opportunities?

3 Do you intend to rent out the property? Short-term holiday lets or long-term residential lets? What is the market for tenants?

4 What is your timeframe for holding onto the property? Do you intend to sell up in the foreseeable future?

5 What exit strategies are currently available to someone owning a property in the area? What exit strategy do you hope to employ? What is the demand for property in the area?

6 What is your attitude to risk?

7 How much capital have you got available to purchase? What is your attitude to borrowing?

As well as your personal objectives and situation, you also need to consider all aspects of the location:

Economic factors

1 What are the future political and economic forecasts for the country? Is it politically stable?

2 What are interest rates? Is the trend downwards?

3 What is the rate of inflation?

4 What is the employment situation?

5 What level of Foreign Direct Investment (FDI) is there? Large amounts of FDI will create jobs and local wealth.

Tourism factors

1 Is it a popular destination? What happens if tastes change and somewhere else becomes the latest hotspot?

2 What tourism trends is the country experiencing?

3 What is access like? Can you visit the property easily? Are there regular flights from the UK or the tourism market which the country serves? (i.e. it's not just the British that go on holiday to other countries – other nationalities have their own holiday hotspots.)

4 Is there tourism year round? How long is the season?

5 What kind of tourism does the area offer? Bucket & spade brigade, cheap package holidays, spa, golf or skiing holidays?

6 What is the average weekly or nightly rental for similar properties?

7 How many hotels are in the area? What are the relative costs of hotels versus self-catering?

Property factors

1 What is the attitude to foreigners owning property there? Do you need to take extra steps to actually own property there, such as setting up a company?

2 What are the build standards like in the country? If you are buying a new build property, what guarantees from the developer are there?

3 Are there services and utilities in place? How reliable are they?

4 How safe is your money? If you are sending money across before taking legal title (i.e. in the case of an off plan purchase) what bank guarantees are in place? How easy is it to get your money out of the country?

5 What is the current rate of property inflation? What is the future performance of property predicted to be?

6 What are the appropriate tax rates in the country on the property and you as an owner?

7 Where is the demand for property coming from? Foreigners or locals?

8 What are the local planning laws? Is the property at risk of being affected adversely by new construction?

Legal factors

1 What is the legal process of buying in this destination? Is it legally robust?
2 What is the legal position if you rent the property. Is the law pro-tenant or pro-landlord?
3 Is the practice of making 'under the table' or 'black money' transactions common?
4 What kind of legal jurisdiction is prevalent?
5 What tax rates apply to the property and to you as a property owner?
6 Is there a double-taxation treaty with the UK in place?
7 Is freehold available to foreigners? If not is there a satisfactory workaround?

Miscellaneous factors

1 Are there geographical factors to consider? For example, is the property in an earthquake zone?
2 Do you speak the language? Or is English widely spoken in the country?

In short, there is a lot to consider and some careful thought about what you hope to achieve from the property, before you go on your spending spree, could make that actual search far more focused and successful. For companies that can help you, visit www.makingmoneyfromproperty.tv.

Spanish land grab

There has been a lot of press coverage about 'Land Grab' in Spain, whereby developers have effectively 'compulsorily purchased' land and property from unsuspecting owners. It occurs when land is rezoned from rural or 'rustico' to land for development or urban use. However, the practice is illegal and is almost entirely limited to the Spanish region of Valencia.

Land which lies close to existing urbanization is the most likely to be affected – so a farmhouse with bags of charm and development potential, conveniently located not too far from the facilities of the nearby town could be at risk should the neighbouring urbanization be expanded in the future.

At the time of writing, 'land grab' is in the process of being outlawed, following campaigns by homeowners which have led to intervention by the European Commission. Nevertheless, if you are considering buying land in Valencia (or indeed anywhere) you should make sure you get a thorough search done by a qualified lawyer to establish whether the property or land is at risk.

New build, off plan and second-hand property

The majority of overseas property opportunities that you see advertised in specialist magazines and trade shows are new build or off plan properties within developments of varying sizes. This goes without saying, since it will be only the medium-sized to large developers with multiple units to sell that will be able to afford to market in this way. The individual selling his family home, won't be featured unless he has appointed an agent who advertises his property along with others in this way.

If you are looking to buy overseas property as an investment, then the case for buying off plan is a valid one (as we talked about in Chapter 6). You are able to lock in on a price of a property that you don't have to fully pay for until months or years down the line. In the meantime, you can benefit from the capital growth associated with property ownership. Also by virtue of the fact that many overseas destinations are in developmental stage you are more likely to be able to buy there by acquiring a newly built property – older houses just simply aren't around in sufficient supply. However, depending on your objectives, buying an older or resale property may actually be more beneficial, so don't overlook this. Essentially, the main pros and cons of buying new build or off plan versus resale property are below.

Advantages of 'off plan' or new build

- Buying 'off plan' gives you the opportunity to gear your investment (see Chapter 6 for an example of this).
- If your contract is fully assignable, you may be able to sell or trade the contract prior to completion of the property. This means that you never actually take possession of the completed building, but sell it at the market price at some point during the construction. This is an attractive proposition – you don't complete on the property, there may be tax savings and you aren't trying to sell on a development at a time when other people may be trying to do the same, and yet you can still benefit from the growth. Be aware that this is a high-risk strategy, though, and you need to thoroughly check out the resale market and demand for this type of property before you embark on this approach.

- Build quality and standards will be as modern and up to date as the developer can afford. If you are buying within the EU, then developers have to build to EU regulations – which means that you can guarantee safe electrical and plumbing work. Older properties may have been built many years ago without the same quality checks in place. You may have to replace wiring or plumbing completely if it is unsafe.
- On smaller, more bespoke, developments you may be able to negotiate with the developer on the specification or finish of the property.

Advantages of buying resale property

- You know what you are getting. You can walk in the door and touch and feel the property for yourself. If you are buying for personal reasons, this is a very comforting factor. Many people struggle to visualize what a room will look like from a drawing or artist's impression. No matter how sophisticated the marketing material, there is nothing quite the same as being able to step inside yourself. If you are furnishing the property, you can take precise measurements and plan your furniture to fit exactly within the space.
- You know what your view is like – although if you are buying a resale property in a developing area you will still need to do your checks on what other planning applications are pending in the immediate vicinity.
- It's ready for you to move in. There's no waiting, as there would be with an off plan purchase. Once you complete the purchase of the property, you are able to move in, sell or rent it straight away.
- Depending on the situation of the seller and how motivated they are to sell, you may be able to negotiate a better deal. Some sellers are influenced by factors other than just money. If it is a private individual selling a family property it might be important to them that they *like* you rather than just getting the highest possible price.

The buying process

The process of buying overseas property should always start with research. You need to spend some time carefully evaluating your own goals, objectives and attitudes, and giving careful consideration to the other factors listed above.

⑪ Food for thought

Devise your own scoring system to evaluate different overseas property opportunities using the checklist on the previous pages. There may be other more personal factors that you also want to include, for example you know people who have already bought property there, which may influence your perceived risk.

Once you have narrowed down your choice of country, region and area you can start to look for individual properties that meet your requirements.

The actual buying process may vary depending on the type of property you are buying (i.e. new build, off plan, resale or renovation) the country and its own process of buying, and your personal reasons for buying (if you are buying somewhere to live, there will be lots of other considerations). However, since this book focuses on property investing, the following process is a simple example of the steps you are likely to go through to acquire your property.

Research

Narrow down your choice to the country, region and area that you would like to buy in. Use the checklist to gather as much information as possible about the location. The Internet is a great tool for carrying out research and 'Taking it further' and www.makingmoneyfromproperty.tv lists some useful websites that can help you.

You can also get a wealth of information by attending overseas property exhibitions. For the price of entry, you can have access to agents and developers from all corners of the globe. They will, of course, be wanting to sell you property, so bear that in mind when speaking to them. But professional, well-qualified salespeople can be a great source of general information about an area and the things to be aware of when buying. You can also attend seminars as part of these shows which cover all sorts of topics, from buying in particular countries to property renting and tax and legal issues. Usually these seminars are run by experts in the field and there is often the opportunity for you to pose your own specific questions to them.

You should also buy and read some of the many specialist overseas property magazines and publications. Again, although they will feature articles on a whole variety of topics, you can get a feel for where the hotspots are just by looking at their front covers.

Find properties

Using the same tools, identify properties and/or developments which interest you and then gather as much information as you can about them. Usually, there will be an agent or marketing company appointed to help sell a project on behalf of a developer and these people should have access to full particulars, plans, specifications, prices and purchase contracts for you to review. Request as much information as possible from the agent.

Evaluate

Use your scoring system to compare different projects or properties and narrow down your choice.

Appoint lawyer

To some people this may seem a little premature, but the earlier you appoint a legal representative, the better. You can ask them to review the purchase contracts of properties that you are considering to ensure that there is nothing onerous or unusual about them. There are a few UK-based legal firms who specialize in overseas property, having lawyers from many countries based out of their UK offices. This gives you the opportunity to consult with an expert in the area that you are planning to buy but without the costs, time difference or language barrier of contacting somebody overseas. My company, PropertyQC, works alongside The International Law Partnership (www.lawoverseas.com).

Inspect property

Once you have really narrowed down your choices, at some point you will need to make a site visit to the property, even if it is only to verify that the information contained within the sales particulars is correct! Remember that the overseas property industry is unregulated in the UK, so there is nothing stopping unscrupulous agents or developers 'over-egging' the case. If a property states that it has sea views, for example, you need to know that this isn't just when you stand on the loo and peer out of a top window!

Place reservation

This applies mainly to purchasing property off plan. You can place a reservation deposit on a property to take it off the market for a given length of time while you conclude your research and your lawyer checks out all the paperwork. Usually reservation fees range from a few hundred to a couple of thousand pounds and are non-refundable, although there are companies who allow you to place a reservation fee for a couple of weeks, during which time the fee is refundable. You should make sure you understand whether or not the fee is refundable, and consider how likely it is that you are not going to proceed if you don't want to forfeit your money. It is quite reasonable to place a reservation on a property to hold it off the market while you make arrangements for a site visit, and most developers will allow you to switch to another property on the development if you prefer, without penalty.

Legal checks

If you haven't appointed a lawyer earlier on in the process, now is the time to do so. After placing a reservation on a property, you are usually expected to sign the purchase contracts within 30 days. This is particularly true if you are buying off plan in a rapidly growing market. The developer doesn't want a property held off the market on a reservation fee when he could be selling it to someone else. However, at the same time, you shouldn't feel bullied or pressurized into signing the purchase contract until your lawyer has been able to carry out all the checks to their satisfaction. On conclusion of their work, your lawyer will write to you with a report explaining the purchase contract in layman's terms.

Martin's tip

Purchase contracts

Make sure that the purchase contracts are written in English as well as the local language. Even if you have a good grasp of conversational language in the country where you are buying, legal 'speak' is very different. You need to make sure that you fully understand each and every point in the contract and what it means to you as a buyer. Anything you're not sure about, ask your lawyer to clarify.

Sign contracts

This is, in effect, 'exchange of contracts'. You sign the purchase contract between you and the seller or developer.

Transfer or wire deposit

At the same time as signing the purchase contracts you will make provision for the deposit monies to be electronically transferred to the developer. If you have used a currency exchange broker, they will be holding the money in the local currency for you and you will need to give them written authority to make the transfer. A phone call to them is rarely sufficient. Once the funds have been received by the developer they should issue you with a written receipt or confirmation that they have received your money.

Completion

At some point in the future (maybe in a couple of years if you are buying off plan) you will complete on the property. Your lawyer will take a major role in this and it is usual for you to appoint a lawyer to act as a Power of Attorney to sign to accept the property on your behalf. This is if you don't want to actually fly out and be present at the actual completion. The completions process will usually involve your details being registered on the title of the property and with the land registry (if there is one) and the title deeds and land registry being signed in the presence of a notary. The notary is an official who is there to put on public record the fact that the formal documents recording the sale/purchase have been signed in his or her presence and are understood by the parties concerned. The notary also carries out a number of checks as to the status of the property and/or the buyer and seller. The notary may act for both buyer and seller. The notary will, however, almost always know nothing about UK law and often will have limited English. The use of the notary is, therefore, no substitute for your own independent legal advice.

Raising finance for overseas purchases

As already stated, the mortgage market in many overseas destinations is still in its infancy. This is particularly true of the new 'emerging' destinations such as Central and Eastern European countries. Here, the idea of borrowing money to fund the purchase of a house is often a relatively new concept and banks in these areas have a fairly simplistic approach. A foreign investor wanting to borrow money to purchase a property that they don't intend to live in adds another dimension. You may find that the choice of mortgages available to you in the country where you are buying is very much more limited than if you were buying in the UK. However, borrowing money in the country of the property is only one way of raising finance to fund overseas property purchase; there are other solutions:

1 Buy the property outright – a cash purchase.
2 Borrow money in the UK secured against a UK property.
3 Join forces with other investors.

Paying cash

For cash-rich investors, buying an overseas property doesn't involve any borrowing at all. They have the cash and would like to buy a property with it. These people may not be concerned about gearing or leveraging their capital.

Borrowing money secured against a UK property

If you don't have the cash to buy, borrowing money secured against a UK property may be the only way to buy, due to the fact that mortgages in the country of your purchase are either non-existent or very uncompetitive. Borrowing money against your UK property often proves to be the best way of raising finance anyway for a number of reasons:

- **Interest rates in the UK are stable and relatively low.** Remember that emerging destinations are often still in the early days of a free market economy, and inflation and interest rates can be quite volatile. We are in a period of historically low interest rates in the UK and so money is 'cheap'. This is one factor which has fuelled the whole overseas property market, because coupled with strong house price inflation, it has given people the confidence to equity release from UK property to fund foreign purchases.

- **Set-up costs of taking out a mortgage in the UK are likely to be lower than borrowing in a foreign country.** For some buyers who borrow against their UK property by means of a further advance with their existing lender, the paperwork and process is quite straightforward.

- **Greater choice and competition among lenders.** In going through the process of releasing equity from your UK property to fund your overseas purchase, you may take the opportunity to shop around and see if your existing deal is still competitive. I know of many people who have done this and found a deal that is much better than their existing arrangements to the point that even with the higher amount borrowed (to pay for the overseas purchase) their monthly outlay has remained more or less unchanged.

- **Documentation, terminology and the process are familiar.** If you have a mortgage already, then whether you are extending this or even remortgaging fully with a new lender, you will understand the documentation and process that you go through. The process of borrowing from a foreign bank may be quite different and chances are the paperwork won't be written in English which could make life difficult.
- **More sophisticated products.** The UK mortgage market is one of the most sophisticated in the world and there are lots of different mortgage products to suit different needs of borrowers. You can take out interest only deals, self-certification mortgages, fixed rate loans, and so on, which allow you to be more in control of your monthly outlay.
- **You can borrow higher loan to value.** Even in mature property markets, the ability of foreigners to borrow can be limited by the 'loan to value' (LTV) against the property. This is partly due to the fact that foreign banks don't want to be overexposed in the event that you don't repay the mortgage. Since you may not have a bank account or credit history in the country then it is difficult for the banks to form an opinion on how financially secure you are. They will therefore cover their risk by limiting the amount you can borrow.

Join forces with other investors

If you are buying primarily for investment and don't intend spending very long in the property, then joining forces with other investors means that you can pool your capital. Imagine that you have £50,000 of capital to invest. You have a number of choices:

1 You could buy a property for £50,000 outright.
2 You could use that £50,000 as a deposit against a property worth £150,000 and borrow the rest on a mortgage.
3 You could find four other investors each with £50,000 and pool your money. Now you could buy:
   a 5 × £50,000 properties in different locations giving you greater diversification;
   b 5 × £150,000 properties borrowing the rest on mortgage as with option 2.

The option that is most appealing very much depends on your reasons for purchasing and your attitude to borrowing. But if you are an investor wanting to get leverage on your money, are unemotional about the own-use element of overseas property and like the idea of building a portfolio, then clearly option 3 is best.

Joining forces with other investors to form a 'syndicate' makes a lot of sense and doesn't have to be complicated. A syndicate could be family members, friends or work colleagues or indeed a group of like-minded individuals who are put in contact with one another by means of a mutual acquaintance.

If you do decide to form a syndicate with other people in order to buy property, then you should formalize the relationship with a syndicate agreement or contract. This can cover the eventuality of members wanting to leave or sell up and who gets to use the property (if applicable). A lawyer should be able to draw up a contract for you and it may prevent arguments and disputes further down the line. The other advantages of forming a syndicate are:

- Allows greater diversification and therefore reduction of risk. You could buy different properties in different countries, with different currencies and at different price levels to get the maximum spread of risk.
- Spreads the workload of researching and managing the properties that you buy.
- Draws in other people's experiences and opinions on markets that you might be considering investing in.
- Brings a greater mix of skills and knowledge, for example you may be great at negotiating deals but another member might be stronger on working out finances.

The other benefit, which shouldn't be underestimated, is that it brings an element of fun into overseas property investing. I know of several syndicates who meet regularly (at a suitable watering hole!) to discuss opportunities, and this social aspect is very much enjoyed.

To make contact with people who may be interested in forming a syndicate to buy overseas property, visit www.makingmoneyfromproperty.tv.

Borrow money in the overseas location

Of course, you may be able to borrow money in the overseas location, secured against your property there. This means that apart from the deposit, your UK savings and property can remained untouched. While mortgages aren't commonly available everywhere, the development of the local mortgage market is a key driver of house price inflation in many overseas destinations.

While overseas mortgages tend to be based on the same principles as those in the UK, you should bear in mind that the mortgage market in many foreign countries is far more simplistic than it is here. There are a few things to be aware of:

- The loan to value (LTV) is usually lower than in the UK. It is highly unlikely that you will be able to borrow 90–95 per cent LTV in a foreign country like you can in the UK on your main residence. It is more likely that you will be able to borrow a maximum of 70 per cent, and in some countries it will be even less than that.

- Mortgages are often on a capital repayment basis. Interest only deals either don't exist or are limited to say two to three years at the start of the mortgage – after which it reverts to capital repayment.

- The maximum age at repayment of the loan is often limited to 70 years or younger. So if you are a 55-year-old wanting to borrow, you will be offered a mortgage based on a maximum term of 15 years.

- The concept of a buy to let mortgage is very rare in foreign countries. Your suitability will be assessed on your income and outgoings, without taking into consideration whether the property is going to be rented out.

The other important factor to consider is that if you borrow in the foreign country and you are paying the mortgage interest payments from the UK, you are exposed to a currency risk through fluctuations in the exchange rate. On the other hand, if you are renting out the property and receiving rent in the local currency, it may be preferable that the mortgage is also based in that currency.

☺ Did you know?

Don't automatically assume that you will be able to get a mortgage within the country where you are buying. In some countries, local mortgages do not exist. The only way to buy a property there is to pay for it outright. The ability to borrow against your foreign property may be a factor that influences where you buy, so make sure this is one of the questions that you pose early on in your research.

As well as foreign currency mortgages, the other term you may start to hear more of is 'multicurrency mortgages'. Here you move your mortgage from one currency to another to take into consideration exchange rate fluctuations. They are intended for high net worth individuals since by nature, these types of mortgage are more complicated than a straightforward loan, but you don't have to be an expert on currency markets to have one. Usually you will have a currency manager who works on your behalf and moves your mortgage around in order to maintain the debt in currencies that are expected to weaken against sterling. There is usually a fee for this and very often these types of mortgage are subject to a minimum borrowing amount of, say, £250,000 or equivalent.

If you do want to take out a foreign mortgage on an overseas property, then there are specialist UK-based international mortgage brokers who can research the market and help find the best deal for you. This means that you can deal with someone in the UK who can explain the deal and how it works to you in English. In fact, many of the UK banks and lending institutions are now starting to offer foreign currency mortgages secured on overseas property, and so it could be that your euro mortgage on your property in Spain is provided to you by the international division of your local high street bank.

Visit www.makingmoneyfromproperty.tv for information on all aspects of raising money for UK and overseas property purchases.

Common mistakes when buying overseas and how to avoid them

As more and more people in the UK buy property abroad, the more we hear horror stories of how things have gone wrong. There are even TV programmes dedicated to highlighting some of the disasters that unsuspecting UK purchasers have experienced. Of course, the story of Mr and Mrs Average who have successfully purchased their villa abroad and now spend many happy days there doesn't make good TV or sell newspapers, so it is inevitable that the media will focus on the cases where things haven't worked out as expected. However, it is a sad fact that even level-headed, intelligent people have come unstuck when buying overseas property, so it is worthwhile highlighting some of the most common problems and how to avoid them.

Problems with legal title

As mentioned previously, in some emerging markets, the system of land registry leaves a lot to be desired and so it isn't always easy to find out if a property has good 'title'.

Overcome this by: Using an appropriately qualified lawyer to check out the title of a property before you commit to buy. This will prevent you parting with your hard-earned cash on a property which may have disputed ownership.

---

⑪ Food for thought

Title insurance

If you want extra protection, it is possible to purchase special 'Title Insurance'. Title insurance is protection against loss arising from problems connected with the title to your property. Property typically goes through several ownership changes, and the land on which it stands goes through many more. There may be a weak link at any point in that chain that could emerge to cause trouble. There may be unpaid real estate taxes or someone who feels that they have a right to the land. Title insurance covers the insured party for any claims and legal fees that arise out of such problems. See 'Taking it further' for details of providers.

Problems with the contract

If you are buying a property off plan, you must get the purchase contract checked out by a lawyer. All too often contracts are written with an unfair bias in favour of the developer or builder, leaving the buyer with few rights or little choice to take action in the event that they are late with the completion of the build or deliver a property that is substandard.

Overcome this by: Ensuring that all contracts relating to the sale are written in English as well as the local language and get them fully checked out by an independent lawyer before you sign anything. Make sure that anything you have been promised and that is important to you – such as a clear sea view – is written into the contract.

Problems with security of money

Again, if you are buying off plan and are required to pay a deposit on the property, you must ensure that the money passed over is either held in Escrow (a protected bank account) pending final planning permission or is protected by a bank guarantee. This is effectively an insurance policy taken out by the developer to cover your deposit in the event that they go into liquidation or can't meet their obligations under the terms of the purchase contract. The insurance policy would be called upon to either provide you with a refund of your deposit or to instruct another developer to take over the project.

Problems with planning

Whether you are buying an off plan property from a developer or planning to build or renovate yourself, the process of applying for and obtaining full planning permission can be very drawn out and unpredictable. Be very careful if you are buying property off plan and make sure you understand at what stage in the planning process the developer is. I know of people who have paid deposits on property that was due to be completed by now, but instead find the build has only just begun due to delays in obtaining the appropriate planning. While on the one hand, you are still getting the growth associated with buying off plan, if you have borrowed money to pay the deposit you will be paying interest on this borrowing for which you may not have budgeted.

Problems with security

If you are resident in your property for only a few weeks of the year, even if you rent the property out, it is going to be standing vacant for long periods of time. This makes it easy prey for thieves. Adequate security measures on windows and doors should be a high priority, and, if possible, buy property that is within a gated community so that you won't get casual passersby who may become casual thieves.

Martin's tip

If you are buying a new build property or just completing on an off plan project, make sure one of the first things you do is change the locks. You may not be aware of the number of tradespeople and contractors who have had access to your property during the final stages of build. For all you know, there may be several keys floating around in strangers' hands. Change the locks and entrust your keys only to your managing agent. This may be a requirement of your overseas property insurance.

Problems with finances

Some buyers are unaware of the amount of taxes and fees that they are due to pay on a property until the bill lands on their doorstep and then it comes as a rather unwelcome surprise. As part of your research, make sure you understand the full cost of ownership so that you can account for this in your calculations.

Problems with rental expectations

It's fair to say that many buyers have unrealistic expectations of the number of weeks' rent they can expect from their holiday home. This may be due to over-enthusiastic agents overegging the case in order to secure a sale and buyers not doing their research well enough. Whatever the reason, it is a bitter pill to swallow when a holiday home that was purchased with the intention of being self-funding starts to cost money each month to maintain because the overheads aren't covered by the net rental income. Sadly, all too many buyers are in this position. Owing a holiday home and renting it out isn't a licence to print money, it is hard work and can be time-consuming. So unless you have the time and energy to achieve maximum rental bookings, you should probably set your expectations of rental income at the lower end of any estimates you are given.

Overcome this by: Maximizing your rental opportunities by buying a pretty property that has something about it that differentiates it from others. If you are buying in a large complex where there are lots of identical properties, do what you can to find out how many of them are bought with the intention of renting. Get comparables on rental data and if it doesn't financially stack up consider another property that does.

Make sure you have heating and/or air conditioning to extend the 'season'. Even Mediterranean countries get chilly in winter, and any property in a hot climate that doesn't have air conditioning will struggle to get repeat bookings.

🍴 Food for thought

Overseas Property Insurance

It is important that you take out adequate insurance for your overseas property. This should include building and contents, and should also cover you for short-term holiday lets, if this is what you intend to do. You may have to arrange for someone to visit and check the property on a regular basis, as part of the conditions of insurance.

Most problems can be avoided easily by doing proper research before buying, and making sure you consult your lawyer and tax specialist early on in the decision making process. If you get it right, owning overseas property can not only prove to be a very worthwhile investment, but you have the added bonus of 'free' holidays as well – remember, that your annual trip out to the property will be tax deductible since you can quite legitimately charge it as a business expense!

As the world becomes an ever smaller place, more and more people will buy in more and more locations, so I imagine that in 10 years' time, you may well be the owner of foreign property if you're not already. What a nice thought!

💷 Martin's tip

Investment versus own use balance

Even the most hard-nosed investors get swayed towards buying property overseas for the added bonus of having a home abroad that they can use themselves. Even though the primary objective is investment, the personal aspects of a decision very often come into play. And why not? If you can find a property that stacks up as an investment, located in an area that you like to visit, then this is a real 'lifestyle investment'. What value do you put on the joy of nipping off to your own property for a few days of rest and relaxation in a foreign country? However, the risk is that you allow the 'own use' aspects take over the investment decision. A classic case of the heart ruling the head. If you are susceptible to this in the UK, add in a great view, a dose of warm sun on your back and a glass of sangria … and you'll find it very easy to get carried away. Be clear about your objectives and review them regularly during your research and buying process so you don't forget what it's all about.

Summary

In this chapter we have looked at:

- The case for buying overseas property.
- The risks of buying overseas property.
- Where to buy – factors to consider.
- New build, off plan and second-hand property.
- The buying process.
- Raising finance for overseas purchases.
- Common mistakes when buying overseas.

14
raising finance ...

In this chapter you will learn:
- ways to raise finance
- to understand gearing
- to understand mortgages
- mortgage jargon busters
- about your credit rating and how to improve it
- about 'low money down' deals – what to look out for

... begging and borrowing the expert way

Most property investors will either need or want to raise some finance to assist them with their property purchases. Even those people who are lucky enough to be able to buy the property with their own cash may need to raise finance to cover refurbishment costs or unforeseen expenses. They may also prefer to borrow capital rather than using all their own money so that they can make their finances work harder for them and benefit from *leveraging* on a deal.

One of the unique aspects of property as an asset class is that you can readily use it as security for borrowing money. This is something that we shouldn't take for granted; while shares, bonds and gilts might be good investment vehicles, you can't easily borrow, say, 80 per cent of their value to allow you to buy more! This is one of the most appealing aspects of property. Because it is tangible and has a use as a home for someone, aside from the investment return, you can go to any number of banks, building societies and mortgage lenders who will provide you with a loan secured against the property.

When reading the following chapter, please bear in mind that I am not qualified to provide specific financial or mortgage advice nor regulated to do so. Before making any financial commitment you should consult with a suitably qualified professional intermediary such as an IFA or mortgage broker. Visit www.makingmoneyfromproperty.tv for suggestions.

Ways to raise finance

When contemplating raising finance for a property purchase, most people will think of traditional mortgages. Here in the UK, we have one of the world's most sophisticated mortgage markets – with a whole range of different products designed to meet a whole range of needs and requirements. Later in this chapter, we will take a closer look at the types of mortgage available and give you a 'jargon buster' for some of the commonly used terms. However, mortgages aren't the only way to raise finance. If you think 'outside the box', you may come up with your own, innovative ways to get the money together to fund your purchases.

Investment by an individual

You may know of capital rich individuals who will lend you the money to buy property in return for either a share of the property or interest on the loan. If the latter is the case, you may be able to negotiate that all the interest is paid at some point in the future (i.e. on completion of refurbishment work or onward sale of the property) so you don't have to make the monthly payments.

Equity release

If you own property already, you may wish to take a further advance or mortgage against this asset to give you the money required to buy further properties. The climate of low interest rates in the UK and the level of equity in UK property has been a major factor driving the buy to let or investment market (including overseas). Homeowners have recognized that they can potentially make a better return on the capital that they have tied up in the bricks and mortar of their own home by releasing it and investing in other properties.

Bank loans, overdrafts and credit cards

If you don't have existing property which you can remortgage to release capital for your property purchase, then you may be able to raise deposit money by unsecured bank loans or overdrafts. In particular, if you are investing in low money down schemes (more on this later), then you might be able to take your first step into property investing by borrowing the initial deposit on a credit card. While the rate of interest being charged is higher than a mortgage, the availability of this money is often immediate.

Bridging finance

There are specialist companies that will provide short-term finance to enable you to purchase a property – with a view to quickly swapping to a less expensive form of borrowing. This can enable creative purchasing and refinancing to release equity in property bought below market value. However, bridging finance comes with high interest rates – usually around 1–2 per cent per month, and high set-up charges – usually 1–2 per cent of the amount borrowed.

Sell things

You might be surprised how much money you could raise just by selling things you own – something from the attic, an unused car or family heirlooms. Internet auction sites and free-ad newspapers are a great way to sell things fast.

Understanding mortgages

For most people, borrowing money using a traditional mortgage is the most straightforward and cheapest way to buy property. The lender advances you money as a loan and takes a charge on the property as security. This means that in effect, although you are the registered owner of the property on the title deeds, the lender will have their interest also registered and you will therefore have to pay back the loan when you sell the property. Years ago, lenders often insisted on actually holding the physical mortgage deeds as security, although this practice is no longer necessary.

Next you need to decide on which mortgage type is best for you – interest only or capital repayment.

Interest only

Each month, you pay back just the interest on the loan. The amount advanced to you doesn't reduce, no matter how long you have the mortgage. If you want the property to end up mortgage free, you will have to make alternative arrangements to save up a sum of money sufficient to pay back the loan. However, property investors don't worry about this, since they will work on the basis that the value of their properties will rise over time sufficiently enough that, by selling some of their portfolio, they can repay the mortgages at the end of the term.

Take an example where an investor buys five properties at £100,000 today and borrows 85 per cent loan to value (LTV) on all of them for a mortgage term of 25 years. If we assume that house prices rise by 7 per cent per annum during that period (which is conservative), then at the end of the mortgage term, selling just one of the five properties will be enough to repay all the mortgages.

	For each property	Total for five properties
Property purchase cost	£100,000	£500,000
Mortgage	£85,000	£425,000
Value after 25 years	£543,000 (approx)	£2,714,000 (approx)

Selling just one property at a final value of approximately £543,000 is sufficient to repay the total mortgages of £425,000 and would leave the investor with more than £2 million in equity.

Property investors tend to prefer interest only mortgages for three reasons:

1 They are cheaper than capital repayment loans on a month-by-month basis and therefore it is easy to make a buy to let property have positive cashflow using interest only. This means you have cash available each month to be put to other uses.
2 They can be more suitable if you are buying and selling frequently and swapping mortgages on a regular basis to keep up with the best deals.
3 The interest part of the mortgage payment can be written down as an expense against your gross rent and therefore used to offset your income on a property for tax purposes. This only applies to the interest element – not the capital repayment part if you have a capital repayment mortgage (see below).

Capital repayment

Each month you pay back the interest and some of the capital borrowed. This means that at the end of the mortgage term, you have repaid all that you borrowed. Of course, the amount that you have to pay each month is more than an interest only deal, but you have the benefit of the fact that the loan actually gets paid off. The proportion of capital repaid in the early years is low compared with the latter years of the mortgage term.

Mortgage jargon buster

There are some other terms relating to mortgages that you should be aware of:

Standard variable rate

Here your mortgage is based on the standard rate of interest on offer by the lender. Your monthly payments will go up and down as the lender's mortgage rate changes, which is usually in line with the Bank of England base rate.

Discounted variable rate

These deals are usually offered by lenders to attract new borrowers. Essentially they offer a discount off the standard variable rate for a set period of time. Your monthly payments go up and down as with a standard variable rate mortgage, but you will be paying less. Interestingly, the rate offered for new borrowers is often less than for existing customers, so you might be better off swapping lenders if you can do so without incurring large penalty charges.

Good points – You pay less each month than if you are on a standard variable rate.

Bad points – You can be locked into the deal for the agreed term and if interest rates rise, then your payments will go up and you're stuck with it. Generally, the shorter the term, the better. You can then swap to the next deal on offer.

Fixed interest rate

Here your repayments are fixed at a certain level for a set period of time. No matter what happens to base rates, your mortgage payments will remain unchanged during the term of the fixed rate. Fixed rate deals have traditionally been for two, three or five years, after which time the mortgage will revert back to the standard variable rate. However, deals which have fixed rates for much longer periods of time (10 and even up to 25 years) are now starting to appear on the market.

Good points – You know exactly what your monthly repayments are going to be, and if you think that interest rates are going to rise, you can lock in on a fixed rate deal where your payments will be unaffected by changes in base rates during the fixed rate term.

Bad points – If interest rates fall, you won't benefit from this, and you might end up paying more than you need to for months or even years. If you decide to sell or change the mortgage during the term of the fixed rate, you can face hefty 'early redemption penalties' – fines for coming out of the deal early. These can be as much as 6 per cent of the total amount borrowed.

Tracker rate

Here the interest rate tracks the Bank of England base rate with a constant differential over a set period of time. It's a variable rate loan which means that your monthly mortgage payments will go up and down along with changes in the base rate.

Good points – You benefit from falls in interest rates quickly as your mortgage interest rate will adjust as base rates change.

Bad points – You can't fix your monthly outgoings unlike a fixed rate.

Capped rate

These are supposed to offer the best of both variable and fixed rate deals. Your mortgage will have a limit, a 'cap' on the maximum rate of interest that you will pay over a particular period of time. If base rates fall, then your mortgage rate will fall as on a standard variable rate arrangement, but if they rise, your mortgage payments will not go over a maximum limit.

Good points – You get the best of both worlds, so you can benefit from falling interest rates but are protected from rate rises.

Bad points – There are fewer deals on the market and the rates are not necessarily competitive because the interest rate you'll be paying is higher than some fixed or discounted rates.

All these definitions relate to the actual rate of interest that you pay, but there are other mortgage terms that you are likely to come across:

'Self-certification' mortgages

Most lenders will want proof of your income before they will offer you a mortgage. This can be a problem for people who are self-employed or for people whose income cannot be guaranteed or documented. Self-certification mortgages provide a solution to this since you do not have to prove your income to the lender – just certify that it is what you say it is. They are ideal for self-employed people whose accounts are optimized for tax saving, salespeople whose earnings are mostly commission based and employed people who also have self-employed earnings (i.e. they have their own part-time business).

Flexible mortgages

These are deals that allow you to alter your monthly payments to suit your changing circumstances, without penalty. They are often attached to a specialist 'all in one' bank account that includes your mortgage, current and savings accounts. You can take payment holidays, make underpayments and make regular or occasional overpayments to suit your financial situation. They can offer great flexibility and enable you to pay off the mortgage much quicker – with significant savings as a result. However, if you take a payment holiday or underpay, the amount owing will quickly grow.

Lifetime rate mortgages

An increasing number of lenders now offer lifetime rate mortgages where the rate of interest is fixed for the entire term of the mortgage. Traditionally this has been 25 years, but nowadays, some lenders will allow you to borrow for up to 40 years. Many of these deals also offer some flexible features which means that you can make regular or occasional penalty-free overpayments in order to reduce the debt and pay off the mortgage more quickly.

💰 Martin's tip

Top tips on finding a mortgage

1 Shop around: there's a lot of competition between the mortgage providers and at different times mortgage companies are actively looking to attract new business. They'll offer 'loss leader' deals to get new customers. These can be really competitive offers which don't generally stay around for long. Make sure you compare at least three different deals and look out for extra charges or conditions that are compulsory.

2 Read the small print. When you take out a mortgage you have a legally binding agreement with the lender. This will cover the terms and conditions of the mortgage and have an illustration of the amount you will need to pay each month. Look out for special terms and conditions, particularly if you are on a fixed rate deal, as you may find that there are hefty penalties if you change your mortgage. Similarly 'overhanging lock-ins' are penalties that apply even after a special deal interest rate has come to an end.

3 Don't be overly swayed by a low sounding initial interest rates. This is known as the headline rate. Very low rates often come with restrictions and long-term 'tie ins' which are very costly to

get out of if you want to remortgage. Once the initial 'honeymoon' period is over you may revert to a rate which is uncompetitive and you're stuck with it. An indicator of how much a loan will actually cost is the APR.

4 Keep an open mind and call on the expertise of a mortgage broker who will be able to assess the whole market, not just traditional lenders.

5 Don't undervalue the importance of flexibility. A mortgage with no tie-ins or fixed rates may cost more in interest payments but the ability to change, cancel or refinance without penalty may be vital for your chosen investment strategy.

Loan to value (LTV)

The abbreviation LTV is commonly used to describe the percentage of borrowed money against the value of a property. If you have a property worth £100,000 and you have a mortgage on that property of £80,000, then the LTV is 80 per cent.

Higher lending charge (HLC)

These charges are applied by some lenders to borrowers seeking a loan of 90 per cent or more of the value of their property. It can also be referred to as a **mortgage indemnity guarantee (MIG)** and can cost a considerable amount. It's an insurance policy that is designed to reimburse the lender if you can't keep up the repayments and they end up selling the property for less than you owe on your mortgage. Some lenders allow you to add the charge to the mortgage so you don't have to find the cash upfront to cover it – but then you are paying interest on this amount for the term of the loan and in the long term it will therefore cost even more.

Agreement in principle

This is a written quotation from a lender confirming that they are willing to give you a mortgage and the basis on which the loan will be made. You can get an agreement in principle on the web, over the phone, or in person, and this is usually followed up by a written quotation.

This is a useful document to have. It shows any prospective vendor that you are serious and can actually get a mortgage to cover the purchase price. It also provides a reference for some of the key features of your mortgage, and indicates what your repayments will be.

£ Martin's tip

Use a mortgage broker or independent financial adviser (IFA)

There are so many different mortgage products available these days that it would be nigh-on impossible to keep pace with them all unless you concentrated on the subject full time. Use a qualified mortgage broker or IFA – because that is exactly what they do! Good ones will have close relationships with local representatives of the various lending companies, or the local branch manager in the case of banks, and may be able to use personal connections to get your mortgage sorted out quickly or to allow some flexibility in their requirements. Mortgages and mortgage brokers are now regulated under the Financial Services Authority, so anyone advising on mortgages will have had to pass certain exams to prove that they are competent to do so. Some may charge you a fee for their advice, while others will receive a fee from the lender for introducing your business or sometimes both. However, if they secure you a good deal, you will get back many times their fee over the term of the mortgage.

Details of where to look to find a qualified mortgage broker or IFA are given in 'Taking it further' and on www.makingmoney fromproperty.tv.

Understanding gearing

Now that you understand a bit more about mortgages, it's worth looking at how borrowing money against a property can increase your investment return. First, 'gearing' is the term used to describe the proportion of borrowed money against a property value. If you own a property worth £100,000 and you have a 90 per cent LTV mortgage on it, then you would be considered to be highly geared. Conversely, if the same property had a mortgage of just £40,000 against it, this would represent a 40 per cent LTV and would have low gearing.

At this stage it is also worth going back to the basics of return on investment (ROI) or return on capital employed. Using borrowing, you can make your money work harder for you.

Example of ROI with low gearing

The property price is £100,000. The amount of capital that I put into the deal is £50,000. The remaining £50,000 is on a 50 per cent LTV mortgage. Five years later, I sell the property for £200,000 giving me a profit of £100,000.

$$\text{ROI} = \frac{£100,000 \text{ (profit)}}{£50,000 \text{ (capital employed)}} \times 100\% = 200\% \text{ ROI}$$

Example of ROI with high gearing

I buy the same property costing £100,000, except this time I take out an 85 per cent LTV mortgage, leaving me with just £15,000 of my own capital to put into the deal. Five years later, I sell the property for £200,000 giving me a profit of £100,000.

$$\text{ROI} = \frac{£100,000 \text{ (profit)}}{£15,000 \text{ (capital employed)}} \times 100\% = 667\% \text{ ROI}$$

Gearing is also referred to as 'leveraging' because what, in fact, you are doing is borrowing money to increase your buying power. You are 'leveraging the capital' that you have available. We've already talked about how you can use mortgages to help you buy more property – and if you believe that property is going to increase in value, then you can get a better return on your money. This is why even wealthy property investors who could afford to pay cash for properties still choose to take out mortgages. We can take this concept one step further and illustrate how you can really make a big difference to your investment return using gearing.

Suppose I have £100,000 of cash available to me. I could:

1 Buy one property worth £100,000 with no mortgage. If we assume that I sell it in five years' time, for £200,000, then I make a profit of £100,000. My ROI is 100%.

$$\text{ROI} = \frac{£100,000 \text{ (profit)}}{£100,000 \text{ (capital employed)}} \times 100\% = 100\% \text{ ROI}$$

This is a 'no gearing' strategy. I make £100k profit.

2 Buy two properties worth £100,000 by putting £50,000 into each property and taking the balance on a 50 per cent LTV mortgage. Again, I sell both properties in five years' time for £200,000 each. My ROI is now 200%.

$$\text{ROI} = \frac{£200,000 \text{ (profit)}}{£100,000 \text{ (capital employed)}} \times 100\% = 200\% \text{ ROI}$$

This is a 'low gearing' strategy. I make £200k profit.

3 Buy five properties worth £100,000 by putting £20,000 into each property and taking the balance on a 80 per cent LTV mortgage. I sell all five properties in five years' time for £200,000 each. My ROI is now 500%.

ROI = <u>£500,000</u> (profit) − 5 × £100,000 × 100% = 500% ROI
$\quad$ £100,000 (capital employed)

This is a 'higher gearing' strategy. I make £500k profit.

4 Buy 10 properties worth £100,000 by putting £10,000 into each property and taking the balance on a 90 per cent LTV mortgage. I sell all 10 properties in 5 years' time for £200,000 each. My ROI is now 1000%!

ROI = <u>£1,000,000</u> (profit) − 10 × £100,000 × 100% = 1000% ROI
$\quad$ £100,000 (capital employed)

This is a very 'high gearing' strategy. I make £1million profit.

This is a simplified example and doesn't take into consideration the cost of borrowing which would, in effect, reduce the amount of profit over a five-year term, but it does illustrate how leveraging your money can have dramatic effects.

Gearing, of course, does have its risks and it's not for everyone. If the properties I buy in scenario number 4 above actually fall in value, then I have a greater deficit to cover. I also have to service the debt which puts me at a cashflow risk, but in rising markets gearing is a property investor's best friend.

Your credit rating and how to protect it

You will soon discover, as a property investor, that your credit rating is a precious thing. It determines your ability to borrow money and if you want to buy property, you will probably need to borrow money. Mess up your credit rating and you'll suffer the consequences because you will find that lenders will refuse to lend to you – or they will lend at higher rates of interest. You should protect your credit rating as if your livelihood depends on it – because in effect, it does.

So, how do you know what kind of credit rating you have? There are companies that collect and manage data about your credit history. They store information provided to them by banks, mortgage companies and credit card companies in respect of your credit history – how much money you borrow and, most importantly, what you are like at paying it back! They also keep information on the electoral roll and records of any County Court Judgments (CCJs) made against you. This could be as a result of not repaying a debt or bill that was owed.

> ☺ **Did you know?**
>
> County court judgments (CCJs) will be recorded for six years from the date of the judgment – unless the judgment was paid in full within one month of judgment being given, when the court can remove the record if you contact them. If a CCJ is paid after more than one month, it can be marked as 'satisfied' once it has been repaid.

Details of credit reference agencies in the UK can be found in 'Taking it further'. They will hold details of you at your main residence but also at 'linked' addresses such as other properties that you own.

How to improve your credit rating

You might think that by not having credit cards and loans you will be considered a safer bet and as a result will have a better credit rating, but this is not true. Provided that you pay the interest and other monies due on your loans and credit cards in a timely manner, owing money and having credit cards actually improves your credit rating. The number one rule is to make sure you always make at least the minimum monthly payment within the month that it is due. If you miss a payment, it will be registered on your credit file and used as an indication of poor credit history.

There are other simple measures that you can employ to improve your credit rating:

1 Make sure you are on the Electoral Roll at your current address. If necessary register online at www.rolling-registration.co.uk or contact your local authority directly.
2 If you have incurred county court judgments make sure that they are marked as 'satisfied' when you pay them off. A certificate should be requested from the county court that issued the judgment and forwarded to the major credit reference agencies listed in 'Taking it further'.

3 When you apply for credit and it is refused, it leaves a footprint on your credit history, so don't keep applying for credit if you've been previously refused. If you continue to apply, and keep getting refused, you will leave too many credit search footprints on your file, which will suggest to future lenders that you are financially overcommitted and desperate for credit.

4 You have the right to state your case and defend your position if you have genuine reasons for any credit slip-ups. If you need to explain your financial circumstances you can place a 'notice of correction' on your credit file. Similarly, you can dispute any information which you feel is wrong or inaccurate. You can make a statement of up to 200 words, which will be viewed by the lender when searching your credit file.

☺ **Did you know?**

If you apply for a mortgage or loan and it is rejected because you have a poor credit rating, this rejection itself can be recorded as part of your credit history, making it even more difficult to secure a loan or mortgage in the future. This seems a bit unfair. If you believe that you have a poor credit rating, you are better off consulting a specialist mortgage broker early in the process. They can help you find a lender that will possibly be more accommodating to your particular requirements or circumstances, for example if you are self-employed.

'No or low money down' deals

A 'no money down deal' is a property purchase which involves using very little of your own money. You construct a deal using financing from other sources. You may have to source money from different lenders/investors, but not have to use your own funds. This is often referred to as a 'no money down loan'. To many people this is the Holy Grail of property financing – buying a property without using any of your own money.

Obtaining these no money down loan funds can be done by using all sorts of different facilities, some of which are listed below, but remember the old adage – in general, you don't get something for nothing.

Using credit cards

You might want to consider applying for credit cards. Although the rate of interest is higher, the lender will not require you to state what the money is being spent on and once you have the credit limit agreed, you can access it very quickly. Investors apply for credit cards then build up the credit limits to use these funds as deposits. If you use each one regularly for a while, you will be able to increase your limits and once you have proved yourself to the credit card company, you are often offered an increase to your limits. After a while you can build up a considerable credit facility. You can ask for cheques linked to some cards, making it easier to release cash from them.

Once you have a balance on your card it is a good idea to transfer it over to another card for an interest-free period if this facility is being offered. It might take you some time, but if you can learn to juggle the balances, you can take advantage of the best rates of interest available and often go for long periods without paying any interest at all. However, it can be a time-consuming process.

Using loans

An unsecured loan is a loan which you do not have to secure on your assets. There are many companies that will provide these kinds of loans, although the interest rates will generally be higher than with a secured loan.

Using 100 per cent plus mortgages

A 100 per cent mortgage is usually a residential mortgage provided by a lender for 100 per cent of the cost of your purchase. It may sometimes include your solicitor's fees and MIG (mortgage indemnity insurance). One of the easiest ways of undertaking no money down deals is with a regular residential mortgage. You can obtain 100 per cent to 125 per cent residential mortgages from some lenders.

You must intend to live in the property in order to obtain a residential mortgage. However, you can build up your portfolio by buying a property, moving into it, then, when you have been there for a reasonable period, buy another one, move into that then convert the mortgage of the one you move out of into a buy to let mortgage, providing you can meet the repayments.

Using draw down facilities

A draw down mortgage is a facility secured against a property whereby you can have a cash release system (i.e. cheque book or current account) linked to your mortgage account. This enables you to release equity when you need to without the need to go through the whole process of applying for a new mortgage or further advance each time.

Using a gifted deposit

A gifted deposit means that someone has given you the money or paid the deposit on a property you are buying from them. Builders sometimes offer gifted deposits on new developments. Some lenders will accept a gifted deposit from a builder, but they prefer to see some commitment from you.

If you are buying and selling property privately, there is also a scenario whereby in order to facilitate the deal, the seller will agree to contribute to the cost of the deposit.

Using loan to value lenders

Some lenders will lend LTV and not loan to purchase price. For instance, if a property is valued at £100,000 and you are buying it at, say £70,000, you should be able to get funding for 85 per cent of the value, not the purchase price you have negotiated (£85,000) – releasing £15,000 out of the deal.

Completing a re-mortgage as soon as you have bought property

If you have sourced a property and it is worth more than you paid for it, it is possible to remortgage it as soon as you have bought it. This can be achieved using bridging loan finance. You use a bridging loan based on the purchase price to buy the property. You then immediately remortgage based on the true market value and not the purchase price.

This can also be effective if you have bought a property and quickly done some work on it, thereby increasing its value.

For more information on all aspects of raising finance, visit www.makingmoneyfromproperty.tv.

Martin's tip

Don't forget all the other costs associated with buying and selling property such as legal fees, Stamp Duty, Capital Gains Tax, estate agent's fees, mortgage broker fees and survey fees, etc.

Summary

In this chapter we have looked at:

- Ways to raise finance.
- Understanding gearing.
- Understanding mortgages.
- Mortgage jargon busters.
- Your credit rating and how to improve it.
- 'No and low money down' deals.

15 indirect property investment ...

In this chapter you will learn about:
- owning property through REITs
- owning property through SIPPs
- investing in property funds
- syndicates

... the armchair investor's dream

So far, we have talked mainly about owning property directly. However, there are ways of making money from property that don't involve direct investment.

If you are attracted to the idea of making money from property, but don't have the capital required or the desire to own property directly, then there are plenty of products and initiatives now available for indirect property investment. Here, rather than buying property yourself, you buy a stake in a company or entity that in turn owns property. As a strategy, indirect investment is often overlooked in favour of direct ownership; however, as this chapter will show, depending on your circumstances, it may be prove to be beneficial.

This is a very specialized area of investment, and I am not qualified to advise on it. However, I can give you an overview of the opportunities available. You should then seek professional advice from a suitably qualified and regulated professional. Rules and regulations governing this area of the market are changing all the time, so you should consult with your adviser for the latest position.

There are a number of vehicles available today that facilitate the private individual in owning property indirectly:

1 Real Estate Investment Trusts (REITs)
2 Self Invested Personal Pensions (SIPPs)
3 Property funds
4 Syndicates

Owning property through a REIT

What is a REIT?

A REIT (pronounced 'reet') is a quoted company that owns and manages income producing property. It can invest in both residential and commercial property and most of its taxable income (at least 90 per cent) is distributed to shareholders through dividends – in return for which the company is largely exempt from Corporation Tax.

REITs are designed to offer investors income and capital appreciation from rented property in a tax-efficient way, with a return closely aligned to that offered by direct property investment. This is achieved by taking away the 'double taxation' (Corporation Tax plus the tax on dividends) that you get if you invest into ordinary property funds.

REITs have been on the agenda since 1997 when the government at that time announced its intention to launch them in the UK. Their introduction is partly intended to align the UK with other key markets that already have a bespoke property investment vehicle – including the USA, Australia, Belgium, Canada, Singapore, Japan and France. REITs were finally introduced in the UK on 1 January 2007, and their introduction creates a great opportunity for property investors by creating a more liquid and tax-efficient vehicle.

The case for UK REITs

One of the main reasons for the government introducing UK REITs was the desire to encourage investments that are potentially more secure than direct residential buy to let, and to enable private investors to share in the same attractive returns from commercial property that are arguably available only to bigger investors. At the heart of the new policy is the creation of an investment vehicle that allows UK investors to access property returns without tax being a factor.

Features of REITs

- It is a UK tax-resident company which is listed on one of the UK government's recognized stock exchanges.
- UK REITs do not pay tax on property rental income or chargeable gains.
- UK REITs do have to distribute at least 90 per cent of rental profits to investors, who will pay tax at their normal rates.
- There are additional conditions that a UK REIT must satisfy, including some which limit the amount of debt financing (UK REITs will have to have rental profits of at least 1.25 times their loan interest payable).

One of the drawbacks of direct property investment is that it lacks liquidity (i.e. you can't sell property quickly). UK REITs get around this by enabling investors to buy and sell easily traded units.

Why invest in REITs?

The introduction of REITs opens up exciting new opportunities for small investors in the UK, where access to property investments has always been limited. There are a number of reasons why investment in property via REITs is a good thing:

It allows individual investors to invest indirectly in a diversified property portfolio, buying low-cost and easily tradable units instead of having to finance the purchase of whole properties. Other investors in UK REITs are likely to be pension funds, endowment funds and foundations, insurance companies, bank trust departments and mutual funds. These institutions tend to have a cautious approach to investment, so private individuals can benefit from this level of protection.

They are very tax efficient – investors avoid the double taxation that any normal investor in property company shares faces, as tax won't be payable on rental or capital gains earned within a REIT (as the REIT organization is exempt from Corporation Tax on qualifying property income and gains). One of the current problems with investing in stock market listed property companies is that investors effectively pay tax twice on the same income – first, when the company pays Corporation Tax on its profits, and again when the investor receives a dividend. By contrast, there will be no Corporation Tax on gains arising from the disposal of properties forming part of a UK REIT. Investors will be liable only for the tax due on income received as dividends.

☺ Did you know?

This double layer of tax suffered by most investors is one of the reasons why shares in property companies have historically traded at a discount to the 'net asset value' of their property assets. The relative lack of liquidity of the underlying property assets is also a factor. UK REITs, however, do not attract tax on rental or capital gains and are exempt from Corporation Tax on qualifying property. REITs can therefore regularly trade at a 10–20 per cent premium to the value of their underlying assets.

Another advantage of UK REITs is that compared with unit trusts and open-ended investment companies (OEICs), the liquidity challenges associated with property mean that for the latter, a significant proportion of funds held cannot be directly invested in property (in case investors want to sell). Liquidity is not an issue with UK REITs, since investors can buy or sell easily tradable units. Finally, because UK REITs pay out such a large portion (90 per cent) of their profits in dividends, they're also particularly attractive to income seeking investors.

REITs versus direct property investment

As well as the tax advantages, UK REITs offer several investment benefits which are not available to those investing directly in bricks and mortar:

- Rather than owning a single property in its entirety, an investor in a UK REIT would own a piece of a professionally managed property portfolio. This is less hassle than direct ownership and more suited to armchair investors who don't want to get involved in managing properties themselves.
- UK REITs offer greater liquidity than buying a house, which can be time-consuming and expensive to sell. It is usually easy to buy and sell shares in a property fund.
- Through a UK REIT, an investor may have access to parts of the property sector previously unavailable to them because of the costs of entry. For example, some of the more attractive, high-yielding properties, such as industrial buildings and shopping centres, are beyond the reach of most private investors.
- Investing in UK REITs offers the potential for a diverse portfolio of property assets in a variety of sectors and geographical locations. This offers far greater diversification and therefore a reduced level of risk than having 'all your eggs in one basket'.

Key benefits for investors
- Tax transparency (tax payable only on income dividends)
- Regular high-yield returns
- Access to property investment for minimal outlay
- Portfolio diversification (low correlation to equities and bonds)
- Liquidity – easy to buy/sell
- Lower transaction costs compared with buying property directly (Stamp Duty on direct property is up to 4 per cent, whereas buying shares in a UK REIT will be subject to stamp duty of only 0.5 per cent)
- Low/controlled gearing

- Access to property investment in a variety of sectors and geographical locations.

Owning property through a SIPP

A SIPP or 'Self Invested Personal Pension' is a special type of pension arrangement where the owner of the 'policy' has greater control over the range of assets in which the money is invested. The portfolio therefore may include a range of mutual funds from different managers and may also include individual share holdings and other allowable assets. This differs from traditional pension schemes where the investment options are usually limited only to the funds that are available from the pension provider company.

There are strict rules surrounding the type of assets that are allowed to be held within a SIPP, and UK and overseas commercial property are such assets. This ability for a commercial property to be purchased with pension fund money has led to lots of small- to medium-sized businesses buying their work premises by means of a SIPP. However, in terms of the overall property market, the number of transactions that this accounts for is very small.

Another option for those seeking to invest in property via a SIPP is to consider the relatively wide definition of 'commercial property' used by HM Revenue and Customs (HMRC). Hotel rooms, nursing homes and student halls of residence are classed as commercial properties which can be held directly by a SIPP. However, you need to stay on the right side of the taxman since a 55 per cent tax charge can be levied on any pension fund that invests directly in what HMRC sees as a residential property.

One of the big stories in the property sector back in late 2005 was the expectation that the rules surrounding SIPPs were to be relaxed and that among other things, investment in residential property including buy to let, holiday homes and overseas property would be permitted.

However, as the clock ticked towards 'A Day' (which was 6 April 2006), there were signs that the previous proposals would be changed and we are now at a point where direct investment into holiday homes or residential property from a SIPP is not permitted, but you *can* invest *indirectly* through what is termed by the taxman as a 'genuinely diverse commercial vehicle' (GDCV). This sounds technical, but essentially it means that if you want to invest money held in your SIPP into residential property, you must do so by way of investment into a 'unitized' fund. In other words, you can't buy property directly, but you can buy shares in a fund or company that in turn invests in property. There are some other rules too:

- The GDCV must be unitised or have a corporate structure. Unit trusts and open-ended investment companies (OEICs) are examples of unitized funds, while unlisted or listed shares can be held in corporate structures.
- It must have at least £1 million in investment in at least three residential properties.
- No single property can represent more than 40 per cent of the value of the fund.
- No single pension fund or person can hold more than 10 per cent of its shares or units.

Specialist funds set up to meet these criteria are now benefiting from the huge interest in residential property as a possible pension fund asset.

Bear in mind that the objective of a pension is to provide income in retirement. The trustees of the pension scheme (these are the people who oversee all the investments made and act in the interests of the person whose pension fund it is) tend to take a very cautious view on investments that can be made. Their job is to protect the money in the SIPP from being squandered away on high-risk investments. By forcing investors to invest in property by means of a fund rather than direct investment allows for a greater scope for investment diversification across a portfolio of properties – even for relatively modest investments – which reduces risk. It also opens up a way to enable management companies to handle the day-to-day running of the property and deal with the tenants.

In addition, certain types of overseas property will qualify for inclusion in a SIPP. This will include commercial property and units in hotel complexes, such as condo hotels – but no own use will be permitted.

Why invest in SIPPs?

By way of an incentive for people to save for their own retirement, investment into a SIPP or any other pension policy attracts tax relief at your highest marginal rate. This means that if you are a higher rate taxpayer, for every £1 that you invest, the government will give you tax relief of 40 per cent. This is clearly extremely advantageous since in this example, for every £1 going into the pension fund, you would only have to pay 60p of it – the government would contribute the rest. What's more, all assets held within the pension are able to grow free of Capital Gains and Income Tax. So, you can expect your returns to be better than if you made exactly the same investments outside a pension.

Investing in property funds

Another form of indirect investment is to buy units in a specialist property fund. These are generally regarded as being more suited to sophisticated investors. A fact that is reinforced by the knowledge that a minimum investment of around £25,000 may be required and these funds often use gearing, or borrowing, to boost returns.

On the plus side, funds can pick particular residential property markets where strong rental demand and healthy capital gains are expected. For example, a specialist fund was recently set up to invest in the residential market in major Polish cities, where economic growth may lead to greater demand for properties. This is an example of how a residential property fund can focus on a particular overseas market, where prices and returns are expected to rise due to specific local factors.

But property prices can fall as well as rise, and past performance is not a guide to the future. Investors must be aware that it may be very difficult to sell their holding if they need to before the fund's life cycle is completed. Nevertheless, the prospects of extremely attractive returns make the risks worth taking for many.

In addition, new funds are coming onto the market with guaranteed returns and a low entry point.

Syndicates

In Chapter 13, we discussed the advantages of syndicates for overseas purchases, but clearly this can be applied to any property market. In fact, through syndication you may find you can buy UK residential, UK commercial, overseas residential and land giving you maximum diversification.

For details of REITs, SIPPs, property funds, and to link up with people who may be interested in forming a syndicate, visit www.makingmoneyfromproperty.tv.

Summary

In this chapter we have looked at:

- Owning property through REITs
  - What is a REIT?
  - The case for investing in a REIT
  - REITs versus direct property investment
  - A summary of the key benefits for investors.
- Owning property through a SIPP
  - What are the benefits of buying through a SIPP?
- Owning property by way of a property fund.
- Owning property in a syndicate.

16

making money in a market downturn ...

In this chapter you will learn:
- how to protect yourself from a downturn in the market
- which properties perform better in a slow market
- about balancing a portfolio – the importance of diversification

... ways to ride the storm

What happens when the market takes a downturn and property prices stagnate or fall? What happens if interest rates rise? This chapter helps to address some of the concerns voiced by would-be property investors and shows how to turn a seemingly negative situation into a positive.

All markets move in cycles with periods of expansion and contraction. Property markets are no different, and it is absolutely normal that prices peak and then level, contract and bottom out before recovering and growing again. The UK property market was in a period of decline in the early 1990s and more or less bottomed out by 1995. Since then, it has experienced a long period of expansion, so it is possible that there will be some contraction in the market following this. This doesn't mean that there will be a property crash! But some forecasters predict that prices will only increase by very marginal amounts and in some areas they may fall back, so undoubtedly we are entering a period of time when it is a 'buyer's market'.

As property investors, we should take a medium- to long-term view of any transaction and so periods of contraction should be entirely expected and, in actual fact, can be welcomed. While prices are reducing, it creates a buying opportunity, and provided that we believe that all the other factors about the property stack up, you can expect that prices will increase again in the future.

If you already have a portfolio of property, the downturn in prices will affect you only if you need to sell. Many people lost money during the early 1990s when house prices fell dramatically, but these people were those who had to or chose to sell up. While many other homeowners had 'negative equity' on paper, they stayed put and in time prices recovered again. Let me ask you: If you had the chance now to buy, even at the 'inflated' prices just before the 1990s crash, would you?

How to protect yourself from a downturn in the market if you own buy to let property

Shop around

You should be doing this anyway, but in tougher market conditions, it becomes even more important to shop around for all your products and services relating to the ongoing upkeep and management of property. Review everything from your buildings insurance to services and utilities, and if necessary switch providers. Do read the small print though, and make sure that just because another company's product is much cheaper than your current cover, that it isn't massively inferior. A bit of time invested shopping around when it comes to the renewal date could save you £££ over the year. The biggest expense is usually your mortgage, so keep abreast of the rate and type of deal that you are on and if necessary consider switching to another lender if you can get a lower interest rate. Of course, you will need to weigh up the annual savings that you will make against the costs of switching but, unbelievably, many home owners could be paying less on their mortgage each month, simply by switching to another deal on offer by their existing lender. Banks and building societies won't generally come to you to ask 'Do you want to change to another product and reduce your mortgage?', they will wait for you to threaten to move your business elsewhere before they recommend other deals in their product range to you. Diarize a review of your mortgage every six months, and contact them as your first port of call.

Get help from the taxman

All the repair and maintenance work that you carry out on your properties can be written down as tax-deductible expenses, so for the sake of keeping decent records and filing receipts and paperwork, you could save yourself money on your tax bill. A good accountant will be invaluable in this respect.

Go interest only

If your mortgage isn't already on an interest only basis, consider switching to this type of deal. The monthly repayments will be lower than with a capital repayment mortgage (although you won't actually be paying back any of the loan itself) and this could help you during tighter times. Don't forget that the interest element of your mortgage repayments can also be offset against your rental income on your tax return.

Review agency fees

You may have to take on more administration yourself, but if you can go without your rental agent charging you a proportion of each month's rent for property management, then you could make a big saving. Most lettings agents offer a service where they find the tenants, reference them, sort out the tenancy agreement and compile the list of contents of the property for an upfront fee. Once all this has been sorted out and the tenant is in place, you may find you can manage things quite happily from there on.

Reduce your rent

You may have to accept that to reduce voids in a crowded rental market, you have to reduce your rent to become more competitive. If you cut £50 per month off the rent that you have been charging and which comparable properties are achieving, you are taking a hit but if this means that you avoid a long void period where you could be benefiting from £600 per month rent, then the financial case for doing so stacks up.

Stand out from the crowd

When the market is going through a difficult phase, it is more important for you to differentiate your properties from others that would-be tenants could rent or from others that are on sale. At the very least, make sure they are well maintained and everything is in good working order, but equally a small investment into replacing old white goods with new shiny ones could pay you back in making your property more attractive. Likewise, adopt all the principles in other chapters of this book to help create a property that stands out from the crowd.

Get organized

If you haven't already done so, when tough market conditions arrive this is the time to start keeping proper records. The last thing you want to do is to pay tax unnecessarily, and keeping proper accounts allows you to keep a close eye on budgets. By maintaining proper updated records, you might also spot areas where you can save money.

Have an emergency fund

Again, this is something that in an ideal world you will have in place anyway, but during difficult market conditions, it is more likely that you have to cover void periods or take a 'hit' on the rent. By keeping an emergency fund of money set aside, an unexpected expense won't break the bank. It's worth making a point of taking a small percentage of the rent each month and putting it into a savings account for this reason – this way you won't notice the small amount that you siphon off, and you could be glad of this buffer. An amount equal to three of four month's rent is a sensible figure to have as a contingency fund.

Cut outgoings

Analyse your own spending. Aside from reducing outgoings associated with your buy to let properties, there may be ways of saving within your own home. By curbing your spending, you may be able to take the heat off any deficit in your property investments.

Don't panic

When there is a downturn in the market, it is absolutely *not* the time to panic and sell up. Remember that even if house prices fall, you haven't actually made a loss until such time as you sell. Investing in property should be for the long term, and you are far better off hanging in there and riding out the storm than cashing in. By employing some cost saving strategies, hopefully you will be able to afford to stay invested and this is by far the best thing to do in the long run.

How to turn a slowdown in the market into a positive

Buy in regeneration areas

We've already talked about the fact that regeneration areas are good for maximizing capital growth, but they are also safer locations to buy in during slower markets. The reason is that investment into the area is being made by local, regional or national government, the EU or large corporations. They will have worked out their budgets and committed to the expenditure long before the slowdown has started to bite and so they will still follow through with the capital injection. These areas will therefore still develop without the need for private investors and individual buyers to drive values.

Go large

The sector of the market that tends to get hit hardest during contraction is the large, expensive properties. The family house worth between £1 million and £3 million is identified as the weakest part of the market. Quite simply, there are fewer people in a position to be able to afford these kinds of properties, so the demand for them is limited. Sellers, therefore, will have to reduce prices more substantially than other sectors of the property market and so potentially there will be more bargains to be had. Some of these properties may be suitable for alternative strategies, such as conversion into flats.

Buy property with a difference

During difficult market conditions the riskiest market is the monoculture, monotenure developments of flats where they all look the same and chances are a good percentage of them will have been bought by investors wanting to rent them out. This results in an over-supply of very similar properties. To attract tenants, try to buy properties that are individual or quirky – since these will stand out from the crowd. Property in traditionally popular areas will always cope with a downturn in the market better than that in less popular areas.

Become the housebuilders' best customer

Even large housebuilders will feel the pinch during a general slowdown and very often will reduce prices on new build developments in order to get rid of remaining inventory or free up capital. In particular, approaching the end of the trading year, these companies may want to secure extra sales and will be willing to make substantial price cuts in order to do so. This is a great buying opportunity.

Know your marbles

Better to stick at what you know and buy in your comfort zone rather than using a downturn to 'experiment' with new areas or new markets. As always, research is the key. While in buoyant times even people who buy unwisely can still do okay and make a profit, it won't be the case during a slowdown and you could be paying for your hasty purchases for many years to come.

Cut out the estate agent

If you do sell, then you may wish to consider listing your property yourself. With the Internet now so readily used by purchasers to find properties, you could find that listing the property yourself saves a lot of money. Many of the biggest property portal sites do not accept advertisements from individuals, forcing you to use an estate agent, but there are sites that allow you advertise your property as a private individual.

See 'Taking it further' and www.makingmoneyfromproperty.tv for websites that offer to list your home directly.

Consider investing in other countries

While the UK housing market pauses for breath, other markets worldwide are going full steam ahead. Research other countries to find out whether they could be home to your property investment funds – short or long term.

Which properties perform better in a slow market

If the market is slowing, then all the principles of sensible property investing become even more important. The old rule of 'location, location, location' becomes critical. In a slowdown, people still need or want to buy property – you just have to make sure that yours stands out to get the best possible price. At the end of the day, well presented, attractive properties that are well located will always be in demand, so if you have purchased well, you will still be able to sell at a fair price.

There is no property that will remain untouched by a general slowdown in the property market, but there are sectors which will be affected more than others. The riskier properties are:

- city centre flats and apartments in large developments where there are hundreds of almost identical properties
- properties that are in rundown neighbourhoods or have difficult access
- properties that lack crucial elements for the market that they are aimed at (i.e. family homes that have no parking or garden)
- large family homes with a £1 million to £3 million price tag.

So, the properties which are likely to perform better in a slow market are:

- individual properties that are one-offs or have particular character and features
- properties that are located within regeneration zones
- homes worth more than £3 million. Research suggests that these tend to buck the trend as buyers are wealthy overseas investors
- properties in traditionally popular areas
- first-time buyer level houses, such as terraced properties. Even if there is a percentage reduction, if the property is valued less it will be less of a reduction in absolute terms.

Balancing a portfolio – the importance of diversification

I've already talked about the fact that diversification in a property portfolio is a sensible thing. It reduces risk on all sorts of levels – one of which being if a property market or sector starts to slow. If you have all your 'eggs in one basket', then your entire portfolio could lose value in the event of a slowdown or contraction, but if you have invested wisely and spread your property choices around then this won't be so catastrophic. If we accept that markets move in cycles and, so at some point, any property market will stagnate or contract, then by diversifying your portfolio you can buy properties that are at different stages in the cycle. While the price of one property may fall, another may be experiencing strong growth and so the overall effect on your portfolio is less marked.

The effect of interest rates

Quite understandably, one of the fears of many property investors is rising interest rates. Whether you are an investor or just a straightforward homeowner, if you have a mortgage, then rises in interest rates will have a knock-on effect on mortgage rates. As mortgage rates rise, so does the monthly cost of servicing the loan and while a one-quarter per cent here or there is manageable, those who have high levels of borrowing could face problems if interest rates increase any more than a couple of percentage points.

However, every cloud has a silver lining and whilst rises in interest rates are generally unwelcome, the flipside is that interest rate rises make property less affordable for first-time buyers which will have a knock-on effect of increased rental demand. This is good news if you are a buy to let investor.

The trick is to not become overexposed to interest rate rises, and that means keeping the amount you borrow within sensible limits.

The overriding piece of advice is 'DON'T PANIC'. Write these words on a big piece of paper and stick it on your fridge!

Summary

In this chapter, we have looked at:

- How to protect yourself from downturn in the market.
- Which properties perform better in a slow market.
- Balancing a portfolio – the importance of diversification.

taking it further

In this section, I have listed a selection of useful websites covering all aspects of property investment, developing and renovation. There are many more listed on **www.making moneyfromproperty.tv**, but these should give you a starting point for information gathering.

www.makingmoneyfromproperty.tv

The accompanying website to this book. The site contains a whole host of information including:

- Useful contacts and up-to-date information on everything to do with the world of property.
- Up-to-the-minute news and views of what is happening in the property market.
- Invaluable and downloadable 'How To' guides to give you further practical instruction on applying some of the techniques covered in this book.
- Discussion forums and special tips from experts in the property industry.
- Networking opportunities and a chance to meet fellow investors for potential joint ventures and syndicated purchases.
- Listings of property auctions taking place in the UK and details of property lots.
- Behind the scenes information and reports from location during the filming of *Homes Under the Hammer*.
- An ideas and experiences forum for you to 'talk' to other property investors and developers and pass on your experiences.

- Special property purchase opportunities in the UK and abroad.
- Up-to-date sources of info and links to many other relevant websites.
- Plus loads of other stuff...!

Finding UK properties to buy

www.naea.co.uk – is the website for the National Association of Estate Agents (NAEA) – the largest estate agency organization in the UK. Contains contact details of all registered estate agents.

The following sites all list properties for sale or rent throughout the UK. They may also have the facility to search for Estate Agents in a given area and offer other products and services:

www.fish4homes.co.uk
www.rightmove.co.uk
www.propertyfinder.com
www.home.co.uk
www.primelocation.com
www.findaproperty.com

www.google.co.uk – use the incredible 'Google Earth' facility to zoom in on satellite images of an area you are considering buying in to check it out.

UK property auctions

www.makingmoneyfromproperty.tv – has an up-to-date list of auctions taking place in the UK, and details of specific properties coming up for sale.

Auctions featured on *Homes Under the Hammer* include:

www.westcountrypropertyauctions.co.uk
www.grahampenny.com
www.fss4property.co.uk
www.savills.co.uk
www.cliveemson.co.uk
www.mellerbraggins.com
www.buttersjohnbee.com
www.romans.co.uk

www.pugh-company.co.uk
www.strakergi.co.uk
www.symondsandsampson.co.uk
www.vtj.co.uk
www.rhseel.co.uk

UK property market data

www.landregistry.gov.uk – information about average house prices throughout England and Wales.

www.mouseprice.com – a great source of online property market information. A whole range of comprehensive housing data, such as local property market statistics, comparable transaction data and a current valuation estimate.

www.upmystreet.co.uk – helps you find out everything you could want to know about an area – from actual property prices to the neighbourhood's favourite newspaper.

www.nationwide.co.uk – contains information about house prices across the UK. You can also view forecasts and it has a house price calculator that allows you to find out how the value of a property has changed over the past few years.

www.hometrack.co.uk – provides comprehensive data on all aspects of house buying and selling. There are also various articles that you can download.

www.nethouseprices.com – has useful information about prices of property that has actually sold. Based on information provided by the Land Registry, you can type in a postcode and it will give you data on property sales in the surrounding area.

Property letting and becoming a landlord

www.rla.org.uk – the website of the Residential Landlords Association.

www.landlords.org.uk – the website of the National Association of Landlords

www.rentright.co.uk – gives you the latest rental price statistics taken from the RRPI (Residential Rental Price Index). The RRPI can give you the average rental prices down to town level across the UK. If you are looking to rent property this is a valuable resource to help assist in giving a guide to the market in different areas of the country.

www.tenant-reference.co.uk – offers a Tenant Reference service for landlords.

Finance

www.unbiased.co.uk – website of IFA Promotion Ltd, the industry body responsible for promoting independent financial advice in the UK. Search for an Independent Financial Adviser in your area.

www.searchifa.co.uk – helps you find an Independent Financial Adviser in your area.

www.thisismoney.co.uk – good financial advisory website.

www.bbc.co.uk – contains a wealth of information on financial and other property related issues.

www.fool.co.uk – compares a variety of financial services products including credit cards, mortgages and personal loans.

www.mortgages.co.uk – contains lots of information about mortgages including Buy to Let, First Time Buyer, Equity Release, Commercial mortgages and International mortgages. Also has a directory of UK mortgage brokers.

www.moneysupermarket.com – a price comparison site comparing various products including mortgages.

www.kelland.co.uk – independent financial advice firm with a national network of offices.

www.mwpensions.co.uk – specialist SIPP (Self Invested Personal Pension) providers and trustees.

Credit reference agencies

www.equifax.co.uk
www.experian.co.uk
www.callcredit.co.uk

Accountancy services

www.icaewfirms.co.uk – the official website of the Chartered Institute of Accountants in England & Wales.

www.robsontaylor.co.uk – highly regarded accountancy firm.

Tax information

www.hmrc.gov.uk – the official website of the Inland Revenue giving information on all taxes including stamp duty, capital gains tax etc.

www.direct.gov.uk – government website listing information on numerous relevant topics.

Solicitors

www.thelawsociety.org.uk – official website of the Law Society in England & Wales. If you want to find a solicitor in your area use the 'Find Solicitor' feature.

www.kirbysimcox.co.uk – Mark Delahoy comes recommended.

www.fklaw.co.uk – Fursdon Knapper. Charles Knapper is also recommended.

Website design, build and hosting

www.webromtv.com – a leading edge website design, build and hosting company specializing in multimedia content.

www.wsbinteractive.com – a Do It Yourself web based website building tool.

www.123-reg.co.uk – a good domain name registration site.

Renovation projects

www.planningportal.gov.uk – an online planning and building regulations site to help you learn about planning and building regulations, apply for planning permission, find out about development near you, appeal against a decision and research government policy.

www.buildstore.co.uk – National Self Build & Renovation Centre. A huge permanent display of all the products, services, inspiration and advice required for self build or renovation.

www.fmb.org.uk – the official website of the Federation of Master Builders.

www.consumerprotectionagency.co.uk – lists recommended tradespeople who meet recognized standards.

www.rics.org – official website of the Royal Institution of Chartered Surveyors. Loads of information and advice on all aspects of land purchase, property construction and renovation projects.

www.ribafind.org – the official website of the Royal Institute of British Architects. Lists qualified architects and associated services.

Overseas property

www.propertyqc.com – PropertyQC Ltd – my overseas property investment company offering advice and guidance on all aspects of buying abroad.

www.globalpropertyguide.com – gives useful information about property in countries all over the world.

www.cia.gov – the CIA World Fact Book gives general information about countries all over the world.

www.worldtravelguide.net – comprehensive site with worldwide travel and country information.

www.bbc.co.uk/weather – information on weather in countries around the world.

Currency exchange

www.xe.com – up-to-date currency exchange rates.

The following companies are specialist currency exchange brokers:

www.hifx.co.uk
www.moneycorp.co.uk
www.gcsexpress.com
www.purefx.co.uk

International property lawyers

www.lawoverseas.com – The International Law Partnership – with senior partner John Howell.

www.internationalpropertylaw.com – The International Property Law Centre.

Specialist insurance

www.overseas-property-club.co.uk – Providers of Title Insurance and other services for overseas property.

www.lloydwhyteintl.com – specialist overseas property insurance.

www.schofields.ltd.uk – insurance for UK holiday lets and property abroad.

Miscellaneous

www.companieshouse.gov.uk – the official website of UK Companies House. Information on setting up a limited company.

www.fcls.co.uk – one of the many law firms that can help with setting up a limited company.

www.homeinformationpacks.gov.uk – details about HIPs.

www.rollingregistration.co.uk – online electoral roll completion.

www.hse.gov.uk/asbestos – vital information about regonizing and dealing with asbestos.

www.communities.gov.uk – lots of useful info, including legalities of Party Walls.

index

teach
yourself

entrepreneurship
alex mcmillan

- Do you want to become a successful entrepreneur?
- Do you need to find the right opportunities?
- Do you want to beat the competition?

Entrepreneurship tells you what makes a successful entrepreneur, how to set a clear vision of the sort of entrepreneur you are and how to motivate yourself and others to get the results you want. Full of practical 'streetwise' tips, this book also features interviews with successful entrepreneurs with a wealth of experience to share. If you want to turn your ideas into reality then this is the book to guide you!

Alex McMillan is a writer, consultant, trainer and mentor to entrepreneurs. He is also founder of Club Entrepreneur, a community for people interested in running their own business.